NEWE HUPIA

SHOSHONI POETRY SONGS

NEWE HUPIA
SHOSHONI POETRY SONGS

Beverly Crum   Earl Crum   Jon P. Dayley

Utah State University Press
Logan, Utah

Utah State University Press
Logan, Utah 84322-7800

Manufactured in the United States of America
Printed on acid-free paper

08 07 06 05 04 03 02 01   1 2 3 4 5 6 7 8

Library of Congress Cataloging-in-Publication Data

Crum, Beverly.
    Newe Hupia : Shoshoni poetry songs / Beverly Crum, Earl Crum, Jon P. Dayley.
        p.cm.
Includes bibliographical references.
        ISBN 0-87421-413-0 (pbk. : alk. paper) — 0-87421-433-5 (cloth : alk. paper)
        1. Shoshoni poetry—History and criticism. 2. Shoshoni Indians—Songs and
music. I. Crum, Earl, 1923– II. Dayley, Jon P.(Jon Phillip), 1944– III. Title.
        PM2321 .Z77 C78 2001
        897'.45–dc21
                                                    2001006301

To the many *Newe hupiakantee* 'Shoshoni singers' who have already *nekkamaihku* 'gone dancing' (i.e., passed away). They have been our teachers. Their generosity has enabled us to make this collection of poetry songs possible.

CONTENTS

Songs   27

CD Track

Music   161

Glossary   167

ILLUSTRATIONS

Acknowledgments

Many people have contributed to make this collection of *Newe hupia* 'Shoshoni poetry songs' possible. First, we would like to thank the Shoshoni people who kept reminding us of how important it is to preserve our songs in written form and on CD.

We are indebted to the late Wick R. Miller, who developed the writing system that we use for writing Shoshoni (see Crum and Miller 1987; Crum and Dayley 1993).

We want to thank Johann Helton for recording the poetry songs on CD and Jon Fransen, the audio engineer who remixed and edited the final copy of the CD.

We would like to give our deepest gratitude to Ken Kuchler, music director and conductor of the Wasatch Community Symphony Orchestra in Salt Lake City, who, working with Earl Crum, put a number of the songs in this collection to musical notation. Two of the songs here, along with other Native American songs, were played by members of the orchestra in a concert in Salt Lake City in May 2000.

We thank Professor Charles Greenhaw at the Great Basin College in Elko, Nevada, for giving us an initial critique of the manuscript and encouraging us to continue. We also thank several anonymous readers for their many helpful suggestions.

Finally, we want to thank members of our families for their patience and encouragement during the long process of putting this book together. Jon Dayley would especially like to thank his wife Dana Logan for her support in this effort.

ABBREVIATIONS

ADJ	adjective	NP	noun phrase
ADV	adverb	O	object
AUX	auxiliary verb	ø	no objective case suffix
CONJ	conjunction	obj	object/objective case
DEM	demonstrative	P	postposition
distrib	distributive	pass	passive
dl	dual	perf	perfective
dub	dubitative	pl	plural
dur	durative	poss	possessive
EMPH	emphatic	PRFX	prefix
excl	exclusive	PRO	pronoun
flex	flexible	Q	yes/no question particle
hab	habitual	QUANT	quantifier
incl	inclusive	quote	quotative particle
INCORP	object incorporating verb	rcprcl	reciprocal
INSTR	instrumental	REL	relative
INTER	interrogative	RFLX	reflexive
INTRJCT	interjection	sg	singular
IV	intransitive verb	state	stative
LINK	linking	sub	subordinate, subordinating
LOC	locative	subj	subject/subjective case
N	noun	TOP	toponym
NEG	negative	TV	transitive verb
NO	number	V	verb

INTRODUCTION

This work is a collection of *Newe hupia* 'Shoshoni poetry songs', which celebrate the traditional Shoshoni hunting and gathering lifeway and world view. For centuries the ancestors of the Shoshoni lived in the Great Basin and surrounding areas of what is now the western United States, moving seasonally from place to place harvesting various roots, berries, grains, pinenuts, herbs, and game animals. The poetry songs are rich in describing this way of life, which is intimately connected to the natural world. Today, Shoshoni people still sing these songs celebrating the traditional lifeway.

From the Shoshoni perspective, nearly everything in life and nature is sacred and worthy of being put to song. Thus, many songs are about specific details of nature such as animals, plants, and geographical and meteorological phenomena. They are also about traditional human activities such as hunting game and gathering and preparing foods, as well as spiritual practices and themes. On the one hand, the poetry songs are a traditional art form for the enjoyment of all who sing and hear them. On the other hand, they are used to help people learn about the specific details of nature, which are extremely important for people living in a hunting and gathering lifeway.

The themes of Shoshoni poetry songs are often not what either songs or poetry might be about in the modern Western tradition. The beauty of the lyrics of the songs lies in their simplicity and their power to capture details of nature and human existence that some of us may overlook or not pay much attention to. The poetry songs offer us a fresh look at the world, making the familiar vivid and alive. They give us insight and invoke clear imagery of the ordinary yet wondrous world we live in, expressing the experience of seeing the world as it is.

The poetry songs invoke imagery rather than describe it. In fact, elaborate description is avoided, and the songs use as few words as possible. Thus, the poetry songs are minimalist, simply illuminating the wonders of everyday life and celebrating its sacredness. The imagery is what is important, and so what is invoked is to some degree individual. Different singers of the same song and different people listening to it may have different interpretations. Each person has his or her own experience in the world, and so different interpretations of a given song are possible. What is important is taking delight in the wonders of nature and the world, to see it clearly as it is. The songs help one pay attention to the world and delight in it. In this regard the poetry songs are much like Japanese haiku poetry but without restrictions on numbers of lines and syllables within the line.

However, Shoshoni poetry songs are different from Old World poetry in that they are always sung, never simply recited, and always sung in the context of other activities such as dancing, playing handgame (= stickgame), healing ceremonies, and other rituals. The poetry songs are sung to provide a background invoking energy and power for the other activities, so the same song may be sung over and over again during a particular dance or ceremony before another song is sung. And in some songs the same line is repeated several times for rhythmic effect. The repetition is important in order to emphasize the imagery and power the song invokes for the hearers, whether they are dancers in a dance, players gambling in handgame, or healers and patients in healing ceremonies. The songs serve an important function by invoking *puha* 'supernatural power' in whatever context they are being sung. In this way, the poetry songs play an important role in the lives of the Shoshoni people.

The *Newe* (~ *Neme*) 'Shoshoni (people)' have a rich oral tradition which includes historical narratives and mythological stories as well as songs (see Canonge 1958; Crum 1980, 1985, 1993; Crum and Dayley 1997; Lowie 1909, 1924; Miller 1972; Smith 1993). Traditionally, older singers would teach younger people who wanted to learn the songs, and so the songs were passed down orally from generation to generation as something of especial value. Occasionally, a singer would create his or her own new song. Different singers may sing slightly different versions of the same song, and sometimes the same singer may sing slightly different versions. But as each generation of people who know the songs dies off, fewer and fewer young people have an opportunity to learn them. So, it is with a sense of urgency that we have collected and recorded them.

All of the poetry songs in this work are sung by Beverly and Earl Crum, both native speakers of Western Shoshoni and traditional singers. They live on the Duck Valley Indian Reservation straddling the border between Idaho and Nevada, have been married for fifty-five years, and have three grown children. Earl was born on a hillside near Battle Mountain, Nevada, in 1923 and learned many of the songs from older relatives and friends while growing up. Earl also learned some of the songs by hearing them at dances and other social gatherings and in healing ceremonies and other rituals. In addition, Earl's mother, the late Mabel Rodrigues, tape-recorded many *Newe hupia* that she had learned in her lifetime and gave them to Earl before she passed away to add to his collection. In recent years, Earl and other Shoshonis who enjoy

The authors and others from a training program for Shoshoni writing teachers, who keep the language alive by using it. *From left to right*: the late Alice Eben, Earl Crum, Beverly Crum, Sharon Maldoon, and Jon Dayley. Photograph by Lois Kane.

singing the poetry songs get together to share each of their personal repertoires of the songs. Earl has lived and worked most of his life on the Duck Valley Indian Reservation. He also has lived and worked off the reservation in various periods of his life. As a young boy he went to Stewart Indian School in Nevada. Later he served as a marine in the Pacific in World War II.

Beverly Crum was born on the Duck Valley Indian Reservation in 1926. Throughout her life, she has lived both on and off the reservation. During the years on the reservation, she learned the songs from relatives and friends and at various dances and other social gatherings. Much later in life she lived in Salt Lake City pursuing an M.A. degree at the University of Utah, where she wrote her master's thesis on Shoshoni poetry songs.

For many years, both Earl and Beverly have had a keen interest in the Shoshoni language and have recorded, transcribed, and translated various oral traditions in the language, including myths and stories, histories, and poetry songs, as well as the everyday speech of elderly Shoshoni speakers. They have also spent many years teaching how to read, write, and speak Shoshoni on the Duck Valley Indian Reservation to many tribal members as well as to some non-Indians who work and live there. Their hope has always been that *Newe* will continue as a viable language.

This collection of *hupia* or poetry songs represents only a small fraction of the Shoshoni poetry songs known in the past and still sung today. The poetry songs presented here are a gift and legacy from the Shoshoni people to the world. They are also a means of preserving a small but important part of the Shoshoni language for future generations, for the Shoshoni people, and also for all who appreciate music, poetry, culture, and language. The songs are wonderful pieces of music, often with rhythms and melodies that differ from the classical European tradition. They can only be fully appreciated as pieces of sung verse, not simply printed on a page. For this reason, we have included a CD of the songs being sung in Shoshoni so readers can appreciate them as music even if they don't understand the Shoshoni words.

Song and Dance Types

The Shoshoni tradition offers several different kinds of *hupia* or poetry songs. The first three songs presented here are *natayaa hupia*, which are sung in the ritual called *natayaa* performed especially before the round dance. In this ritual, an elder or several elders lead a procession of people singing the songs. The people march counterclockwise to the dance ground, which has a pinenut tree or an aspen planted in its center. Then they offer prayers to the 'Maker of People', *Newi Manemenaippehkante*, for a good harvest in the current year and for harvests to come in the future. The people then purify themselves, *nampuisitai*, by washing themselves and putting red ochre or white clay on their bodies. Afterwards, the round dance begins.

The ceremonies during the harvesting of pinenuts are typical of combining dance with poetry songs and music. Recalling the rituals that went along with the pinenut harvesting festival, one elderly Shoshoni woman narrated the following:

> Our old people used to work very hard during the warm months before the cold winter months set in. That's the way it was with gathering pinenuts. Some years the pinenuts were plentiful; other years there were hardly any. The times when the pinenuts were plentiful, we would choose a *tepattaik-wahni* 'pinenut chief'. He would tell us to purify ourselves before we went to gather the pinenuts. So with prayerful thoughts we would wash our bodies. Then we would put on *pisappi* 'red ochre' or *aipi* 'white chalky clay'. We did this so the pinenuts would not be wormy, and so we would have strong healthy bodies. Only then would we go and gather the pinenuts. When we finished, our pinenut chief would ask us to get ourselves ready for the dances. Right away, the old women would grind up some of their pinenuts into flour and make pinenut pudding with it. Then, we would begin our dance with a special one called *natayaa*. This dance had its own

special songs [namely, *Totsantsi* 'Cleansing', the first song in this collection]. They would sing these songs as the old women took spoonfuls of pinenut pudding and walked circling the dance place. In this way we celebrated the harvesting of pinenuts.

After the ritual *natayaa* dance, the people would join together for social dances. The dance performed most often during festive occasions was the round dance. In the round dance, men, women, and children dance in a circle, intertwining their arms and holding hands while moving in short measured steps to one side. As one elderly woman laughingly remarked:

Tammen	nanah	kwi'naa	wa'ihku	yotikkinna.
we (incl)	just	bird	like	fly (pl) along

'We just fly along like birds.'

Taking part in the round dance is fun and energizing, and everybody enjoys it.

Songs sung during dances in general are called *nehka hupia* 'dance songs', and those sung at round dances are called *nua hupia* 'movement songs'. Most of the songs we present in this work are round dance songs. Traditionally, people begin dancing in round dances in the evening and dance all night until daybreak. Throughout the night various songs are sung by different singers. During the day other activities go on, such as handgame, races, and other activities for everyone, young and old. The celebration goes on for several days and nights, and on the last day people dance until noon and then begin to go home.

Another kind of dance performed during the round dance is called *ta aipuntu nuan nekkanna* 'this direction round dance'. This dance is different from the regular round dance in that the music is faster, the dancers hold hands and move in a peppy jog. When the singer says "*aipuntu*" the dancers stop and start moving in the opposite direction. The change in direction is signaled by songs called *aipuntu hupia* which are transitional songs that singers sing when people have been dancing for two or more hours, to change the direction (clockwise or counterclockwise) in which people are dancing. The *aipuntu* songs give the dancers a break to relieve tired legs and hips. *Aipuntu* literally means 'this way' or 'this direction'. An *aipuntu* song is sung and then the word *aipuntu* is repeated several times, which is the signal to turn and change directions, and then the song may be sung again several times.

Another Shoshoni dance is called *ta wehe'neki nekkanna* 'the rasping dance', named in reference to the noise made by a rasping instrument which beats the rhythm for the dance. Nowadays this dance is commonly called the bear dance in English. In this dance, participants dance with a

An early twentieth century round dance. The Shoshoni people called this dance *tan tapai nekkanna* 'the day time dance'. Beverly Crum's sister Laura Townsend, 90 years old, said the tribal elders did this round dance on the last day after several nights of dancing. Laura remembers seeing the last performance of it when she was a small girl.

partner, moving back and forth in a linear fashion. Songs sung during the bear dance are called *wehe'neki hupia*, literally meaning 'rasping song'.

Other traditional songs are *puha hupia*, literally 'power songs'. These songs are also called *nanisuntehai hupia* 'prayer songs' or *nattahsu'u hupia* 'medicine songs' and are used in various kinds of ceremonies and healing services to invoke *puha* or supernatural power.

Handgame songs are also traditional songs sung to invoke luck while playing handgame (or stickgame), a very old traditional gambling game among many North American groups. However, handgame songs are not represented in this selection.

Finally, there are more contemporary songs that Shoshonis sing at pow-wows, which are modern nontraditional intertribal gatherings with dancing, singing, and drumming, as well as competitions for all of these. Pow-wow songs include flag songs like one presented at the end of this volume. It should be noted, however, that a few flag songs are traditional, and they might better be called banner songs since they are about banners identifying different groups of people. Other modern pow-wow songs not included here are honoring songs and songs sung during what are called the war dance in English, but called *tan tase'yekinna* 'moving the feet' in Shoshoni. These are

This picture was taken during the Ruby Valley Fandango in 1972. Note the changes in dance style from the *tan tapai nekkanna* 'the day time dance' some 57 years earlier. Photograph by Steve Crum.

not traditional to the Western Shoshoni but rather had their origins in Native American Plains culture, then spread to many North American Indian groups in the nineteenth and twentieth centuries. These songs differ from traditional ones in rhythm, cadence, and lyrics.

Other more contemporary songs are peyote songs sung in Native American Church services. The Native American Church movement began among the Kiowa and Comanche in Oklahoma in the 1890s and spread to most other North American Indian tribes at the end of the nineteenth century and during the first part of the twentieth century. The church was formally incorporated in 1918. Members of the Native American Church consider peyote a very sacred medicine and take it as sacrament in church ritual. Peyote songs are considered *nattahsu'u hupia* 'medicine songs' much like traditional medicine songs. One peyote song is included near the end of this book.[1]

THE SHOSHONI LANGUAGE

Since the *hupia* or poetry songs presented here are sung in Shoshoni, a few words about the language are in order. Here, we simply present a short sketch of the language in general and also mention special characteristics of the language used in poetry songs.

Before Europeans began colonizing western North America, Shoshoni was spoken by several thousand people in the valleys and mountains of the Great Basin area, the Snake River Plain, and the northern Rocky Mountains. Shoshoni territory included a large triangle-shaped area stretching out from a point in southeastern California through central Nevada and into southern Idaho and northern Utah and on into southwestern Wyoming. There are still several thousand Shoshoni people living on Indian reservations and in towns and cities scattered throughout the same area today. However, the number of people who still speak the language fluently has been dwindling fairly rapidly in the last few decades, so there are only a few hundred people who use the language on a day-to-day basis as their first language, although a few thousand still know it to one degree or another.

Shoshoni belongs to a large family of genetically related languages called Uto-Aztecan, which includes some thirty languages whose speakers aboriginally inhabited a vast territory stretching from the Salmon River in central Idaho, southward through the Great Basin and Southwest, into much of northern and central Mexico, and with colonies of speakers in Central America in parts of present-day Guatemala, El Salvador, and Nicaragua. Aztec (or Nahuatl, called Pipil in Central America) is the southernmost member of the family, and Shoshoni is the northernmost member. Other languages scattered in between are listed below. The language family gets its name from combining Ute and Aztec. Shoshoni belongs to a subbranch or subfamily of Uto-Aztecan called Numic (much like English belongs to the Germanic subbranch of the Indo-European language family). The word Numic in English is borrowed from cognate words in all the Numic languages meaning 'Indian, person' and the name of the language in each of the Numic languages. For example, in Shoshoni *neme* (~ *newe*) means 'Shoshoni, Indian, person' and also 'the Shoshoni language'; and similarly in Panamint Shoshoni, *nümü* means 'Tümpisa Shoshoni, Indian, person' and also 'the Tümpisa Shoshoni language'.

Uto-Aztecan Language Family

Northern Division

Numic
Central Numic
Shoshoni, Panamint (= Tümpisa Shoshoni), Comanche
Western Numic
Mono, Northern Paiute (= Paviotso and Bannock)
Southern Numic
Kawaiisu, Chemehuevi-Southern Paiute-Ute

Takic
  Serrano-Kitanemuk
  Cupan
    Luiseño-Juaneño, Gabrielino-Fernandiño, Cupeño, Cahuilla

Tubatulabal

Hopi

Southern Division

Sonoran
  Corachol
    Cora, Huichol
  Tarahumaran
    Tarahumara, Guarijio
  Tepiman
    Pima-Papago, Pima Bajo, Northern Tepehuan, Southern Tepehuan
    Tepecano
  Opatan
    Opata-Jova, Eudeve-Heve
  Mayo-Yaqui isolate
  Tubar isolate

Aztecan
  Pochutec
  Nahua(tl) Pipil

In terms of grammar, Shoshoni is quite different from English. Its words, especially verbs, tend to be quite complex with several morphemes or meaningful elements strung together agglutinatively. For example, note the complex internal structure of the verbs below, which are taken from the poetry songs:

manemenaippehkanten 'created people'

<	ma-	'by hand' instrumental prefix
	neme	'person'
	-nai	'make, create' incorporating verb
	ppehkanten	remote past compound suffix
	< -ppeh	past participle suffix
	-kan	stative suffix
	-ten	habitual suffix

namapataatsikiyukwainna 'be glazing oneself all over'

<	na-	reflexive prefix
	ma-	'by hand' instrumental prefix
	pataatsiki	'glaze, shine' verb
	-yu	progressive suffix
	-kwain	'all over' directional suffix
	-nna	general tense/aspect suffix

namattsiwenenemmi	'stand by itself pointed alive'
< na-	reflexive prefix
ma-	'by hand' instrumental prefix
tsi"-	'pointed object' instrumental prefix
wene"	'stand' verb
-nemmi	'living' auxiliary verb

As the examples above illustrate, verbs often have prefixes indicating grammatical voice and the type of instrument with which the action is done. They also often have one or more suffixes indicating directional and adverbial notions as well as tense and aspect. And some verbs (like *-nai* 'make, create' and *-pa'in* 'have') incorporate (direct) object nouns into the verb stem (e.g., *manemenaippehkanten* above).

With respect to sentence structure and word order, Shoshoni is much more like Japanese, Turkish, and Basque than English because the basic word order in Shoshoni is Subject + Object + Verb (sov). For example:

s	o	v	
Ne	hunanna	puinnu.	'I saw a badger.'
I	badger-o	saw	

Andy	punkunii	pamakannu.	'Andy watered the horses.'
Andy	horses-o	watered	

En	nemmi	manemenaippehkante.	'You created us.'
you	us (excl)	by hand-people-make-remote past	

Not only direct objects but also indirect objects go before verbs, as the sentences below illustrate.

s	io	do	v
Puhakante	hepitsoo'a	nattahsu'unna	uttunnu.
doctor	old lady-o	medicine-o	gave

'The doctor gave the old lady some medicine.'

	s	do	io	v
Ne	pii	sikka	ne	mapaiankannu.
my	mother	this-o	me	made

'My mother made this for me.'

Shoshoni and other languages like it with basic sov word order (about 40 percent of the world's 5,000 languages) usually have a number of syntactic characteristics in common which are often mirror image of their English counterparts. Thus, instead of prepositions Shoshoni has postpositions which go after nouns or noun phrases (rather than before nouns or noun phrases as prepositions do in English). For example:

Ne   kentu   kahni   tukkanku   tsippiha   puinnu.
I   yesterday house   under   squirrel-o   saw
'I saw a squirrel under the house yesterday.'

Newe   nehe   *munnai*   mi'akinna.
Indian   us two   ahead of   walk
'An Indian was walking ahead of us two.'

Hepitsoo'an   kahni   *kuppanten*   kai   tottsapa'i.
old lady's   house   in   not   dirt-have
'There isn't any dirt in the old lady's house.'

And auxiliary or helping verbs follow main verbs instead of preceding them, as the sentences below illustrate.

Ne   ekise   awe   koitsoih-*teki-to'i*.
I   soon   dish-o   wash-start-will
'I'll start to wash the dishes pretty soon.'

Bill   tammi   tenitlo'inkahan-*to'i*.
Bill   us (incl)   sing for-will
'Bill will sing for us.'

Also, subordinate clauses usually precede the main verb as well. For example:

Pei *ta*   *kahnlnainkanuhka*   sote   hepitsoo   tsaan   nisuanna.
her   someone   house-made for-when   that   old lady   good   express
'The old lady expressed happiness when a house was built for her.'

Soten tainna *kai* *pei* *ta*   *wookkahteaku*   sukkuh mannai mi'annu.
that   man   not   him   someone   work-ask to-when   there   from   went
'That man went away from there when he wasn't given a job.'

Even though the basic word order in Shoshoni is sov, other orders are possible. This freedom of word order is possible because nouns and pronouns, as well as adjectives modifying nouns, are inflected for grammatical case (as they are in Latin, Russian, German, and Japanese, and many other languages). In other words, from the endings on nouns and pronouns, one can always tell whether they are subjects or objects no matter what order they occur in. Therefore, word order is not as crucial in Shoshoni as it is in English. In Shoshoni nouns and pronouns are inflected for subjective, objective, and possessive cases. Compare the nouns below.

Nouns

Subjective	Objective	Possessive	
newe	newi	newen	'person, Indian, Shoshoni (language)'

pii	pii'a	pii'an	'mother'
wa'ippe	wa'ippe'a	wa'ippe'an	'woman'
pohopin	pohopitta	pohopittan	'sagebrush'
hupia	hupiai	hupian	'poetry song'
hupiakanten	hupiakanti	hupiakantennan	'singer'

Nouns and pronouns are also inflected for singular, dual, and plural numbers, each with their own subjective, objective, and possessive forms. For example:

	Subjective	Objective	Possessive	
sg	wa'ippe	wa'ippe'a	wa'ippe'an	'woman'
dl	wa'ippeneweh	wa'ippenihi	wa'ippenehen	'two women'
pl	wa'ippeneen	wa'ippenii	wa'ippeneen	'women'

Some nouns have irregular or unpredictable forms in the dual or plural. For example:

	Subjective	Objective	Possessive	
sg	tei	tei'a	tei'an	'friend'
dl	tetteyanneweh	tetteyannihi	tetteyannehen	'two friends'
pl	tetteyanneen	tetteyannii	tetteyanneen	'friends'

Personal pronouns are inflected for subjective, objective, and possessive cases; singular, dual, and plural numbers; and for first, second, and third persons. For example:

Personal Pronouns

	Subjective	Objective		Possessive	
sg					
1st	ne	nei	~ ne	nean	~ ne
2nd	en	emmi	~ en	en	~ emmen
3rd	__	ma	~ u	man	~ un
dl					
1st incl	taweh	tahi		tahan	
1st excl	neweh	nehi		nehen	
2nd	meweh	mehi		mehen	
pl					
1st incl	tammen	tammi	~ tai	tammen	
1st excl	nemmen	nemmi		nemmen	
2nd	memmen	memmi	~ mei	memmen	

However, in the dual and plural numbers and in the singular subjective case, there are no third person personal pronouns per se. Rather, demonstratives are used instead. Shoshoni demonstratives are composed of a demonstrative-locative base indicating relative distance from the speaker or place thought of, followed by a stem ending. Most of the demonstrative-locative bases come in two forms, one with initial s- followed by a vowel, and one with a vowel alone without s-. The bases without s- are used to introduce new or indefinite information into the discourse, or to indicate that a given discourse participant is not the topic. The forms beginning in s- are used to signal given or definite information and continuing topics. There is also another base, *ma-*, which indicates given and definite information like the forms beginning with s-, and it always indicates nearness. Thus, demonstratives in *ma-* cover the range of the *si-* and *sai-* forms. Since the forms in s- and *ma-* are used to track topics in discourse, they are referred to as the proximates; the forms without s- or *ma-* are never used to track continuing topics in discourse so they are called obviatives. For example:

Demonstrative-Locative Bases

Obviative	Proximate	
i-	si-	'this right here'
ai-	sai-	'this nearby'
o-	so	'that'
a-	sa-	'that (yonder)'
u-	su-	'that (not visible)'
	ma-	'this'

The demonstratives are presented below. Note that there are no forms in *ma-* in the singular subjective case (i.e., *mate* is not used and is ungrammatical).

Demonstratives

	Subjective	Objective	Possessive
sg	(s)iten	(s)ikka	(s)ikkan
	(s)aiten	(s)aikka	(s)aikkan
	(s)oten	(s)okka	(s)okkan
	(s)aten	(s)akka	(s)akkan
	(s)uten	(s)ukka ~ (s)ukki	(s)ukkan
		makka ~ makki	makkan
dl	(s)iteweh	(s)itehi	(s)itehen
	(s)aiteweh	(s)aitehi	(s)aitehen
	(s)oteweh	(s)otehi	(s)otehen
	(s)ateweh	(s)atehi	(s)atehen
	(s)uteweh	(s)utehi	(s)utehen
		matehi	matehen
pl	(s)iteen	(s)itii	(s)iteen
	(s)aiteen	(s)altii	(s)aiteen
	(s)oteen	(s)otii	(s)oteen
	(s)ateen	(s)atii	(s)ateen

(s)uteen	(s)utii	(s)uteen
	matii	mateen

The demonstratives are used as third person pronouns, where in English we would have to use he, him, his; she, her(s); it, its; as well as they, them, and their; but in Shoshoni there are no gender distinctions, much like the plural in English. The demonstratives are also used before nouns like demonstratives in English, except that Shoshoni demonstratives must agree with the nouns they modify in case and number. The demonstratives are also used much like English articles, since Shoshoni has no definite and indefinite articles. The demonstratives beginning with s- are always definite, but the demonstratives without s- may be interpreted as definite or indefinite depending on the context, though they are never used with the immediate discourse topic. It should also be noted that in Shoshoni, nouns do not require demonstratives or some other determiner, so that nouns may often occur alone without any kind of determiner (such as articles, demonstratives, or possessives). In these cases, nouns have to be determined in context.

One other characteristic feature of Shoshoni syntax different from English is that in running discourse, subjects of sentences are often omitted if they are understood in context. This is especially the case if the subject is the ongoing topic of the discourse. In Shoshoni poetry songs, the subject is often presumed as the topic even though it hasn't been mentioned at all, so the subject is often omitted altogether because it is understood in the context of the song.

THE SHOSHONI ALPHABET AND SOUND SYSTEM

We write Shoshoni with the following letters, all of which are from the Roman alphabet except for the last:

A   AI   E   H   I   K   KW   M   N   O   P   S   T   TS   U   W   Y   '

The Roman alphabet is used to write many languages in the world including English, German, Spanish, Italian, Navajo, Turkish, Vietnamese, Mayan languages, and many others. In each language, the letters often represent different sounds. For example, the letter p in Shoshoni represents a sound different from the p in English, which is also different from the p in Spanish. What this means is that the letters in Shoshoni have their own values and Shoshoni words are pronounced in their own way, not like in English or in any other language.

The one letter that isn't part of the Roman alphabet is ', which represents a consonant called the glottal stop. English doesn't write the glottal stop at all. But many languages such as Arabic and Hebrew do, and when these languages are written with Roman letters they use ' for the glottal stop. It occurs only in the middle of Shoshoni words and is like the gap where the hyphen is in English oh-oh. E.g.:

wa'ippe	'woman'		so'o	'cheek'
ka'i	'forehead'		mo'o	'hand'

The six vowels in Shoshoni, *a*, *i*, *u*, *o*, *ai* and *e*, can be short or long. If they are long, they are written double and are pronounced holding the vowel about twice as long as the corresponding short vowel. Thus, short *a* is pronounced like the *a* in English father (e.g., *ata* 'uncle'), and the long *aa* is pronounced the same way but held twice as long (e.g., *ohaa* 'baby'). The short *i* is pronounced as the vowel sound in English eat or peep (e.g., *itsappe* 'coyote'), and long *ii* is pronounced the same way but held twice as long (e.g., *siippeh* 'urine'). The short *u* is pronounced as the vowel sound in English rule or suit (e.g., *punku* 'horse'), and the long *uu* is pronounced the same way but held twice as long (e.g., *huuppi(n)* 'stick'). The short *o* is pronounced somewhat like the vowel sound in English horse but articulated with the tongue slightly lower and with the mouth more open (e.g., *tommo* 'winter', *oo'o* 'cheek'), and the long *oo* is pronounced the same way but held twice as long (e.g., *tooppeh* 'cloud', *oo(n)* 'leg').

The Shoshoni vowel written with *e* is rare in English, only occurring in a few words, for example, the vowel in just, in one pronunciation of "he just left." It is pronounced like the *u* except without any lip rounding (e.g., *teheya* 'deer'). Long *ee* is pronounced the same way but held twice as long (e.g., *kweettsi* 'wife', *peeppi(n)* 'blood').

The vowel written *ai* usually can be pronounced in two ways, either like the vowel sound in English ate or bait, or like English I or the vowel sound in bite. Some people may say *ai* one way one time and the other way another time, and some people may say a particular word with *ai* only one way while others may say it in the other way. And in different dialects of Shoshoni a given word with *ai* may usually be pronounced one way or the other. A few words are only spoken with the vowel as in English ate, in which case we write it with an underlined *ai*, and a few words seem to be pronounced only with the vowel as in English I, but most words with *ai* may be pronounced either way depending on the individual speaker or dialect.

Like English ate		Like English I		Like English ate or I	
p<u>ai</u>nkwi	'fish'	haintseh	'friend'	aiti	'gun'
h<u>ai</u>wi	'dove'	haih	'crow'	taipo	'Caucasian'
<u>ai</u>te(n)	'this'	akai	'salmon'	aipi(n)	'chalky clay'

When the vowel *ai* is long, it is written *aai* as in the following words:

m<u>aai</u>kkuh	'OK; now'	naaiyawi	'play handgame'

Some Shoshoni words have vowel clusters. When vowels come together like this, each is pronounced the same as when alone. E.g.:

mea	'moon'	hupia	'poetry song'
tokoa	'snake'	tua	'child'
tei	'friend'	puih	'eye'

Many consonants (i.e., *k, kw, m, n, p, t,* and *ts*) in Shoshoni can be single or double (although *h, s, w, y,* and ' are never double). When consonants are single, they can occur at the beginning or in the middle of words. When they are double, they only occur in the middle. Single consonants at the beginning of words are pronounced as in English except that *k, kw, p,* and *t* don't have any aspiration or puff of air after them as the corresponding English consonants usually do at the beginning of words.

However, in the middle of words single *k, kw, p, t,* and *ts* are normally voiced, pronounced with the vocal chords vibrating. So, in the middle of the following words, *k* sounds like English g, *kw* like English gw, *p* like English b, *t* like English d, and *ts* like English dz.

nankahi	'listen'	kentu	'yesterday'
p<u>a</u>inkwi	'fish'	wantsi	'buck antelope'
nampai	'foot'		

In the middle of the words above, the consonants are preceded by nasals. When *k, kw, p, t,* and *ts* are between two vowels, they are not only voiced but also softened, having a fricative or spirant quality, meaning the air is not stopped completely in their pronunciation (much like some consonants in Spanish). So, *k* and *kw* sound like Spanish g and gu between vowels, *p* sounds a little like English v but more like Spanish b between vowels, *t* more like a single Spanish r between vowels, and *ts* like English z. In the words below, the consonants between vowels are pronounced in this softened manner.

sokopi	'earth'	satee	'dog'
okw<u>ai</u>te	'stream'	tatsa	'summer'
tepa"	'pinenut'		

Double consonants *kk, kkw, mm, nn, pp, tt,* and *tts* only occur in the middle of words and are pronounced much like their English counterparts but held slightly longer as double consonants are in Italian. Single *m, n, w,* and *y* are pronounced like their English correspondents at the beginning of words and in the middle, although for some speakers *m* between vowels is also softened and so it is pronounced with the lips slightly open, more like a nasalized w.

The consonants *s, t, ts,* and *tts* change their pronunciation when following short *i* or long *ii*. Thus, after *i* or *ii, s* sounds like English sh, *t* like th in English *the*, *ts* like English j, and *tts* like English ch. In the words below s, t, *ts*, and *tts* have these special pronunciations after the *i*.

| pisippeh | 'rotten' | pitsi | 'breast' |
| pite | 'arrive' | kuittseh | 'throat' |

Shoshoni words may end in four distinctive ways, either in (1) a final vowel, (2) a final -*n*, (3) a final -*h*, or (4) a final -". Each of these word endings have differing effects. When words end in a final vowel, the initial consonants *k*, *kw*, *p*, *t*, and *ts* of following words are softened, exactly as described above when they occur between vowels in the middle of words. So, for example, when the noun-incorporating verb *pa'i* 'have' is added to words ending in a vowel (e.g., *kahni* 'house', *punku* 'horse', *mukua* 'soul', and *mo'o* 'hand'), the *p* is softened, sounding like Spanish b between vowels. E.g.:

| kahnipa'i | 'have a house' | mukuapa'i | 'have a soul' |
| punkupa'i | 'have a horse' | mo'opa'i | 'have a hand' |

Also, when the word *kuppa* 'inside, in' follows another word ending in a vowel, its *k* is softened, sounding like Spanish g between vowels. E.g.:

| kahni kuppa | 'inside the house' | wittua kuppa | 'in the bucket/drum' |
| tempai kuppa | 'in the mouth' | hupa kuppa | 'in the broth' |

Similarly, when the word *tukka(n)* 'under, below' follows a word ending in a vowel, its *t* is softened. After *i* it sounds like th in English *the* and after other vowels like a single Spanish r between vowels. E.g.:

| kahni tukka | 'under the house' | wittua tukka | 'under a bucket/drum' |
| tempai tukka | 'under the mouth' | punku tukka | 'under the horse' |

Words ending in final -*n* lose the -*n* completely when spoken in isolation or at the end of a phrase or sentence, and also before the consonants *h*, *s*, *w*, and *y*. The final -*n* disappears in these situations altogether. For example, the word *e(n)* 'you, your' has a final -*n*, which disappears altogether in the examples below.

e	'you, your'	e wika	'your blanket'
e hupia	'your song'	e yantu(n)	'your winnowing tray'
e sappeh	'your stomach'		

The final -*n* appears if the word is in the middle of a phrase and if the next word begins with *k*, *kw*, *n*, *t*, or *ts*. E.g.:

en kahni	'your house'	en nampeh	'your shoe'
en kwehe	'your wife'	en tsuhni	'your bone'
en tami	'your younger brother'		

A later use of the *yantu* 'winnowing basket' was for winnowing wheat, that is, separating the chaff from the kernels. In the early twentieth century, elderly women went from grain field to grain field on the reservation gathering leftover wheat kernels for their own use. Photograph from the Earl Crum collection.

However, the final *-n* becomes an *m* when the next word begins with *m* or *p*. E.g.:

em mo'o	'your hand'	em papi	'your older brother'

Also, compare the pronunciation of the word *yantu(n)* 'winnowing basket', ending in final *-n*. When said in isolation or at the end of a phrase or sentence, it is *yantu*, without the final *-n*. But the *-n* appears in *yantun kuppa* 'in the winnowing basket' and *yantun tukka* 'under the winnowing basket', and it becomes *-m* in *yantumpa'i* 'have a winnowing basket'.

When a word ends with final *-h*, the vowel before it is normally voiceless or whispered. In the following words the vowel before the *-h* is always whispered.

isampeh	'liar'	maaikkuh	'OK; now'
e'attsih	'sore'	ta'wah	'flour'
tipoh	'table'	kwiippeh	'smoke'

Final *-h* also influences the pronunciation of following *k*, *kw*, *p*, and *t*. Normally, the *hk*, *hkw*, *hp*, and *ht* combinations merge forming single voiceless fricatives. For example, when a *p* follows *h*, the two sounds merge to make a sound that is somewhat like the English f, phonetically a [ɸ]. So, for example, when the noun-incorporating verb *pa'i* 'have' follows the words *ahtahpeh*, *e'attsih*, and *tipoh*, all ending in final *-h*, the *hp* combination is pronounced as [ɸ]. E.g.:

ahtahpehpa'i	'have a jaw'	e'attsihpa'i	'have a sore'
tipohpa'i	'have a table'		

Similarly, *h+k* and *h+kw* become phonetically [x] and [xw], respectively. The [x] is the same as the sound spelled ch in German as in nacht 'night'. Also, *h+t* becomes [Θ], the same as th in English thin, if the vowel preceding the *h* is *i*; otherwise, *h+t* is pronounced like a voiceless [R]. E.g.:

haih kuppa	'in a raven'	haih tukka	'under a raven'
e'attsih kuppa	'in a sore'	tipoh tukka	'under a table'

Some Shoshoni words end in final *-"*. This *-"* is not a normal consonant having a pronunciation of its own, but rather it has the effect of causing the first consonant of a following word to be doubled if it is *k, kw, m, n, p, t,* or *ts*. Thus, when *pa'i* 'have' is added to the words *kuna"* 'firewood', *kwee"* 'wife', *tua"* 'son', and *tepa"* 'pinenuts', the *p* of *pa'i* is doubled.

kunappa'i	'have firewood'	tuappa'i	'have a son'
kweeppa'i	'have a wife'	tepappa'i	'have pinenuts'

Similarly, the *k* of *kuppa* and the *t* of *tukka* are doubled after these words. E.g.:

kunakkuppa	'inside firewood'	kunattukka	'under firewood'
kweekkuppa	'inside of a wife'	kweettukka	'under a wife'
tuakkuppa	'in a son'	tuattukka	'under a son'
tepakkuppa	'inside pinenuts'	tepattukka	'under a pinenut tree'

SPECIAL POETRY SONG LANGUAGE

The language in poetry songs may differ substantially from ordinary speech in a number of ways. Grammatically the songs are usually attenuated in that case suffixes on nouns and adjectives are often not marked, verbs usually have no or very few tense, aspect, and adverbial suffixes, and determiners like demonstratives are almost never used. And normal word orders may change. Thus, normal subject-object-verb order may become subject-verb-object order, or even more commonly the subject is not mentioned at all but is either understood or left for listeners to interpret for themselves. In some cases, normal noun phrase–plus-postposition order may become preposition-plus–noun phrase order, and sometimes the postposition is omitted altogether.

The diminutive-affectionate suffix -*ttsi* often used on nouns and adjectives is usually changed to -*ntsi* in poetry songs. It commonly indicates special emphasis denoting endearment, high esteem, reverence, affection, and warm feelings, as well as the notion of smallness. In both poetry songs and ordinary speech, Shoshonis often add the suffix to nouns to express their warm feelings for things in nature like *yehne(ttsi)* 'porcupine', *yaha(ttsi)* 'ground hog', and *kwi'naa(ttsi)* 'bird', and for domestic animals like *satee(ttsi)* 'dog' and *punku(ttsi)* 'horse'.

Poetry songs are also distinguished by the use of many obscure or obsolete words that are not used in ordinary speech and which many people do not know or understand, although some of the unique poetry song words may be understood in the context of the songs. However, sometimes even the singer doesn't know their meaning.

Other words like *hainna*, *ha̲inneh*, *haainna*, *hainah*, *hainai*, *nai*, *yanna*, *ho*, and *noowaineh* are song words without meaning used to fill in and complement the rhythm and cadence, although some are also used somewhat like mantras to bless or make sacred the situation in which they are sung. And finally, sometimes *haiya wainna* and also less commonly *yaaya wainna* are used by singers at the end of songs to bless them, making them sacred.

In addition, many ordinary words used in poetry songs undergo various degrees of change in pronunciation. The most typical changes are described and illustrated below. One common change is that nasals pop into ordinary words, especially replacing the first consonant of an identical consonant cluster. For example:

song word		*ordinary word*	
waimpentsi	<	wa'ippe(ttsi)	'woman'
tuantsi	<	tuattsi	'baby, child, young'
huumpi	<	huuppi(n)	'stick, wood'
waanka(n)	<	waakka(n)	'at the junipers'
huintsaantsi	<	huittsaa(ttsi)	'sage hen'

Often geminate or double consonants between vowels become single, and therefore voiced. For example:

potoo(n)	<	potto(n)	'grinding stone'
waaka(n)	<	waakka(n)	'at the junipers'
tepana	<	teppanna	'on the side of'

Ss between vowels often become *ts*, phonetically [z]. For example:

watsempi(n)	<	waseppi(n)	'mountain sheep'
totsa"	<	tosa"	'white'

Glottal stops almost always disappear. For example:

waimpentsi	<	wa'ippe(ttsi)	'woman'
patui	<	pato'ih	'wade'
toi	<	to'ih	'emerge, go out, come up'
pomia	<	pomi'ah	'migrate'

Short vowels become long, even extra long, in syllables where the note is held. For example:

yotii(i)	<	yoti"	'fly, arise (pl)'
opii	<	opi	'there about'
potoo(n)	<	potto(n)	'grinding stone'

Vowel clusters are often broken with semivowels intervening. For example:

| wiya | < | wia | 'mountain pass' |
| mukuwa | < | mukua | 'soul' |

All of these changes in pronunciation are used to make the song words more melodious and rhythmical.

In the pages that follow, the poetry songs are first presented in the original Shoshoni, then a figurative English translation is given, followed by the Shoshoni again but this time with an interlinear literal word-by-word translation. We give both figurative and literal translations to accomplish two sometimes contradictory goals. The figurative translation is given in an attempt to capture a sense of the poetic beauty of the Shoshoni lyrics, while the interlinear word-by-word translation is given so the reader can see exactly what the Shoshoni words say literally, even if they may not make (aesthetic) sense in English. After each of the poetry songs and their translations, we then make short comments about particular aspects of the songs.

After all the poetry songs are presented, there follows a Shoshoni to English glossary containing several thousand Shoshoni words with their English translations, as well as grammatical information such as parts of speech, paradigmatic forms, and irregularities. Then, an English to Shoshoni glossary is given.

If readers wish to know more about the Shoshoni language, they should consult Crapo 1976, Crum and Dayley 1993, and Miller 1996. They might also consult informative works on two closely related languages: Panamint (Dayley 1989a, 1989b) and Comanche (Charney 1993; Robinson and Armagost 1990). The most important works on Shoshoni culture and ethnology are Harris 1940, Steward 1938, and Thomas, Pendleton, and Cappannari 1986. Vennum's article (1986) on Great Basin music is a good introduction to the kinds of music found among aboriginal Great Basin peoples. Also, an excellent book on Native North American poetry songs in general is Soens 1999.

Problems in Translating the Poetry Songs

Translating from one language to another is never easy. It is impossible to capture all the meaning(s) in a given linguistic expression in one language in translating to another. Any linguistic expression always has several layers of meaning expressed simultaneously depending on a whole range of factors such as: (1) the literal meanings of each word in a sentence and then the literal interpretation of the whole sentence; (2) how the words and sentence are interpreted given the context of the immediately preceding discourse in the given social situation in which the discourse occurs; (3) the cultural setting, lifeway, and world view of the people using the language; and (4) the things alluded to metaphorically, humorously, satirically, and ironically given the entire cultural, social, linguistic, and discourse context. Not only is there a problem in expressing all the meaning in translation, but there is also the problem of capturing the aesthetics or beauty of a linguistic expression in one language in translating to another. This problem is magnified immensely when translating from a language used in a cultural context vastly different from the one in which the target language is normally spoken.

As noted earlier, the traditional Shoshoni lifeway was one of a hunting and gathering society in which the people lived intimately tied to nature, very different from modern Western society with its elaborate social institutions and technology which actually distance people a great deal from the natural world. Shoshoni poetry songs are most often about nature and the people's warm and intimate feelings about the plants, animals, and the geographical terrain in which the Shoshoni lived. So, often a certain amount of meaning contained in the poetry songs is lost in the English translation, since people speaking English as their native language usually no longer live so closely tied to nature nor feel the intimacy with it that a people with a hunting and gathering lifeway do.

For example, the Shoshoni words in song 52, *Tamme Yampa Sateettsi*, offer a lighthearted picture for native listeners, but the words in the English translation, 'Our Wild Carrot Pet', sound flat. In Shoshoni, the word *sateettsi* can mean either 'little dog' or 'pet', but in the context of this bear dance song, the word is normally interpreted by native speakers as a bear that hung around in the wild carrot fields when the people were harvesting *yampa*, 'wild carrots', an important staple food source in the Shoshoni diet. In fact, *yampa* was a favorite food for the Shoshoni and a number of poetry songs make reference to it. In times past, the Shoshoni camped in places where the wild carrots grew, and their campsites were surrounded by various curious animals. *Tamme Yampa Sateettsi* was probably one such animal. Nowadays, most modern Americans have probably never even heard of wild carrots.

Translating the Shoshoni of the poetry songs can be particularly difficult for other reasons as well: (1) often obscure and obsolete words are open to interpretation; (2) the imagery is open to interpretation; and (3) there are levels of meaning invoked on the literal level as well as on the spiritual level. In fact, some poetry songs can have different interpretations even by native speakers. For example, song 27 presented here, entitled *Oyon Tempi* 'Every Rock', has two completely different interpretations. The two different interpretations are possible because the song contains words that are not used in ordinary language but are similar to different everyday words with completely different meanings. As is the case with speakers of all languages, every speaker carries a mental dictionary in their heads, but when they hear words of their own language that they don't know, they automatically attempt to decode them in the best way they can, given the context. However, this process doesn't always result in the same outcome.

So, the English translations presented here may not capture all of the possible interpretations of the poetry songs, or their aesthetic beauty as experienced by native speakers hearing them in Shoshoni. The important thing is for one to allow the poetry songs to invoke a sense of the wonder and sacredness of the world we live in.

NOTE

1. Judith Vander, in her book *Songprints* (1988) on five Eastern Shoshoni women singers from the Wind River Indian Reservation in Wyoming, lists fourteen different genres of Shoshoni songs. They include all of the ones we have noted except bear dance songs, which either do not occur with the Eastern Shoshoni or she simply didn't record any. Also, she lists *natayaa* songs as ghost dance songs, but *natayaa hupia* are very traditional songs long predating the ghost dance revival movement in the nineteenth century. Vander also lists sun dance songs, called *takowene hupia* 'standing thirsty songs' in Shoshoni, but not practiced in the Western Shoshoni area, and crow hop songs, an intertribal genre sung in some pow-wows under the influence of Plains Indian culture. She also notes other Shoshoni genres such as hymns sung in Christian congregations, country and western songs, and "forty-nine" (love) songs. These are all nontraditional songs sung in English. Vander also lists lullabies and children's songs as genres of the Eastern Shoshoni. The Western Shoshoni do not have children's songs as a separate genre, and lullabies are individual songs made up by mothers on the spot singing to their own children, so they are not culture-wide songs among the Western Shoshoni but rather individual creations. Vander also has a book entirely devoted to Shoshoni ghost dance songs (1997).

Works Cited

Canonge, Elliott. 1958. *Comanche Texts*. Summer Institute of Linguistics and University of Texas at Arlington Publications in Linguistics 1. Norman, Oklahoma: Summer Institute of Linguistics.

Charney, Jean Omrsbee. 1993. *A Grammar of Comanche*. Studies in the Anthropology of North American Indians. Lincoln: University of Nebraska Press.

Crapo, Richley H. 1976. *Big Smokey Valley Shoshoni*. Desert Research Institute Publications in the Social Sciences, no. 10. Reno, Nevada: DRI.

Crum, Beverly. 1980. Newe Hupia—Shoshoni Poetry Songs. *Journal of California and Great Basin Anthropology Papers in Linguistics* 2:3–23.

———. 1985. *Markhan Te'ahwaippeh: Tammen Appean Teniwaahtaikwappeh*. With three tapes in Shoshoni. Elko, Nevada: Humboldt Printer Publisher.

———. 1993. Afterword. In *Shoshoni Tales*. Collected by Anne M. Smith. Salt Lake City: University of Utah Press.

Crum, Beverly, and Jon P. Dayley. 1993. *Western Shoshoni Grammar*. Occasional Papers and Monographs in Cultural Anthropology and Linguistics, vol. 1. Boise, Idaho: Boise State University, Department of Anthropology.

———. 1997. *Shoshoni Texts*. Occasional Papers and Monographs in Cultural Anthropology and Linguistics, vol. 2. Boise, Idaho: Boise State University, Department of Anthropology.

Crum, Beverly, and Wick R. Miller. 1987. *How to Read and Write Shoshoni: A Book of Spelling Lessons, Readings, and Glossary for Shoshoni Speakers*. With three tapes in Shoshoni. Elko, Nevada: Humboldt Printer Publisher.

Dayley, Jon P. 1989a. *Tümpisa (Panamint) Shoshone Grammar*. University of California Publications in Linguistics 115. Berkeley: University of California Press.

———. 1989b. *Tümpisa (Panamint) Shoshone Dictionary*. University of California Publications in Linguistics 116. Berkeley: University of California Press.

Harris, Jack. 1940. The White Knife Shoshone of Nevada. In *Acculturation in Seven American Indian Tribes*, ed. Ralph Linton. New York: Appleton-Century.

Lowie, Robert H. 1909. *The Northern Shoshone*. Anthropological Papers of the American Museum of Natural History 2 (2): 169–306.

———. 1924. Shoshonean tales. *Journal of American Folklore* 37:92–200.

Miller, Wick R. 1972. *Newe Natekwinappeh: Shoshoni Stories and Dictionary*. University of Utah Anthropological Papers 94. Salt Lake City: University of Utah Press.

———. 1996. Sketch of Shoshone, a Uto-Aztecan Language. In *Handbook of American Indians*. Ed. William C. Sturtevant. Vol. 17, *Languages*, ed. Ives Goddard. Washington, D.C.: Smithsonian Institution.

Robinson, Lila Wistrand, and James Armagost. 1990. *Comanche Dictionary and Grammar*. Summer Institute of Linguistics and University of Texas at Arlington Publications in Linguistics 92. Dallas, Texas: Summer Institute of Linguistics.

Smith, Anne M. 1993. *Shoshoni Tales*. Salt Lake City: University of Utah Press.

Soens, A.L. 1999. *I, the Song: Classical Poetry of Native North America*. Salt Lake City: University of Utah Press.

Steward, Julian H. 1938. *Basin-Plateau Aboriginal Socio-Political Groups*. Bureau of American Ethnology, Bulletin 120. Washington, D.C.: Smithsonian Institution.

Thomas, David H., Lorann S. A. Pendleton, and Stephen C. Cappannari. 1986. Western Shoshone. In *Handbook of North American Indians*. Ed. William C. Sturtevant. Vol. 11, *Great Basin*, ed. Warren L. D'Azevedo. Washington, D.C.: Smithsonian Institution.

Vander, Judith. 1988. *Songprints: The Musical Experience of Five Shoshone Women*. Urbana: University of Illinois Press.

———. 1997. *Shoshoni Ghost Dance Religion: Poetry Songs and Great Basin Context*. Urbana: University of Illinois Press.

Vennum, Thomas, Jr. 1986. Music. In *Handbook of North American Indians*. Ed. William C. Sturtevant. Vol. 11, *Great Basin*, ed. Warren L. D'Azevedo. Washington, D.C.: Smithsonian Institution.

Songs

NATAYAA SONGS

Totsantsi 'Cleansing'
Earl Crum

Totsantsi

> Haaiyuh waihna,   1st Version
> Haaiyuh waihnah.
> Haaiyuh waihna,
> Haaiyuh waihnah.
>
> Totsantsii totsantsi nanasokoppentsi,
> Totsantsii totsantsi nanasokoppentsi.
>
> Haaiyuh waihna,   2nd Version
> Haaiyuh waihnah.
> Haaiyuh waihna,
> Haaiyuh waihnah.
>
> Totsantsii totsantsi nanapunuhakinna,
> Totsantsii totsantsi nanapunuhakinna.

Cleansing

> *Haaiyuh waihna,*   1st Version
> *Haaiyuh waihnah.*
> *Haaiyuh waihna,*
> *Haaiyuh waihnah.*
>
> Cleansing, cleansing the blessed earth,
> Cleansing, cleansing the blessed earth.
>
> *Haaiyuh waihna,*   2nd Version
> *Haaiyuh waihnah.*
> *Haaiyuh waihna,*
> *Haaiyuh waihnah.*
>
> Cleansing, cleansing, energizing!
> Cleansing, cleansing, energizing!

Totsantsi
Cleansing

Haaiyuh waihna, rhythmical song words		1st Version

Haaiyuh waihnah.
rhythmical song words

Haaiyuh waihna,
rhythmical song words

Haaiyuh waihnah.
rhythmical song words

Totsantsii cleansing	totsantsi cleansing	nanasokoppentsi, reciprocal-earth-blessed
Totsantsii cleansing	totsantsi cleansing	nanasokoppentsi. reciprocal-earth blessed

Haaiyuh waihna, rhythmical song words		2nd Version

Haaiyuh waihnah.
Haaiyuh waihna,
Haaiyuh waihnah.

Totsantsii cleansing	totsantsi cleansing	nanapunuhakinna, being energized
Totsantsii cleansing	totsantsi cleansing	nanapunuhakinna. being energized

COMMENTS

This is a *natayaa* song. *Totsantsi(i)* is a song form meaning 'cleansing'. It is based on the root *tosa"*- 'white', which has the song form *totsa*, plus *-ntsi*, the song form of the diminutive-affectionate and nominalizing suffix *-ttsi*. Either of the two versions of this song is sung repeatedly, especially as the opening ceremony of the pinenut festival traditionally held in the fall when pinenuts were harvested. Pinenuts were one of the most important staple food sources for the Western Shoshoni people.

Ainkappata 'Red Currants'
Earl Crum

A̲inkappata

A̲inkappata yoowennekinna,
A̲inkappata yoowennekinna.
A̲iyoo wainna a̲iyoo wainna,
A̲iyoo wainna a̲iyoo wainna.

A̲inkappata yoowennekinna,
A̲inkappata yoowennekinna.
A̲iyoo wainna a̲iyoo wainna,
A̲iyoo wainna a̲iyoo wainna.

Red Currants

Red currants swaying gently,
Red currants swaying gently.
A̲iyoo wainna a̲iyoo wainna,
A̲iyoo wainna a̲iyoo wainna.

Red currants swaying gently,
Red currants swaying gently.
A̲iyoo wainna a̲iyoo wainna,
A̲iyoo wainna a̲iyoo wainna.

Ainkappata
Red Currant

A̲inkappata	yoowennekinna,
red currant	gently-stand (dur)-moving
A̲inkappata	yoowennekinna.
red currant	gently-stand (dur)-moving

A̲iyoo wainna a̲iyoo wainna,
rhythmical song words

A̲iyoo wainna a̲iyoo wainna.
rhythmical song words

A̲inkappata	yoowennekinna,
red currant	gently-stand (dur)-moving

A̲inkappata	yoowennekinna.
red currant	gently-stand (dur)-moving

A̲iyoo wainna a̲iyoo wainna,
rhythmical song words

A̲iyoo wainna a̲iyoo wainna.
rhythmical song words

COMMENTS

This is a *natayaa* song. *Yoo* is the song form of the root *yuu(n)* 'gentle, peaceful, still'. *A̲inkappata* is a medicinal plant.

Puisenna 'Green Aspen'
Earl Crum

Puisenna

Puisenna totowaantsi.
Wainna haiyaho wainna,
Wainna haiyaho.

Puisenna totowaantsi,
Puisenna totowaantsi.
Wainna haiyaho wainna,
Wainna haiyaho wainna.
Puisenna totowaantsi,
Puisenna totowaantsi.

Green Aspen

Green aspen grove.
Wainna haiyaho wainna,
Wainna haiyaho wainna.

Green aspen grove,
Green aspen grove.
Wainna haiyaho wainna,
Wainna haiyaho wainna.
Green aspen grove,
Green aspen grove.

Puisenna
Green Aspen

Puisenna	totowaantsi.
green-aspen	stand (pl)

Wainna h<u>a</u>iyaho wainna,
rhythmical song words

Wainna h<u>a</u>iyaho wainna.
rhythmical song words

Puisenna	totowaantsi,
green-aspen	stand (pl)

Puisenna	totowaantsi.
green-aspen	stand (pl)

Wainna h<u>a</u>iyaho wainna,
rhythmical song words

Wainna h<u>a</u>iyaho wainna.
rhythmical song words

Puisenna	totowaantsi,
green-aspen	stand (pl)

Puisenna	totowaantsi.
green-aspen	stand (pl)

Comments

This is a *nataya'a* song. *Totowaantsi* is a song word related to *topo'ih(ka)* 'stand, be upright (pl)'. But, *totowaantsi* has the song form with the nominalizing diminutive and affectionate suffix *-ntsi* (normal *-ttsi*) on it, which makes it a noun meaning 'stand, grove'. *Puisenna* 'green aspen' here means aspen that is leafing, as in the springtime.

ROUND DANCE SONGS

Sai Paa Hupia 'Boat and Water Song'
Beverly Crum

Sai Paa Hupia

> Sai paa weyaa,
> Sai paa weyaa,
> Sai paa weyaa,
> Sai paa weyaa.
>
> Piaa toyaakatete mantu,
> Toyaatu mantu,
> Tewekkwintoote.
>
> Piaa toyaakatete mantu,
> Toyaatu mantu,
> Tewekkwintoote.

Boat and Water Song

> Water carries the boat,
> Water carries the boat,
> Water carries the boat,
> Water carries the boat.
>
> Towards the big mountain range,
> Towards the mountains,
> Swirling.
>
> Towards the big mountain range,
> Towards the mountains,
> Swirling.

Sai	Paa	Hupia
Boat	Water	Song

Sai	paa	weyaa,
boat	water	carry

Sai	paa	weyaa,
boat	water	carry

Sai	paa	weyaa,
boat	water	carry

Sai	paa	weyaa.
boat	water	carry

Piaa	toyaakatete	mantu,
big	mountain range	towards

Toyaatu	mantu,
mountain-through	towards

Tewekkwintoote.
swirling/churning

Piaa	toyaakatete	mantu,
big	mountain range	towards

Toyaatu	mantu,
mountain-through	towards

Tewekkwintoote.
swirling/churning

COMMENTS

This is a nua hupia 'round dance song'. Tewekkwintoote is the song form of tewekkwintuih 'swirl, churn'.

5

Waseppittsian Nahupia
'Song of the Mountain Sheep'
Earl Crum

Waseppittsian Nahupia

> Watsempin nampatui,
> Ainkam paa tu,
> Nointsai,
> Hainna.

> Watsempin nampatui,
> Ainkam paa tu,
> Nointsai.

> Hainna,
> Wonkotetsii tepanayu.
> Wainna,
> Wonkotetsii tepanayu.
> Wainnah.

> Haiya wainna.

Song of the Mountain Sheep

> Mountain sheep wading
> Through red water,
> Trudging in the mud.

> Mountain sheep wading
> Through red water,
> Trudging in the mud.

> Beside the pine grass,
> Behold.
> Beside the pine grass,
> Behold.

> *Haiya wainna.*

| Waseppittsian | Nahupia |
| Mountain Sheep's | RFLX-Song |

| Watsempin | nampatui, | |
| mountain sheep | foot-wade | |

| Ainkam | paa | tu, |
| red | water | through |

Nointsai,
stickily

Hainna.
rhythmical song word

| Watsempin | nampatui, | |
| mountain sheep | foot-wade | |

| Ainkam | paa | tu, |
| red | water | through |

Nointsai.
stickily

Hainna,
behold

| Wonkotetsii | tepanayu. |
| pine grass | be on the side of |

Wainna,
behold

| Wonkotetsii | tepanayu. |
| pine grass | be on the side of |

Wainnah.
rhythmical song word

Haiya wainna.

COMMENTS

This is a nua hupia 'round dance song'. *Watsempi(n)* is the song form of *waseppi(n)* ~ *waseppeh* 'mountain sheep', and nointsai is the song form of noitsai 'sticky, stickily'. The ordinary word for '(on the) side (of)' is *teppanna*. Here, a song word *tepanayu(n)* has been formed with the verbalizing suffix -yu.

Tahmani Hupia 'Spring Song'
Earl Crum

Tahmani Hupia

Sokopinna puipaa tuattsi kimman tuu,
Sokopinna puipaa tuattsi kimman tuu.

Tatsaw<u>ai</u> h<u>aai</u>,
Tatsaw<u>ai</u> h<u>aai</u>.

Sokopinna puipaa tuattsi kimman tuu,
Sokopinna puipaa tuattsi kimman tuu.

Tatsaw<u>ai</u> h<u>aai</u>,
Tatsaw<u>ai</u> h<u>aai</u>.

Spring Song

The earth's newborn green grass is coming forth,
The earth's newborn green grass is coming forth.

It's becoming summer, ho!
It's becoming summer, ho!

The earth's newborn green grass is coming forth,
The earth's newborn green grass is coming forth.

It's becoming summer, ho!
It's becoming summer, ho!

Tahmani	Hupia	
Spring	Song	
Sokopinna	puipaa	tuattsi
earth's	green grass-on	newborn
kimman	tuu,	
come	song syllable	

38

Sokopinna	puipaa	tuattsi
earth's	green grass-on	newborn
kimman	tuu.	
come	song syllable	

Tatsaw<u>ai</u>		h<u>aai</u>,
become summer		ho

Tatsaw<u>ai</u>		h<u>aai</u>.
become summer		ho

Sokopinna	puipaa	tuattsi
earth's	green grass-on	newborn
kimman	tuu,	
come	song syllable	

Sokopinna	puipaa	tuattsi
earth's	green grass-on	newborn
kimman	tuu.	
come	song syllable	

Tatsaw<u>ai</u>		h<u>aai</u>,
become summer		ho

Tatsaw<u>ai</u>		h<u>aai</u>.
become summer		ho

COMMENTS

This is a *nua hupia* 'round dance song'. Earl Crum says, "This song is about the coming of spring, when the first blades of green grass start to come up. That's what it's about."

7

Hunnita Ma'ai A'ninna Nahupia
'Red Ants and Black Ants Song'
Earl Crum

Hunnita Ma'ai A'ninna Nahupia

Hunnitan kuu annitan kuu,
Hunnitan kuu annitan kuu.

Nakennaaw<u>aai</u> akennaaw<u>ai</u>,
H<u>ai</u>nnah.
Nakennaaw<u>aai</u> akennaaw<u>ai</u>,
H<u>ai</u>nnah.

Hunnitan kuu annitan kuu,
Hunnitan kuu annitan kuu.

Nakennaaw<u>aai</u> akennaaw<u>ai</u>,
H<u>ai</u>nnah.
Nakennaaw<u>aai</u> akennaaw<u>ai</u>,
H<u>ai</u>nnah.

Red Ants and Black Ants Song

Bury the red ants, bury the black ants [together],
Bury the red ants, bury the black ants [together].

And they'll snap at each other with their mouths,
H<u>ai</u>nnah.
And they'll snap at each other with their mouths.
H<u>ai</u>nnah.

Bury the red ants, bury the black ants [together],
Bury the red ants, bury the black ants [together].

And they'll snap at each other with their mouths,
H<u>ai</u>nnah.
And they'll snap at each other with their mouths.
H<u>ai</u>nnah.

Hunnita	Ma'ai	A'ninna	Nahupia
Red Ant	and	Black Ant	RFLX-Song

Hunnitan	kuu	annitan	kuu,
red ant	bury	black ant	bury

Hunnitan	kuu	annitan	kuu.
red ant	bury	black ant	bury

Nakennaaw<u>aa</u>i   akennaaw<u>ai</u>,
be done with mouth   be done with mouth

H<u>ai</u>nnah.
rhythmical song word

Nakennaaw<u>aa</u>i   akennaaw<u>ai</u>,
be done with mouth   be done with mouth

H<u>ai</u>nnah.
rhythmical song word

COMMENTS

This is a *nua hupia* 'round dance song'. Earl Crum says, "You know, a long time ago before children had toys like they do now, the children used to play with anything that they could find. So anyway, this song is about when children were playing, they would sit there with red fire ants and the pissants and mix them together. Then, they would watch them fight. That's what this song is about."

The normal word for black ant is *a'ni(n)*. Here, the song form *annitan* is used to rhyme and keep rhythm with *hunnitan (~ hu'nitan)* 'red ant'. Similarly, *akennaawai* is not really a word, but is used to rhyme and keep rhythm with *nakennaawai*.

Teheya'an Kuhan Nahupia 'Song of the Buck Deer'
Earl Crum

Teheya'an Kuhan Nahupia

> Aan kuantsi,
> Aan kuantsi
> Imaayu toowenete mantu
> natsapaikkantoote,
> natsapaikkantoote,
> natsapaikkantoote.

> Aan kuantsi,
> Aan kuantsi
> Imaayu toowenete mantu
> natsapaikkantoote,
> natsapaikkantoote,
> natsapaikkantoote.

Song of the Buck Deer

> Buck deer,
> Buck deer
> Grazing in the early morning,
> Is killed with a bow,
> Is killed with a bow,
> Is killed with a bow.

> Buck deer,
> Buck deer
> Grazing in the early morning,
> Is killed with a bow,
> Is killed with a bow,
> Is killed with a bow.

Jode "Shorty" Jake, *left*, and Jim Crum, *right*, with a recently killed buck deer, about 1938. Photograph from the Earl Crum Collection.

Teheya'an	Kuhan	Nahupia	
Deer's	Male's	RFLX-Song	

Aan		kuantsi,	
horn		male = buck	

Aan		kuantsi	
horn		male = buck	

Imaayu		toowenete	mantu
become morning		grazing	towards

natsap<u>ai</u>kkantoote,
be killed with bow

natsap<u>ai</u>kkantoote,
be killed with bow

natsap<u>ai</u>kkantoote.
be killed with bow

COMMENTS

This is a *nua hupia* 'round dance song'. Earl Crum says, "This song is about a buck deer standing on the side of a hill early in the morning. And the hunter killed it with a bow and arrow." *Aan kuantsi* is the song form of *aan kuha* 'buck, stag' (< *aan* 'horn', *kuha* ~ *kuhma* 'male').

Pia Teheya'an Kuhan Nahupia 'Stag Song'
Earl Crum

Pia Teheya'an Kuhan Nahupia

Pia teheya'an kuantsi
Opi ipu maapinna.
Pia teheya'an kuantsi
Opi ipu maapinna.

Toyatepaka
Pia tuu wennete
Hainna.
Toyatepaka
Pia tuu wennete
Hainna.

Stag Song

Over there,
Big stag climbs up this way.
Over there,
Big stag climbs up this way.

On the side of the mountain
Stands a big dark silhouette.
Behold.
On the side of the mountain
Stands a big dark silhouette.
Behold.

Pia	Teheya'an	Kuhan	Nahupia
Big	Deer	Male's	RFLX-Song

Pia		teheya'an	kuantsi
big		deer	male = stag

45

Opi	ipu	maapinna.
around there	this way	climb up

Pia	teheya'an	kuantsi
big	deer	male = stag

Opi	ipu	maapinna.
around there	this way	climb up

Toyatepaka
mountain side-on

Pia	tuu	wennete
big	dark	stand (dur)

Hai̱nna.
rhythmical song word

Toyatepaka
mountain side-on

Pia	tuu	wennete
big	dark	stand (dur)

Hai̱nna.
rhythmical song word

COMMENTS

This is a *nua hupia* 'round dance song'. Earl Crum says, "This song is about a big buck deer. When a deer gets that big, some people call it a stag." *Maapi(nna)* is the song form of *maape(nna)* 'climb'. And *tepa* is the song form of *teppanna* '(on the) side (of)'.

Yepani Hupia 'Fall Song'
Earl Crum

Yepani Hupia

> Tamme yepatu,
> Tamme tuintsi,
> Tamme yepatu,
> Tamme tuintsi,
> Huuntukkantu
> Tap<u>aa</u>i pintoi pipuntu.
> Huuntukkantu
> Tap<u>aa</u>i pintsi pipuntu.
>
> Haiya wainna.

Fall Song

> Our fall,
> Our rebirth,
> Our fall,
> Our rebirth,
> But under the trees,
> The sun heads back (south).
> But under the trees,
> The sun heads back (south).
>
> *Haiya wainna.*

Yepani	Hupia
Fall	Song

Tamme	yepatu,
our (incl)	fall
Tamme	tuintsi,
our (incl)	rebirth

47

| Tamme | yepatu, |
| our (incl) | fall |

| Tamme | tuintsi, |
| our (incl) | rebirth |

Huuntukkantu
tree-under

| Tap<u>aai</u> | pintsi | pipuntu. |
| sun | but | go back |

Huuntukkantu
tree-under

| Tap<u>aai</u> | pintsi | pipuntu. |
| sun | but | go back |

Haiya wainna.

COMMENTS

This is a *nua hupia* 'round dance song'. Earl Crum says, "This song is about the beginning of fall. You know, the Indian calender is different from the white man's calender. When the sun reaches its highest point in the summer and starts to go back towards south, and the nights start to be colder, to the Indians, that is the beginning of fall. That's what this song is about."

The normal word for 'fall' is *yepani*, instead of the song word *yepatu* used here. The normal word for 'but' is *pinnah*, instead of *pintsi*. And *pipuntu* is not an ordinary word for 'go back' but is related to *pimpippu* 'backwards'. The suffix *-tu* found on *yepatu*, *pipuntu*, and *huuntukkantu* in this song, and on many other words in other songs, is a song suffix used for rhythm.

11
Kwahatenna Kuhan Nahupia
'Song of the Buck Antelope'
Earl Crum

Kwahatenna Kuhan Nahupia

> Wantsi nani naniyuu.
> Hainnaa.
> Wantsi naniyuu.
> Hainneh.
>
> Wantsi nani naniyuu.
> Hainnaa.
> Wantsi naniyuu.
> Hainneh.
>
> Tsaam puiwan kematu,
> Hainnaa,
> Wantsi naniyuu.
> Hainneh.

Song of the Buck Antelope

> Buck antelope is just at peace with himself.
> Behold!
> Duck antelope is at peace with himself.
>
> Buck antelope is just at peace with himself.
> Behold!
> Buck antelope is at peace with himself.
>
> Next to good green grass,
> Behold,
> Buck antelope is at peace with himself.

Kwahatenna	Kuhan	Nahupia	1st Version
Antelope	Male's	RFLX-Song	

Wantsi	nani	naniyuu.
buck antelope	just	be at peace with self

Hainnaa.
behold

Wantsi	naniyuu.
buck antelope	be at peace with self

Hainneh.
rhythmical song word

Tsaam	puiwan	kematu,
good	green grass's	next to

Hainnaa,
behold

Wantsi	naniyuu.
buck antelope	be at peace with self

Hainneh.
rhythmical song word

COMMENTS

This is a *nua hupia* 'round dance song', with several somewhat different versions. Earl Crum says, "You know, a long time ago when I was a little boy in Battle Mountain, the old people used to sing this song. It sounds like a mèdicine song. It's a song about a buck antelope grazing on green grass." The third version is not recorded on the CD.

Kwahatenna kuha, literally meaning 'antelope male', is a descriptive phrase for buck antelope. *Wantsi* is the normal word for 'buck antelope'. *Nani* is the song form of *nanah* 'just, only', used here to be in rhythm with following *naniyuu*.

Kwahatenna Kuhan Nahupia	2nd Version

Wantsi maniyuu,
Hainnaa.
Wantsi maniyuu,
Hainnaa.

A lone *wantsi* 'buck antelope', out in the sagebrush. Photograph by Earl Crum.

Wantsi maniyuu,
H<u>a</u>inneh.

Wantsi nehen kahnin kematuu,
H<u>a</u>innaa,
Wantsi maniyuu,
H<u>a</u>inneh.

Song of the Buck Antelope

Buck antelope is crossing the water,
H<u>a</u>innaa.
Buck antelope is crossing the water,
H<u>a</u>innaa.
Buck antelope is crossing the water,
H<u>a</u>inneh.

Buck antelope close to our house,
H<u>a</u>innaa,
Is crossing the water.
H<u>a</u>inneh.

Kwahatenna	Kuhan	Nahupia	2nd Version
Antelope	Male's	RFLX-Song	

Wantsi   maniyuu,
buck antelope   is crossing water

H<u>a</u>innaa.
rhythmical song word

Wantsi   maniyuu,
buck antelope   is crossing water

H<u>a</u>innaa.
rhythmical song word

Wantsi   maniyuu,
buck antelope   is crossing water

H<u>a</u>inneh.
rhythmical song word

Wantsi	nehen	kahnin	kematuu,
buck antelope	our (dl excl)	house's	close to

Hainnaa,
rhythmical song word

Wantsi	maniyuu,
buck antelope	is crossing water

Hainneh.
rhythmical song word

Kwahatenna Kuhan Nahupia   3rd Version

Wantsi maniyuu,
Hainnaa.
Wantsi maniyuu,
Hainnaa.
Wantsi maniyuu.
Hainneh.

Tsaam puiwan kematuu.
Hainnaa.
Wantsi maniyuu.
Hainneh.

Song of the Buck Antelope

Buck antelope is crossing the water,
Hainnaa.
Buck antelope is crossing the water,
Hainnaa.
Buck antelope is crossing the water.
Hainneh.

Next to nice green grass,
Hainnaa.
Buck antelope is crossing the water.
Hainneh.

Kwahatenna   Kuhan   Nahupia   3rd Version
Antelope   Male's   RFLX-Song

Wantsi   maniyuu,
buck antelope   be crossing water

Hainnaa.
rhythmical song word

Wantsi   maniyuu,
buck antelope   be crossing water

Hainnaa.
rhythmical song word

Wantsi   maniyuu.
buck antelope   be crossing water

Hainneh.
rhythmical song word

Tsaam   puiwan   kematuu.
good   green grass'   next to

Hainnaa.
rhythmical song word

Wantsi   maniyuu.
buck antelope   be crossing water

Hainneh.
rhythmical song word

Tekaitennan Nahupia 'Song of the Hunter'
Earl Crum

Tekaitennan Nahupia   1st Version

   Watsepin tsukumpe,
   Watsepin tsukumpe,
   Watsepin tsukumpe.

   Watsepin tsukumpe,
   Watsepin tsukumpe,
   Watsepin tsukumpe.

   Huuntoyan kematuu
   Tuu winnookinna,
   Tuu winnookinna.

   Huuntoyan kematuu
   Tuu winnookinna,
   Tuu winnookinna.

Song of the Hunter

   Hunter,
   Hunter,
   Hunter.

   Hunter,
   Hunter,
   Hunter.

   Next to a wooded mountain
   He is a dark shadow walking along,
   A dark shadow walking along.

   Next to a wooded mountain
   He is a dark shadow walking along,
   A dark shadow walking along.

Mi'akinna, mi'akinna 'walk along, walk along'—as Beverly Crum chants these words to the beat of a drum, children at the tribal Head Start center join hands and walk along with her. The children learn the meaning of different action words by listening to the chant and doing as the words say. This is fun time and good exercise as well. Photograph by Sandy Jones.

Tek<u>a</u>itennan   Nahupia   1st Version
Hunter's   RFLX-Song

Watsepin tsukumpe,
hunter

Watsepin tsukumpe,
hunter

Watsepin tsukumpe.
hunter

Huuntoyan   kematuu
wood-mountain   next to

Tuu   winnookinna,
dark   walk along with head bobbing up and down

Tuu   winnookinna.
dark   walk along with head bobbing up and down

Huuntoyan   kematuu
wood-mountain   next to

Tuu   winnookinna,
dark   walk along with head bobbing up and down

Tuu   winnookinna.
dark   walk along with head bobbing up and down

COMMENTS

This is a *nua hupia* 'round dance song'. Earl Crum says, "This song is about a hunter walking at a distance like a shadow." The second version is not recorded on the CD.

Watsempin tsukumpe is the song form of *waseppeh tsukuppe* 'hunter', which is derived from *waseppeh* 'killed (pl)' and *tsukuppe* 'old man'. Another common word for hunter is *tek<u>a</u>ite(n)*.

Tek<u>a</u>itennan Nahupia   2nd Version

Watsepin tsukumpe,
Watsepin tsukumpe,
Watsepin tsukumpe.

Watsepin tsukumpe,
Watsepin tsukumpe,
Watsepin tsukumpe.

Pennan natoyaa pai
Tuu winnookinna,
Tuu winnookinna.

Pennan natoyaa pai
Tuu winnookinna,
Tuu winnookinna.

Haiya wainna.

Song of the Hunter

Hunter,
Hunter,
Hunter.

Hunter,
Hunter,
Hunter.

Over his own mountain
He is a dark shadow walking along,
A dark shadow walking along.

Over his own mountain
He is a dark shadow walking along,
A dark shadow walking along.

Haiya wainna.

Tek<u>ai</u>tennan	Nahupia	2nd Version
Hunter's	RFLX-Song	

Watsepin tsukumpe,
hunter

Watsepin tsukumpe,
hunter

Watsepin tsukumpe.
hunter

Watsepin tsukumpe,
hunter

Watsepin tsukumpe,
hunter

Watsepin tsukumpe.
hunter

Pennan	natoyaa	pai
his own	RFLX-mountain	on

Tuu	winnookinna,
dark	walk along with head bobbing up and down

Tuu	winnookinna.	—
dark	walk along with head bobbing up and down	

Pennan	natoyaa	pai
his own	RFLX-mountain	on

Tuu	winnookinna,
dark	walk along with head bobbing up and down

Tuu	winnookinna.
dark	walk along with head bobbing up and down

Haiya wainna.

Ainkam Pehyen Nahupia 'Song of the Red Duck'
Earl Crum

Ainkam Pehyen Nahupia

Ainkam pehyennan tuantsi,
Ainkam pehye,
Hapin kuukinna,
Oyom paa tu pintsi,
Ainkam paa tu nonowa hapiikinna.

Ainkam pehyennan tuantsi,
Ainkam pehye,
Hapin kuukinna,
Oyom paa tu pintsi,
Ainkam paa tu nonowa hapiikinna.

Haiya wainna.

Song of the Red Duck

Child of a red duck,
Red duck,
Floating along diving,
Always sucking through the water,
Through the red water floating along.

Child of a red duck,
Red duck,
Floating along diving,
Always sucking through the water,
Through the red water floating along.

Haiya wainna.

Ainkam	Pehyen	Nahupia
Red	Duck's	RFLX-Song

Ainkam	pehyennan	tuantsi,
red	duck's	baby

Ainkam	pehye,
red	duck

Hapin	kuukinna,
float	dive along

Oyom	paa	tu	pintsi,
always	water	through	suck

Ainkam	paa	tu	nonowa	hapiikinna.
red	water	through	move (?)	float along

Ainkam	pehyennan	tuantsi,
red	duck's	baby

Ainkam	pehye,
red	duck

Hapin	kuukinna,
float	dive along

Oyom	paa	tu	pintsi,
always	water	through	suck

Ainkam	paa	tu	nonowa	hapiikinna.
red	water	through	move (?)	float along

Haiya wainna.
blessed

COMMENTS

This is a *nua hupia* 'round dance song'. Earl Crum says, "You know a long time ago, the early Indians used to go through a ritual by going through different motions with their hands and with the words they said. And every time you hear in a song where they say *hainna* or *haiya wainna*, they are blessing the song."

Pintsi is the song form of *pitsi* 'suck, suckle'. *Nonowa* is not a normal word but is probably related to the auxiliary verb *nooh* 'move about', itself from the main verb *noo"* 'carry'. *Ainkam pehyen* literally means 'red duck' but it is a kind of teal with a red head. The red water in this song is refering to the water at sunset reflecting the redness of the sky.

Pia Kuittsunnan Nahupia 'Song of the Big Buffalo'
Earl Crum

Pia Kuittsunnan Nahupia

> Pia kuittsunna yewampontsi,
> Yewampontsi.
> Yaaya wainna.
>
> Pia kuittsunna yewampontsi,
> Yewampontsi.
> Yaaya wainna.
>
> Pui'awatsi yunkite,
> Pui'awatsi yunkite.
> Yaaya wainna.
>
> Haiya wainna.

Song of the Big Buffalo

> He was tracking Big Buffalo,
> Tracking him.
> *Yaaya wainna.*
>
> He was tracking Big Buffalo,
> Tracking him.
> *Yaaya wainna.*
>
> But Big Buffalo spied him and sneaked away.
> Big Buffalo spied him and sneaked away.
> *Yaaya wainna.*
>
> *Haiya wainna.*

Pia	Kuittsunnan	Nahupia
Big	Buffalo's	RFLX-Song

Pia	kuittsunna	yewampontsi,
big	buffalo-O	track

Yewampontsi.
track

Yaaya wainna.
rhythmical song words

Pia	kuittsunna	yewampontsi,
big	buffalo-O	track

Yewampontsi.
track

Yaaya wainna.
rhythmical song words

Pui'awatsi	yunkite,
spy	moving away

Pui'awatsi	yunkite.
spy	moving away

Yaaya wainna.
rhythmical song words

Haiya wainna.

COMMENTS

This is a *nua hupia* 'round dance song'. Earl Crum says, "This song is about a big buffalo that a hunter is tracking. And as he goes tracking the buffalo, the buffalo saw him and sneaked away." *Yewampontsi* is the song word for 'track' and 'take aim'. The ordinary words for 'track' are *nampuih* or *nayaa*, and *wapuih* is the normal word for 'take aim'. *Pui'awatsi* is the song word for 'spy (on)'; the ordinary word is *watsippuih*.

Although buffalo were prevalent in massive herds on the Great Plains, they were also not uncommon in small herds on the Snake River Plain and in grassy areas of the Great Basin in aboriginal times.

Huittsaannan Nahupia 'Song of the Sage Hen'
Earl Crum

Huittsaannan Nahupia

Huintsaantsi wian katete mantu
Pomiakwaainna,
Pomiakwaainna,
Huintsaantsi wian katete mantu
Pomiakwaainna,
Pomiakwaainna,
Yuwaa tosam pasiwampaa
O miakwainna.
Yuwaa tosam pasiwampaa
O miakwainna.

Haiya wainna.

Song of the Sage Hen

Sage Hen landing on a mountain pass
Migrating around,
Migrating around,
Sage Hen landing on a mountain pass
Migrating around,
Migrating around,
Walks around there
On warm white sand.
Walks around there
On warm white sand.

Haiya wainna.

Huittsaannan   Nahupia
Sage Hen's   RFLX-Song

Huintsaantsi	wian	katete	mantu
sage hen	pass	landing	towards

Pomiakwaainna,
migrating around

Pomiakwaainna,
migrating around

Huintsaantsi	wian	katete	mantu
sage hen	pass	landing	towards

Pomiakwaainna,
migrating around

Pomiakwaainna,
migrating around

Yuwaa	tosam	pasiwampaa
warm	white	sand-on

O	miakwainna.
there	walk around

Yuwaa	tosam	pasiwampaa
warm	white	sand-on

O	miakwainna.
there	walk around

Haiya wainna.
blessed

COMMENTS

This is a *nua hupia* 'round dance song'. *Huintsaantsi* is the song word for 'sage hen'; the ordinary word is *huittsaa(n)*. *Pomia(kwaai)* is the song form of *pomi'a(kwai)* 'migrate (around) [of birds]'.

A flock of *huittsaan* 'sage hen'. Tribal members of the Duck Valley Reservation consider the meat of *huittsaa* a gourmet treat. People both on and off the reservation have overhunted the *huittsaan*, and their numbers have dwindled at an alarming rate. Tribal members are asking people not to hunt more than they need. Photograph by Earl Crum.

A lone *huittsaa* 'sage hen' in Earl Crum's backyard. Photograph by Earl Crum.

16

Hoakkantennan Nahupia 'Song of the Warrior'
Beverly Crum

Hoakkantennan Nahupia

Hoakkantem punkukante,
Ta taa pawene pawaiyente
Hainneh.

Hoakkantem punkukante,
Ta taa pawene pawaiyente
Hainneh.

Yooti! Yootiii! Yooti! I yooti! Yooti! Yooti!
Hainneh.
Yooti! Yootiii! Yooti! I yooti! Yooti! Yooti!
Hainneh.

Song of the Warrior

Clearly in the early dawn
A warrior, a horseman, stands
High above us.
Behold!

Clearly in the early dawn
A warrior, a horseman, stands
High above us.
Behold!

Arise! Arise! Arise! O arise! Arise! Arise!
Hainneh.
Arise! Arise! Arise! O arise! Arise! Arise!
Hainneh.

Hoakkantennan   Nahupia
Warrior's   RFLX-Song

Hoakkantem		punkukante,	
warrior/bowman		horseman	

Ta	taa	pawene	pawaiyente
us	predawn	clear-stand	high above-from

Hainneh.
rhythmical song word

Hoakkantem		punkukante,	
warrior/bowman		horseman	

Ta	taa	pawene	pawaiyente
us	predawn	clear-stand	high above-from

Hainneh.
rhythmical song word

Yooti!	Yootiii!	Yooti!	I
arise (pl)	arise (pl)	arise (pl)	song word
yooti!	Yooti!	Yooti!	
arise (pl)	arise (pl)	arise	

Hainneh.
rhythmical song word

Yooti!	Yootiii!	Yooti!	I
arise (pl)	arise (pl)	arise (pl)	song word
yooti!	Yooti!	Yooti!	
arise (pl)	arise (pl)	arise	

Hainneh.
rhythmical song word

COMMENTS

This is a *nua hupia* 'round dance song'. Earl Crum says, "This is a song about the warrior . . . Early in the morning before daylight, the singer looked up into the sky and saw the formation of stars, Orion, and sang about it." *Yooti"* is the plural form of the verb 'arise, get up; fly off'. Here it is directed to the singer's listeners, whom she encourages to rise above their problems and the things that hold them down. This offers them a blessing of hope for better things to come. And on a more practical level, it means for them not to be involved in too much sleep, unaware of what is going on around them. *Ta* is a short song form for *tamme(n)* 'us (pl)'.

Tuittsi'an Nahupia 'Song of the Young Man'
Earl Crum

Tuittsi'an Nahupia

> Tammen nemen tuantsi paa nanku
> Punku kate kimmannoo.
> Hainna.

> Tammen nemen tuantsi paa nanku
> Punku kate kimmannoo.
> Hainna.

> Tamme hunupaa seepi
> Pui patewintsi.

> Tammem paa nanku nemen tuantsi
> Punku kate kimmannoo.
> Hainna.

> Tammem paa nanku nemen tuantsi
> Punku kate kimmannoo.
> Hainna.

> Tamme hunupaa seepi
> Pui patewintsi.

> Haiya wainna.

Song of the Young Man

> Our young man from high above
> Comes riding along on a horse.
> Behold!

> Our young man from high above
> Comes riding along on a horse.
> Behold!

Above our canyon to the willows,
To the little green willow shoots.

From high above,
Comes our young man riding along on a horse.
Behold!

From high above,
Comes our young man riding along on a horse.
Behold!

Above our canyon to the willows,
To the little green willow shoots.

Haiya wainna.

Tuittsi'an   Nahupia
Young Man's   RFLX-Song

Tammen	nemen	tuantsi	paa	nanku
our (incl)	person	young	above	from side of

Punku	kate	kimmannoo.		
horse	sit	come-moving along		

Hainna.
rhythmical song word

Tammen	nemen	tuantsi	paa	nanku
our (incl)	person	young	above	from side of

Punku	kate	kimmannoo.		
horse	sit	come-moving along		

Hainna.
rhythmical song word

Tamme	hunupaa	seepi		
our (incl)	canyon-above	willow		

Pui	patewintsi.			
green	willow shoot			

Tammem	paa	nanku	nemen	tuantsi
our (incl)	above	from side of	person	young

Punku	kate	kimmannoo.		
horse	sit	come-moving along		

Ha<u>i</u>nna.
rhythmical song word

Tammem	paa	nanku	nemen	tuantsi
our (incl)	above	from side of	person	young

Punku	kate	kimmannoo.	
horse	sit	come-moving along	

Ha<u>i</u>nna.
rhythmical song word

Tamme	hunupaa	seepi
our (incl)	canyon-above	willow

Pui	patewintsi.
green	willow shoot

Haiya wainna.

Comments

This is a *nua hupia* 'round dance song'. Earl Crum says, "This is a song about a young man coming down from above, riding on a horse." The song can be interpreted both in the physical sense of a young man riding down from higher ground, but also in a more spiritual sense of a youth riding down from the heavens above. *Paa(n)* is the song form of *pa'a(n)* 'over, above, on (top of)'.

Upi Katete 'There She Sits'
Beverly Crum

Upi Katete

Upii katete hunum ma
Tepai yantum ma.
Hainneh.
Upii katete hunum ma
Tepai yantum ma.
Hainneh.

Ainka tempi huutepana
Tepai yantum ma.
Hainneh.
Ainka tempi huutepana
Tepai yantum ma.
Hainneh.

Haiya wainna.

There She Sits

There she sits in a canyon
Winnowing pinenuts.
Hainneh.
There she sits in a canyon
Winnowing pinenuts.
Hainneh.

Near the red rocks by the woods
Winnowing pinenuts.
Hainneh.
Near the red rocks by the woods
Winnowing pinenuts.
Hainneh.

Haiya wainna.

Upi   Katete
There   Sit

| Upii | katete | hunum | ma |
| there out of sight | sit | canyon | in |

| Tepai | yantum | ma. | |
| pine nut-o | winnowing tray | with | |

Hainneh.
rhythmical song word

| Upii | katete | hunum | ma |
| there out of sight | sit | canyon | in |

| Tepai | yantum | ma. | |
| pinenut-o | winnowing tray | with | |

Hainneh.
rhythmical song word

| Ainka | tempi | huutepana | |
| red | rock | wood-on side of | |

| Tepai | yantum | ma. | |
| pinenut-o | winnowing tray | with | |

Hainneh.
rhythmical song word

| Ainka | tempi | huutepana | |
| red | rock | wood-on side of | |

| Tepai | yantum | ma. | |
| pinenut-o | winnowing tray | with | |

Hainneh.
rhythmical song word

Haiya wainna.

COMMENTS

This is a *nua hupia* 'round dance song'. Pinenuts were one of the most important staple foods for the Western Shoshoni. Several families would gather together in the fall to collect and prepare them and celebrate the harvest.

Piatetsii'an Nahupia 'Song of Wild Rice'
Earl Crum

Piatetsii'an Nahupia

> Piatetsii, piatesiii
> Yomman<u>ai</u> piatetsii,
> Yomman<u>ai</u>.
> Piatetsii, piatesiii
> Yomman<u>ai</u> piatetsii.
>
> Yomman<u>ai</u> puittempi puittenkahan katsunka,
> Puittenkahan katsunkante.
> H<u>ai</u>nneh.
> Puittempi puittenkahan katsunka,
> Puittenkahan katsunkante.
> H<u>ai</u>nneh.

Song of Wild Rice

> Wild rice, wild rice,
> Wild rice swaying in the wind,
> Swaying in the wind.
> Wild rice, wild rice,
> Wild rice swaying in the wind.
>
> Swaying on the green rocks at the end of a grassy meadow,
> At the end of a grassy meadow.
> *Hainneh.*
> On the green rocks at the end of a grassy meadow,
> At the end of a grassy meadow.
> *Hainneh.*

Piatetsii'an   Nahupia
Wild Rice's   RFLX-Song

> Piatetsii   piatesiii
> wild rice   wild rice
>
> Yomman<u>ai</u>   piatetsii,
> sway (pl) in the wind   wild rice
>
> Yomman<u>ai</u>.
> sway (pl) in the wind
>
> Piatetsii,   piatesiii
> wild rice   wild rice
>
> Yomman<u>ai</u>   piatetsii.
> sway (pl) in the wind   wild rice
>
> Yomman<u>ai</u>   puittempi   puittenkahan   katsunka,
> sway (pl) in the wind   green rock   grass place's   end of-at
>
> Puittenkahan   katsunkante.
> green place's   end of-at
>
> Hainneh.
> rhythmical song word
>
> Puittempi   puittenkahan   katsunka,
> green rock   grass place's   end of-at
>
> Puittenkahan   katsunkante.
> grass place's   end of-at
>
> H<u>ai</u>nneh.
> rhythmical song word

COMMENTS

This is a *nua hupia* 'round dance song'. Earl Crum says, "A long time ago, the Indians used to go out and harvest this plant, *piatetsii* 'wild rice'. But the plant doesn't grow anymore. The cattle, the sheep, and the horses ate them all up, and the plant just couldn't reproduce itself. It has become extinct. Some people identify it as tall rye grass, which is good to eat too. But that is not as numerous as *piatetsii* used to be."

Toyakaitennan Nahupia 'Thunder Song'
Earl Crum

Toyakaitennan Nahupia

Toyakainnai tuu winkum mantu,
Toyakainnai tuu winkum mantu.
Paa tottsapikka tukkan naitu winkum mantu.

Toyakainnai tuu winkum mantu,
Toyakainnai tuu winkum mantu.
Paa tottsapikka tukkan naitu winkum mantu.

Toyakainnai tuu winkum mantu,
Toyakainnai tuu winkum mantu.
Paa tottsapikka tukkan naitu winkum mantu.

Haiya wainna.

Thunder Song

Rumbling thundering darkness breaks loose,
Rumbling thundering darkness breaks loose.
Water crashing breaks away downward.

Rumbling thundering darkness breaks loose,
Rumbling thundering darkness breaks loose.
Water crashing breaks away downward.

Rumbling thundering darkness breaks loose,
Rumbling thundering darkness breaks loose.
Water crashing breaks away downward.

Haiya wainna.

| Toyaka<u>ai</u>tennan | Nahupia |
| Thunder's | RFLX-Song |

| Toyak<u>ai</u>nnai | tuu | winkum | mantu, |
| thundering | dark | break away | toward |

| Toyak<u>ai</u>nnai | tuu | winkum | mantu. |
| thundering | dark | break away | toward |

Paa	tottsapikka	tukkan	naitu
water	make crashing sound	down	from
winkum	mantu.		
break away	toward		

| Toyak<u>ai</u>nnai | tuu | winkum | mantu, |
| thundering | dark | break away | toward |

| Toyak<u>ai</u>nnai | tuu | winkum | mantu. |
| thundering | dark | break away | toward |

Paa	tottsapikka	tukkan	naitu
water	make crashing sound	down	from
winkum	mantu.		
break away	toward		

| Toyak<u>ai</u>nnai | tuu | winkum | mantu, |
| thundering | dark | break away | toward |

| Toyak<u>ai</u>nnai | tuu | winkum | mantu. |
| thundering | dark | break away | toward |

Paa	tottsapikka	tukkan	naitu
water	make crashing sound	down	from
winkum	mantu.		
break away	toward		

Haiya wainna.
blessed

COMMENTS

This is a *nua hupia* 'round dance song'. It is about the ominous and frightful flash floods that can happen any time in the desert West. *Winkum* is the song form of *wikkah(ku)* 'break away, break loose, give way'.

Pa'emah Hupia 'Rain Song'
Earl Crum

Pa'emah Hupia

> Tammen toya'ana katetenna mannai,
> Kutsiwaa paa nopii.
> Hainneh.
>
> Tammen toya'ana katetenna mannai,
> Kutsiwaa paa nopii.
> Hainneh.
>
> Kutsiwaa ha tammen tuu ha tammen tuu?
> Hainneh.
>
> Kutsiwaa ha tammen tuu ha tammen tuu?
> Hainneh.
>
> Haiya wainna.

Rain Song

> From the top of the mountain
> Dust and rain are coming our way.
> Look!
>
> From the top of the mountain
> Dust and rain are coming our way.
> Look!
>
> Is the dust storm coming our way, coming our way?
> Look!
>
> Is the dust storm coming our way, coming our way?
> Look!

Pa'emah   Hupia
Rain   Song

Tammen	toya'ana	katetenna	mannai,
our (incl)	mountain top	sitting-O	from

Kutsiwaa	paa	nopii.
dust storm	water	arrive

Hainneh.
rhythmical song word

Tammen	toya'ana	katetenna	mannai,
our (incl)	mountain top	sitting-O	from

Kutsiwaa	paa	nopii.
dust storm	water	arrive

Hainneh.
rhythmical song word

Kutsiwaa	ha	tammen	tuu	ha	tammen tuu?
dust storm	Q	us (incl)	through	Q	us (incl) through

Hainneh.
rhythmical song word

Kutsiwaa	ha	tammen	tuu	ha	tammen tuu?
dust storm	Q	us (incl)	through	Q	us (incl) through

Hainneh.
rhythmical song word

Haiya wainna.

COMMENTS

This is a *nua hupia* 'round dance song'. In this song the singer could use *hapite(n)* 'lying' instead of *katete(n)* 'sitting'. *Toyahapite(n)* means 'mountain range', literally, 'mountain lying', while *toyakatete(n)* means a single large 'mountain sitting' alone. *Nopii* is the song form for *noopite* 'arrive'.

22
Tempitta Nemittan Nahupia
'Song of the Rock Walker'
Earl Crum

Tempitta Nemittan Nahupia

> Tempitta nemittan kematuu,
> Tempitta nemittan kematuu
> Tenaa tempi,
> Tempin tuun nuwa,
> Nanka yunkinnoote.
> Tenaa tempi,
> Tempin tuun nuwa,
> Nanka yunkinnoote.
>
> Haiya wainna.

Song of the Rock Walker

> Next to the Rock Walker,
> Next to the Rock Walker,
> Rocks falling away,
> Rocks rolling down,
> Echoing fading away.
> Rocks falling away,
> Rocks rolling down,
> Echoing fading away.
>
> *Haiya wainna.*

Tempitta	Nemittan	Nahupia
Rock-o	Walker's	RFLX-Song
Tempitta	nemittan	kematuu,
rock-o	walker's	next to

Tempitta	nemittan	kematuu
rock-o	walker's	next to

Tenaa	tempi,
down	rock

Tempin	tuun	nuwa,
rock	down	move

Nanka	yunkinnoote.
sounding	move away-moving along

Tenaa	tempi,
down	rock

Tempin	tuun	nuwa,
rock	down	move

Nanka	yunkinnoote.
sounding	move away-moving along

Haiya wainna.

COMMENTS

This is a *nua hupia* 'round dance song'. Earl Crum says, "This song is called 'The Rock Walker'. It is about a person walking on a hill, and he is rolling the rocks down. And as the rock goes rolling down, he listens to it as it goes away from him."

The noun-forming suffix *-tta* on *nemitta* 'walker, wanderer' (< *nemi* 'walk around, wander, roam') is not a normal agentive noun suffix in Western Shoshoni, although it is probably historically related to the regular agentive suffix *-ttü* in Panamint (Tümpisa) Shoshoni (see Dayley 1989, 237). *Tuun* before *nuwa* is a short form of *tenaa* 'down'.

23
Tsaan Napuni Tamme Sokopi
'How Beautiful Is Our Land'
Beverly Crum

Tsaan Napuni Tamme Sokopi

> Tsaan napuni taai sokopii,
> Tsaan napuni taai sokopi,
> Oyom paam paanan kematu.
> Tsaan napuni taai sokopi.
>
> Tsaan napuni taai sokopii,
> Tsaan napuni taai sokopi,
> Sokotontsiyam ma paan kematu
> Tsaan napuni taai sokopi.
>
> Haiya wainna.

How Beautiful Is Our Land

> How beautiful is our land,
> How beautiful is our land,
> Forever near the water, the water.
> How beautiful is our land.
>
> How beautiful is our land,
> How beautiful is our land,
> Earth flowers bloom next to the water.
> How beautiful is our land.
>
> *Haiya wainna.*

Tsaan	Napuni	Tamme	Sokopi
Beautiful	Look	Our	Land

Tsaan	napuni	taai	sokopii,
beautiful	look	our (incl)	land

Tsaan	napuni	taai	sokopi,
beautiful	look	our (incl)	land

Oyom	paam	paanan	kematu.
always	water	water's	next to

Tsaan	napuni	taai	sokopi,
beautiful	look	our (incl)	land

Tsaan	napuni	taai	sokopii,
beautiful	look	our (incl)	land

Tsaan	napuni	taai	sokopi.
beautiful	look	our (incl)	land

Sokotontsiyam	ma	paan	kematu
earth flower	with	water	next to

Tsaan	napuni	taai	sokopi.
beautiful	look	our (incl)	land

Haiya wainna.

Comments

This is a *nua hupia* 'round dance song'. Earl Crum says, "You know, early in the morning when the sun comes up, and a little after, the singer would sing this song. And when he would get through singing this song, having danced all night, the people would go home." *Taai* is the poetic word used in this song for normal *tai(n)* ~ *tamme(n)* 'our (incl)'. Some singers use *tewaai* instead of *taai*.

Sokotontsiyam ma paan kematu / Tsaan napuni tai sokopi, 'Earth flowers bloom forth next to the water / How beautiful is our land'. Here, a grove of quaking aspen stands near a mountain stream flowing down a ravine. Growing on its banks are lupines, lavender, and lavender iris. Photograph by Beverly Crum.

Pia Isan Nahupia 'Wolf Song'
Beverly Crum

Pia Isan Nahupia

Pia Isam peentsi
Pennan kwasin katsunka
U piyaatehki,
Piyaatehki,
Piyaatehki,
Piyaattua noote.
Piyaatehki,
Piyaattua noote.

Haiya wainna.

Wolf Song

Furry Wolf
On his tail
Carries him away,
Carries him away,
Carries him away,
Carries the child away.
Carries him away,
Carries the child away.

Haiya wainna.

Pia Isan	Nahupia
Wolf's	RFLX-Song

Pia Isam	peentsi
wolf	furry

Pennan	kwasin	katsunka
his own	tail's	end of-at

U	piyaatehki,
him	with behind-carry-start

Piyaatehki,
with behind-carry-start

Piyaatehki,
with behind-carry-start

Piyaattua	noote.
with behind-carry-child	carrying on back

Piyaatehki,
with behind-carry-start

Piyaattua	noote.
with behind-carry-child	carrying on back

Haiya wainna.

COMMENTS

This is a *nua hupia* 'round dance song'. The song makes reference to a saying that parents used to say to misbehaving children: *Ukka kai en ten-ankanku, Itsappe en kwasi pinnookkwanto'i.* 'If you don't behave, Coyote will carry you off on his tail.' Another warning to misbehaving children was that *Tsu'apiiiseh*, a mythological monster who ate people, would come from the mountains and carry them off. Both of these sayings are much like when English speaking parents say, "If you don't behave, the boogeyman will get you." Shoshonis say *Pia Isa* 'Wolf' and *Itsappe* 'Coyote' are *nanapapinneweh* 'brothers'. In this song *Pia Isa*, not *Itsappe*, is carrying the child off on his tail.

Kamme Hupia 'Jackrabbit Song'
Earl Crum

Kamme Hupia

> Tammem maananku
> Pohotoyapi.
> Hainna.
> Tammem maananku
> Pohotoyapi.
> Hainna, oyo wia paa
> Kammentsi.
> Hainna.
> Kammentsi.
> Hainna.

Jackrabbit Song

> Before us in the distance
> Is the sage covered mountain.
> Look!
> Before us in the distance
> Is the sage covered mountain.
> Look! On every mountain pass
> Jackrabbits.
> Look!
> Jackrabbits.
> Look!

Kamme	Hupia
Jackrabbit	Song

Tammem	maananku
us (incl)	far away from

Jim Crum with rabbits he hunted, about 1928 or 1929, near Battle Mountain.
Photograph from the Earl Crum Collection.

Pohotoyapi.
sagebrush mountain

Ha̱inna.
rhythmical song word

Tammem	maananku
us (incl)	far away from

Pohotoyapi.
sagebrush mountain

Ha̱inna,	oyo	wia	paa
rhythmical song word	every	mountain pass	on

Kammentsi.
jackrabbit-diminutive

Ha̱inna.
rhythmical song word

Kammentsi.
jackrabbit-diminutive

Ha̱inna.
rhythmical song word

COMMENTS

This is a *nua hupia* 'round dance song'. *Kammentsi* is the affectionate endearing song form of ordinary *kamme ~ kammu* 'jackrabbit'. Jackrabbits were an important food source and also prized for their fur to make rabbit-skin blankets. *Paa* is the song form of *pa'a(n)* 'on (top of)'.

26

Pimmaa Tuintsi 'Young Calves'
Earl Crum

Pimmaa Tuintsi

Pimmaa tuintsi pimma tuintsi,
Pimmaa tuintsi pimma tuintsi,
Paan kemaa tuu.
Tuintsi kwakkwapiikinna.
Paan kemaa tuu.
Tuintsi kwakkwapiikinna.

Pimmaa tuintsi pimma tuintsi,
Pimmaa tuintsi pimma tuintsi,
Paan kemaa tuu,
Tuintsi kwakkwapiikinna.
Paan kemaa tuu.
Tuintsi kwakkwapiikinna.

Young Calves

Young calves, young calves,
Young calves, young calves,
Next to the water,
Young ones lying around,
Next to the water,
Young ones lying around.

Young calves, young calves,
Young calves, young calves,
Next to the water,
Young ones lying around,
Next to the water,
Young ones lying around.

Pimmaa	Tuintsi
bovine	young

Pimmaa	tuintsi	pimma	tuintsi,
bovine	young	bovine	young

Pimmaa	tuintsi	pimma	tuintsi,
bovine	young	bovine	young

Paan	kemaa	tuu.
water's	side of	song word

Tuintsi	kwakkwapiikinna.
young	be lying around (pl distrib)

Paan	kemaa	tuu.
water's	side of	song word

Tuintsi	kwakkwapiikinna.
young	be lying around (pl distrib)

Pimmaa	tuintsi	pimma	tuintsi,
bovine	young	bovine	young

Pimmaa	tuintsi	pimma	tuintsi,
bovine	young	bovine	young

Paan	kemaa	tuu.
water's	side of	song word

Tuintsi	kwakkwapiikinna.
young	be lying around (pl distrib)

Paan	kemaa	tuu.
water's	side of	song word

Tuintsi	kwakkwapiikinna.
young	be lying around (pl distrib)

COMMENTS

This is a *nua hupia* 'round dance song'. *Pimma(a) tuantsi* is related to Comanche *pimmorua* 'calf'. *Pimma(a)* is not an ordinary word in Shoshoni. *Kwakkwapiikinna* is the distributive song form of *kwapi"* 'lie (down)' plural.

Oyon Tempi 'Every Rock'
Earl Crum

Oyon Tempi   1st Interpretation

> Oyon tempi aiwan tempi
> Patemmam pii toi.
> Oyon tempi patemmam pii toi
> Oyon tempi aiwan tempi
> Patemmam pii toi.
>
> Oyon tempi patemmam pii toi
> Totsappaa wooyompa
> Patemmam pii.
> Totsappaa wooyompa
> Patemmam pii.
>
> Oyon tempi aiwan tempi
> Patemmam pii toi.
> Oyon tempi patemmam pii toi
> Totsappaa wooyompa
> Patemmam pii
> Totsappaa wooyompa
> Patemmam pii.

Every Rock   1st Interpretation

> Every rock, rocks like this,
> Throw around in the pool.
> Throw every rock around in the water.
> Every rock, rocks like this,
> Throw around in the pool.
>
> Throw every rock around in the pool.
> They splash around
> In the white water,
> They splash around
> In the white water.

93

Every rock, rocks like this,
Throw around in the pool.
Throw every rock around in the water.
They splash around
In the white water,
They splash around
In the white water.

Oyon	Tempi		1st Interpretation	
Every	Rock			
Oyon	tempi	aiwan	tempi	
every	rock	this-like	rock	
Patemmam	pii	toi.		
pool of water	around	throw		
Oyon	tempi	patemmam	pii	toi
every	rock	pool of water	around	throw
Oyon	tempi	aiwan	tempi	
every	rock	this-like	rock	
Patemmam	pii	toi.		
pool of water	around	throw		
Oyon '	tempi	patemmam	pii	toi
every	rock	pool of water	around	throw
Totsappaa	wooyompa			
white-water	splash			
Patemmam	pii.			
pool of water	around			
Totsappaa	wooyompa			
white-water	splash			
Patemmam	pii.			
pool of water	around			
Oyon	tempi	aiwan	tempi	
every	rock	this-like	rock	

Patemmam	pii	toi.		
pool of water	around	throw		

Oyon	tempi	patemmam	pii	toi
every	rock	pool of water	around	throw

Totsappaa	wooyompa
white-water	splash

Patemmam	pii
pool of water	around

Totsappaa	wooyompa
white-water	splash

Patemmam	pii.
pool of water	around

COMMENTS

This is a *nua hupia* 'round dance song'. The song has two totally different interpretations. The first makes reference to skipping stones, especially small flat cobblestones *patsittempi*, around in the water. The second interpretation is given on the following two pages. In both interpretations *aiwan* is the song form of <u>ai</u>wa'ih 'like this'. In the first version, *toi* is the song form of *tawiih* 'throw'. *Patemmam pii* is a song word from *pakateten* 'body of water, pool' plus the song form *pii* of the postposition *pai* 'around (in an undefined area)'. *Wooyompa* means 'splash' and is a song word but not related to any ordinary word. The normal word for 'splash' is *pakwittsu'ih*.

Oyon Tempi   2nd Interpretation

<u>O</u>yon tempi <u>ai</u>wan tempi
Patemmampii toi.
Oyon tempi patemmampii toi
Oyon tempi <u>ai</u>wan tempi
Patemmampii toi.

Oyon tempi patemmampii toi
Totsappaa wooyompa
Patemmampii
Totsappaa wooyompa
Patemmampii.

Oyon tempi aiwan tempi
Patemmampii toi.
Oyon tempi patemmampii toi
Totsappaa wooyompa
Patemmampii
Totsappaa wooyompa
Patemmampii.

Every Rock   2nd Interpretation

From under every rock, rocks like this,
Water-rock creatures emerge.
From under every rock, water-rock creatures emerge.
From under every rock, rocks like this,
Water-rock creatures emerge.

From under every rock, water-rock creatures emerge,
White water worms,
Water-rock creatures,
White water worms,
Water-rock creatures.

From under every rock, rocks like this,
Water rock creatures emerge.
From under every rock, water-rock creatures emerge.
White water worms,
Water-rock creatures,
White water worms,
Water-rock creatures.

Oyon	Tempi		2nd Interpretation
Every	Rock		
Oyon	tempi	aiwan	tempi
every	rock	this-like	rock
Patemmampii		toi.	
water-rock-creature		emerge	
Oyon	tempi	patemmampii	toi
every	rock	water-rock-creature	emerge

Oyon	tempi	aiwan	tempi
every	rock	this-like	rock

Patemmampii	toi.
water-rock-creature	emerge

Oyon	tempi	patemmampii	toi
every	rock	water-rock-creature	emerge

Totsappaa	wooyompa
white-water	worm

Patemmampii
water-rock-creature

Totsappaa	wooyompa
white-water	worm

Patemmampii.
water-rock-creature

Oyon	tempi	aiwan	tempi
every	rock	this-like	rock

Patemmampii	toi.
water-rock-creature	emerge

Oyon	tempi	patemmampii	toi
every	rock	water-rock-creature	emerge

Totsappaa	wooyompa
white-water	worm

Patemmampii
water-rock-creature

Totsappaa	wooyompa
white-water	worm

Patemmampii.
water-rock-creature

COMMENTS

The second interpretation of the song is about turning rocks over in the water and watching white water worms come out from underneath the rocks. *Toi* is the song form of *to'ih* 'emerge, come up/out'. *Patemmampii* is a song word meaning 'water-rock creature' (< *pa-* 'water', *ten-* 'rock' plus *mampii* 'creature', not an ordinary word). *Wooyompa* is the song word in this interpetation for 'worm', and perhaps related to ordinary *wo'api(n)* 'worm, maggot'.

The two interpretations of the song are both compatible and possible because the song has words that are not used in ordinary language, but some are somewhat similar to different ordinary words, and therefore interpretable in different ways. And the song has two words that don't occur at all in ordinary language (i.e., *patemmampii* and *wooyompa*) and thus are open to interpretation.

28 *Tooppehan Nahupia* 'Cloud Song'
Earl Crum

Tooppehan Nahupia

Haiyon tootompi tootompi,
Hainnah.
Haiyon tootompi tootompi,
Hainnah.
Akka wiya pahan tootompi tootompi,
Hainnah.
Akka wiya pahan tootompi tootompi,
Hainnah.

Haiyon tootompi tootompi,
Hainnah.
Haiyon tootompi tootompi,
Hainnah.
Akka wiya pahan tootompi tootompi,
Hainnah.
Akka wiya pahan tootompi tootompi,
Hainnah.

Cloud Song

O clouds, clouds,
Hainnah.
O clouds, clouds,
Hainnah.
Clouds, clouds over that mountain pass,
Hainnah.
Clouds, clouds over that mountain pass,
Hainnah.

O clouds, clouds,
Hainnah.
O clouds, clouds,
Hainnah.
Clouds, clouds over that mountain pass,
Hainnah.
Clouds, clouds over that mountain pass,
Hainnah.

Tooppehan   Nahupia
Clouds (distrib)   RFLX-Song

Haiyon rhythmical song word			tootompi clouds (distrib)	tootompi, clouds (distrib)
Hainnah. rhythmical song word				
Haiyon rhythmical song word			tootompi clouds (distrib)	tootompi, clouds (distrib)
Hainnah. rhythmical song word				
Akka that	wiya pass	pahan on	tootompi clouds (distrib)	tootompi, clouds (distrib)
Hainnah. rhythmical song word				
Akka that	wiya pass	pahan on	tootompi clouds (distrib)	tootompi, clouds (distrib)
Hainnah. rhythmical song word				

COMMENTS

This is a *nua hupia* 'round dance song'. *Tootompi* is the distributive plural song form of *tooppeh* 'cloud', *wiya* is the song form of *wia* '(mountain) pass', and *paha(n)* is the song form in this song of *pa'a(n)* 'on'.

Pia Pakenappeh 'Heavy Fog'
Earl Crum

Pia Pakenappeh

> Piya pakenna kenna wenkatompi,
> Yaainno.
> Piya pakenna kenna wenkatompi,
> Yaainno.
>
> Totsappakenna wenkato,
> Totsappakenna wenkatompi,
> Yaainneh.
>
> Totsappakenna wenkato,
> Totsappakenna wenkatompi,
> Yaainneh.
>
> Piya pakenna kenna wenkatompi,
> Yaainno.
> Piya pakenna kenna wenkatompi,
> Yaainno.
>
> Totsappakenna wenkato,
> Totsappakenna wenkatompi,
> Yaainneh.

Heavy Fog

> Heavy fog cover rolling in,
> *Yaainno.*
> Heavy fog cover rolling in,
> *Yaainno.*
>
> White fog spreading out,
> White fog spreading out,
> *Yaainneh.*

White fog spreading out,
White fog spreading out,
Yaainneh.

Heavy fog cover rolling in,
Yaainno.
Heavy fog cover rolling in,
Yaainno.

White fog spreading out,
White fog spreading out,
Yaainneh.

Pia   Pakenappeh
Big   Fog

Piya   pakenna   kenna   wenkatompi,
big   fog   cover   spread out

Yaainno.
rhythmical song word

Piya   pakenna   kenna   wenkatompi,
big   fog   cover   spread out

Yaainno.
rhythmical song word

Totsappakenna   wenkato,
white-fog   spread out

Totsappakenna   wenkatompi,
white-fog   spread out

Yaainneh.
rhythmical song word

Totsappakenna   wenkato,
white-fog   spread out

Totsappakenna   wenkatompi,
white-fog   spread out

Yaainneh.
rhythmical song word

Piya	pakenna	kenna	wenkatompi,
big	fog	cover	spread out

Yaainno.
rhythmical song word

Piya	pakenna	kenna	wenkatompi,
big	fog	cover	spread out

Yaainno.
rhythmical song word

Totsappakenna	wenkato,
white-fog	spread out

Totsappakenna	wenkatompi,
white-fog	spread out

Yaainneh.
rhythmical song word

COMMENTS

This is a *nua hupia* 'round dance song'. *Wenkato(mpi)* is the song form of *wekkatookka* 'spread out', *pakenna* is the song form of *pakenappeh* 'fog', and *kenna* is the song form of the instrumental verb *-kenah* 'cover'.

Pasiwakkatetem Manteh 'To the Sand Dunes'
Earl Crum

Pasiwakkatetem Manteh

Patsiwankatetem mantuu,
Pasiwakkatetem manteh.

Patsiwankatetem mantuu,
Pasiwakkatetem manteh.

Patsiwankatetem mantuu,
Pasiwakkatetem manteh.

Patsiwankatetem mantuu,
Pasiwakkatetem manteh.

To the Sand Dunes

Toward the sand dunes,
To the sand dunes.

Toward the sand dunes,
To the sand dunes.

Toward the sand dunes,
To the sand dunes.

Toward the sand dunes,
To the sand dunes.

Pasiwakkatetem	Manteh
Sand Dunes	To
Patsiwankatetem	mantuu,
sand dune	toward
Pasiwakkatetem	manteh.
sand dune	to

Patsiwankatetem	mantuu,
sand dune	toward

Pasiwakkatetem	manteh.
sand dune	to

Patsiwankatetem	mantuu,
sand dune	toward

Pasiwakkatetem	manteh.
sand dune	to

Patsiwankatetem	mantuu,
sand dune	toward

Pasiwakkatetem	manteh.
sand dune	to

COMMENTS

This is a *nua hupia* 'round dance song'. *Patsiwankatte(n)* is one song form of *pasiwakkatete(n)* 'sand dune', also used in this song. *Mantuu* is the song form used in this song of *mantu(n)* 'towards'; *manteh* is the song form used here of *mante(n)*, another ordinary form of 'to', 'towards'.

Yuwannan Totompeentsi 'Heat Wave'
Earl Crum

Yuwannan Totompeentsi

> Yuwannan totompeentsi,
> We'napii we'napii we'napii.
> Hainnah.

> Waattoya yeyekwitem mantu
> Kotsimpoo kotsimpoo kwakkwapiikinna
> Yuwannan totompeentsi,
> We'napii we'napii we'napii.
> Hainnah.

> Waattoya yeyekwitem mantu
> Kotsimpoo kotsimpoo kwakkwapiikinna
> Yuwannan totompeentsi,
> We'napii we'napii we'napii.
> Hainnah.

> Waattoya yeyekwitem mantu
> Kotsimpoo kotsimpoo kwakkwapiikinna.

Heat Wave

> Warm clouds—heat wave,
> From the desert, desert, desert.
> *Hainnah.*

> Toward the two mountains sitting there in the distance,
> Trails of dust, trails of dust coming in low-lying waves.
> Warm clouds—heat wave,
> From the desert, desert, desert.
> *Hainnah.*

Toward the two mountains sitting there in the distance,
Trails of dust, trails of dust coming in low-lying waves.
Warm clouds—heat wave,
From the desert, desert, desert.
H<u>a</u>innah.

Toward the two mountains sitting there in the distance,
Trails of dust, trails of dust coming in low-lying waves.

Yuwannan   Totompeentsi
Warm   Cloud Waves

| Yuwannan
warm | totompeentsi,
cloud waves | |
| We'napii
desert | we'napii
desert | we'napii,
desert |

H<u>a</u>innah.
rhythmical song word

Waattoya two-mountain	yeyekwitem sitting (dl)	mantu towards
Kotsimpoo dust trail	kotsimpoo dust trail	kwakkwapiikinna lying (pl distrib)-coming
Yuwannan warm	totompeentsi, cloud waves	
We'napii desert	we'napii desert	we'napii, desert

H<u>a</u>innah.
rhythmical song word

| Waattoya
two-mountain | yeyekwitem
sitting (dl) | mantu
towards |
| Kotsimpoo
dust trail | kotsimpoo
dust trail | kwakkwapiikinna.
lying (pl distrib)-coming |

COMMENTS

This is a *nua hupia* 'round dance song'. *Yuwannan* is a song form of *yu'aih* 'be warm'. *Totompeentsi* is a distributive song word based on *tooppeh* 'cloud' plus *peesi* 'fine fur'. *Kotsimpoo* 'dust trail' is a compound song form based on the ordinary words *kusippeh* 'dust, ashes' and *po'i"* 'trail, path, road'. *Kwakkwapi* is a distributive song form of *kwapi"* 'lie (down) (pl)'.

Pui Aipin Tempi Tenapoo
'Marks of Blue Chalky Clay'
Earl Crum

Pui Aipin Tempi Tenapoo

> Pui aipin tempi tenapoo tenapoo,
> Hain tenapoo,
> Hainneh.
> Pui aipin tempi tenapoo tenapoo,
> Hain tenapoo,
> Hainneh.

> Toyawaikin nankwa,
> Toyawaikin nankwa,
> Pui aipin namapataatsiyuwainna.
> Hainneh.

> Toyawaikin nankwa,
> Toyawaikin nankwa.
> Pui aipin namapataatsiyuwainna.
> Hainneh.

Marks of Blue Chalky Clay

> Marks, blue chalky clay marks,
> Blessed marks,
> *Hainneh.*
> Marks, blue chalky clay marks,
> Blessed marks,
> *Hainneh.*

> On the side of a mountain,
> On the side of a mountain,
> Glazing one's body all over with blue chalky clay,
> *Hainneh.*

On the side of a mountain,
On the side of a mountain,
Glazing one's body all over with blue chalky clay,
Hainneh.

Pui	Aipin	Tempi	Tenapoo
Blue	Chalky Clay	Rock	Mark

Pui	aipin	tempi	tenapoo	tenapoo,
blue	chalky clay	rock	mark	mark

Hain		tenapoo,
rhythmical song word		mark

Hainneh.
rhythmical song word

Pui	aipin	tempi	tenapoo	tenapoo,
blue	chalky clay	rock	mark	mark

Hain		tenapoo,
rhythmical song word		mark

Hainneh.
rhythmical song word

Toyawaikin		nankwa,
mountain-area		side of

Toyawaikin		nankwa,
mountain-area		side of

Pui	aipin	namapataatsiyuwainna.
blue	chalky clay	self-with hand-shine-all over

Hainneh.
rhythmical song word

COMMENTS

This is a *nua hupia* 'round dance song'. It is about rubbing oneself with wet, shiny, bluish chalky clay as a purification process. *Namapataatsiyuwainna* is a verb built with the reflexive prefix *na-*, plus the instrumental prefix *ma-* 'with the hand', and the verb root *pataatsi* (ordinary form: *patatsiki*) 'shine', followed by the suffixes *-yu* progressive, *-kwain* 'all over' and *-nna* general tense and aspect.

Payampa Yampa Tuu 'Through Wild Carrot Fields'
Earl Crum

Payampa Yampa Tuu

> Hain tempim paa tuu yuwainna,
> Hain tempim paa tuu yuwainna,
> Hain tempim paa tuu yuwainna,
> Hain tempim paa tuu yuwainna.
>
> Payampa yampa tuu,
> Payampa yampa tuu tatsawai,
> Hainneh.
> Payampa yampa tuu,
> Payampa yampa tuu tatsawai.
> Hainneh.

Through Wild Carrot Fields

> O it's warm through the rocks and water,
> O it's warm through the rocks and water,
> O it's warm through the rocks and water,
> O it's warm through the rocks and water.
>
> Crispy wild carrots, through wild carrot fields,
> Crispy wild carrots, through wild carrot fields in early summer.
> *Hainneh.*
> Crispy wild carrots, through wild carrot fields,
> Crispy wild carrots, through wild carrot fields in early summer.
> *Hainneh.*

Payampa		Yampa	Tuu	
Juicy-Wild Carrot		Wild Carrot	Through	
Hain	tempim	paa	tuu	yuwainna,
O	rock	water	through	be warm

III

Hain	tempim	paa	tuu	yuwainna,
O	rock	water	through	be warm

Hain	tempim	paa	tuu	yuwainna,
O	rock	water	through	be warm

Hain	tempim	paa	tuu	yuwainna.
O	rock	water	through	be warm

Payampa	yampa	tuu,
juicy-wild carrot	wild carrot	through

Payampa	yampa	tuu	tatsawai.
juicy-wild carrot	wild carrot	through	be early summer

Hainneh.
rhythmical song work

Payampa	yampa	tuu,
juicy-wild carrot	wild carrot	through

Payampa	yampa	tuu	tatsawai.
juicy-wild carrot	wild carrot	through	be early summer

Hainneh.
rhythmical song word

COMMENTS

This is a *nua hupia* 'round dance song'. It is about walking through the *yampa* 'wild carrot' fields in the summer time. *Payampa* are crispy, juicy wild carrots as they first come out in the early summer. Wild carrots were an important and cherished food source.

Tahma Okwaiteentsi 'Spring Floods'
Earl Crum

Tahma Okwaiteentsi

Tahma okw<u>ai</u>teentsi,
Tahma okw<u>ai</u>teentsi,
Tahma okw<u>ai</u>teentsi,
Tahma okw<u>ai</u>teentsi.

Huuppinnam pantan kantsu himmapi,
Pasaattointsi pampunuuhanniite.
Huuppinnam pantan kantsu himmapi,
Pasaattointsi pampunuuhanniite.

Spring Floods

Spring floods,
Spring floods,
Spring floods,
Spring floods.

Foamy water swirling around and around
Carrying sticks and branches from the water's edge.
Foamy water swirling around and around
Carrying sticks and branches from the water's edge.

Tahma	Okw<u>ai</u>teentsi
Spring	Floods

Tahma	okw<u>ai</u>teentsi,
spring	flood

Tahma	okw<u>ai</u>teentsi,
spring	flood

| Tahma | okw<u>a</u>iteentsi, | | |
| spring | flood | | |

| Tahma | okw<u>a</u>iteentsi. | | |
| spring | flood | | |

| Huuppinnam | pantan | kantsu | himmapi, |
| stick/branch-O | water's | edge | carry (pl) |

| Pasaattointsi | pampunuuhanniite. | | |
| water-foam | water-swirl around | | |

| Huuppinnam | pantan | kantsu | himmapi, |
| stick/branch-O | water's | edge | carry (pl) |

| Pasaattointsi | pampunuuhanniite. | | |
| water-foam | water-swirl around | | |

COMMENTS

This is a *nua hupia* 'round dance song'. *Himmapi* is the song form of *hima"* 'carry, take (pl)', and *kantsu* is the song form of *katsu(n)* 'end, tip, edge'. *Okwaiteentsi* is the song form of *okwaiten* 'flood, flowing' with the addition of the song form *-ntsi* of the diminutive-affectionate suffix *-ttsi*. *Pampunuuhanniite* is the song form of *pampunuaniite(n)* 'swirling water, whirlpool'.

Pakenappeh 'Fog'
Earl Crum

Pakenappeh

>Pakenaa pakenaa pakenaa, tootompi,
>Hainneh.
>Pakenaa pakenaa pakenaa, tootompi,
>Hainneh.
>
>Pennan natempin tui pa'ai pakena tootompi,
>Hainneh.
>Pennan natempin tui pa'ai pakena tootompi,
>Hainneh.

Fog

>Fog, fog, fog—clouds,
>*Hainneh.*
>Fog, fog, fog—clouds,
>*Hainneh.*
>
>Fog and clouds over their kin, the rocks,
>*Hainneh.*
>Fog and clouds over their kin, the rocks,
>*Hainneh.*

Pakenappeh
Fog

Pakenaa	pakenaa	pakenaa,	tootompi,
fog	fog	fog	clouds (distrib)

Hainneh.
rhythmical song word

Pakenaa	pakenaa	pakenaa,	tootompi,		
fog	fog	fog	clouds (distrib)		

Hainneh.
rhythmical song word

Pennan	natempin	tui	pa'ai	pakena	tootompi,
its own	RFLX-rock	kin	over	fog	clouds (distrib)

Hainneh.
rhythmical song word

Pennan	natempin	tui	pa'ai	pakena	tootompi,
its own	RFLX-rock	kin	over	fog	clouds (distrib)

Hainneh.
rhythmical song word

COMMENTS

This is a *nua hupia* 'round dance song'. *Pakena(a)* is a song form of ordinary *pakenappeh* 'fog', *tootompi* is a plural distributive form of *tooppeh* 'cloud', and *natempi* is a possessive form of *tempi* 'rock'.

36 Tekaimmi'a 'Going Hunting'
Earl Crum

Tekaimmi'a

> Piya waanka tokwaimmi,
> Piya tontsin tekaimmiite.
> Piya waanka tokwaimmi,
> Piya tontsin tekaimmiite.
> Namah.
>
> Huumpin namatsawaaikinna,
> Toyapi waaikinna.
> Namah.
> Huumpin namatsawaaikinna,
> Toyapi waaikinna.

Going Hunting

> Climbing in big juniper,
> Hunting for big Indian balsam.
> Climbing in big juniper,
> Hunting for big Indian balsam.
> *Namah.*
>
> Feeling your way through the woods,
> Coming down the mountain.
> *Namah.*
> Feeling your way through the woods,
> Coming down the mountain.

Tekaimmi'a
Hunt-Go

Piya	waanka	tokwaimmi,
big	juniper-at	climb-go

Piya	tontsin	tek<u>a</u>immiite.
big	Indian balsam	hunt for-go

Piya	waanka	tokwaimmi,
big	juniper-at	climb-go

Piya	tontsin	tek<u>a</u>immiite.
big	Indian balsam	hunt for-go

Namah.	
rhymical song word	

Huumpin	namatsaw<u>aa</u>ikinna,
woods	feel one's way down

Toyapi	w<u>aa</u>ikinna.
mountain	come down-hither

Namah.	
rhymical song word	

Huumpin	namatsaw<u>aa</u>ikinna,
woods	feel one's way down

Toyapi	w<u>aa</u>ikinna.
mountain	come down-hither

COMMENTS

This is a *nua hupia* 'round dance song'. *Piya* is the song form of *pia* 'big', *tokwaimmi* is the song form of *tento'immi'a* 'go climbing', *waanka* is the song form of *waakka(n)* 'at the juniper', *toontsin* is the song form of *tootsa* 'Indian balsam', *wa<u>ai</u>(ki)* is the song form of *w<u>ai</u>(kkin)* 'come down (hither)', and *huumpin* is the song form of *huuppi(n)* 'stick, wood(s), tree, log'.

Puiwoo 'Little Green Fish'
Earl Crum

Puiwoo

> Tenaa tei h<u>aa</u>i yaanna,
> Tenaa tei h<u>aa</u>i yaanna,
> Puipaawoo puipaawoo
> Huuntukkantu,
> Puipaawoo huuntukkantu.
>
> Tenaa tei h<u>aa</u>i yaanna,
> Tenaa tei h<u>aa</u>i yaanna,
> Puipaawoo puipaawoo
> Huuntukkantu.
> Puipaawoo huuntukkantu.

Little Green Fish

> Grabbing at something going downward again,
> Grabbing at something going downward again,
> Little green fish, little green fish
> Going under the sticks,
> Little green fish going under the sticks.
>
> Grabbing at something going downward again,
> Grabbing at something going downward again,
> Little green fish, little green fish
> Going under the sticks,
> Little green fish going under the sticks.

Puiwoo
Little Green Fish

Tenaa	tei	h<u>aa</u>i	yaanna,
downward	again	something	grab

Tenaa	tei	h<u>aa</u>i	yaanna,
downward	again	something	grab

Puipaawoo	puipaawoo
little green fish	little green fish

Huuntukkantu,
stick-under-through

Puipaawoo	huuntukkantu.
little green fish	stick-under-through

Tenaa	tei	h<u>aa</u>i	yaanna,
downward	again	something	grab

Tenaa	tei	h<u>aa</u>i	yaanna,
downward	again	something	grab

Puipaawoo	puipaawoo
little green fish	little green fish

Huuntukkantu,
stick-under-through

Puipaawoo	huuntukkantu.
little green fish	stick-under-through

COMMENTS

This is a *nua hupia* 'round dance song'. *Huuntukkantu* is the song form of *huuttukkan tuu* 'through and under the sticks', *tei* is the song form of *tea* 'again, also', and *h<u>aa</u>i* is the song form of *hinna* 'something (obj)'. *Puipaawoo* is the song word for *puiwoo*, which are small green native trout living in streams of northern Nevada and southern Idaho, like Reese's River and the Owyhee River.

Pia Potto(n) 'Big Grinding Stone'
Earl Crum

Pia Potto(n)

> Piankem piankem pennam potoompinna,
> Piankem piankem potoompinna,
> Potoompinna tantsuku yontsakkon tsiyuumantu,
> Tantsukun tsiyuumante.
> H<u>aa</u>inna.
>
> Yuw<u>aa</u> tuankam patewantsii yaanka yunkatu,
> Patewantsiiya,
> Yuw<u>aa</u> tuankam patewantsii
> Tsiyuwaanna patewantsiiya.

Big Grinding Stone

> Her own great big grinding stone,
> A great big grinding stone,
> Pitching seeds in the grinding stone again and again,
> Grinding, softening, grinding seeds, pitching them in the grind-
>   ing stone.
> *H<u>aa</u>inna.*
>
> Taking seeds, tasting and swallowing them,
> Large grass seeds,
> Swallowing them, tasting them
> Savoring big grass seeds.

Pia   Potto(n)
Big   Grinding Stone

Piankem	piankem	pennam	potoompinna,
big	big	her own	grinding stone

Piankem	piankem	potoompinna,	
big	big	grinding stone	

Potoompinna	tantsuku	yontsakkon	tsiyuumantu,
grinding stone	grind	soften	pitch in

Tantsukun	tsiyuumante.
grind	pitch in

Haainna.
rhythmical song word

Yuwaa	tuankam	patewantsii	yaanka	yunkatu,
swallow	taste	large grass seeds	hold	take

Patewantsiiya,
large grass seeds-O

Yuwaa	tuankam	patewantsii
swallow	taste	large grass seeds

Tsiyuwaanna	patewantsiiya.
swallow	large grass seeds-O

COMMENTS

This is a *nua hupia* 'round dance song'. It is about someone pitching large grass seeds in a big grinding stone and reaching in and tasting them every once in a while. *Potoompin* is the song form of *potto(n)* 'grinding stone', *yuwaa* is the song form of *yewe"* 'swallow', *tuankam* is the song form of *temmaih* 'taste', *patewantsii* is the song form of *patuntsi* 'a type of large grass seed', *yaanka* is the song form of *yaakka(n)* 'hold', and *yunka* is the song form of *yunah* 'take'.

Saai Pakantsukkih 'Tule Blackbirds'
Earl Crum

Saai Pakantsukkih

Saai pakantsunkii huummantu,
Saai pakantsunkii huummanteh.
Toyahunupii huummantu,
Toyahunupii huummanteh.

Saai pakantsunkii huummantu,
Saai pakantsunkii huummanteh
Toyahunupii huummantu,
Toyahunupii huummanteh.

Tule Blackbirds

Tule blackbirds toward the woods,
Tule blackbirds through the woods,
Toward the mountain woods and canyons,
Through the mountain woods and canyons.

Tule blackbirds towards the woods,
Tule blackbirds through the woods,
Toward the mountain woods and canyons,
Through the mountain woods and canyons.

Saai	Pakantsukkih	
Tule	Blackbird	
Saai	pakantsunkii	huummantu,
tule	blackbird	trees-toward
Saai	pakantsunkii	huummanteh.
tule	blackbird	trees-to

This variety of *saai pakantsukkih* 'tule blackbird' has a bright yellow breast and head and a black body. Photograph by Earl Crum.

Toyahunupii	huummantu,	
mountain-canyon	trees-toward	
Toyahunupii	huummanteh.	
mountain-canyon	trees-to	
Saai	pakantsunkii	huummantu,
tule	blackbird	trees-toward
Saai	pakantsunkii	huummanteh.
tule	blackbird	trees-to
Toyahunupii	huummantu,	
mountain-canyon	trees-toward	
Toyahunupii	huummanteh.	
mountain-canyon	trees-to	

COMMENTS

This is a *nekka hupia* or *nua hupia* 'round dance song'. *Saai pakantsunkii* is the song form of *sai pakantsukkih* (< *sai* 'tule', *pakantsukkih* 'blackbird'), which refers to both red-winged blackbirds and yellow-headed blackbirds, both of which live in the tules. *Hunupii* is the song form of *hunupi(n)*.

Tosa Weyempih 'White Buffalo Berry'
Earl Crum

Tosa Weyempih

Totsa weyempin, totsa weyempin tokkim paampintsi,
Totsa weyempin, totsa weyempin tokkim paampintsi,
Hupia mukuwa.
Tokkim paampintsi,
Hupia mukuwa.
Tokkim paampintsi.

Totsa weyempin, totsa weyempin tokkim paampintsi,
Totsa weyempin, totsa weyempin tokkim paampintsi,
Hupia mukuwa.
Tokkim paampintsi,
Hupia mukuwa.
Tokkim paampintsi.

White Buffalo Berry

White buffalo berries, white buffalo berries, just nice little berries,
White buffalo berries, white buffalo berries, just nice little berries,
Spirit of the song.
Just nice little berries,
Spirit of the song.
Just nice little berries.

White buffalo berries, white buffalo berries, just nice little berries,
White buffalo berries, white buffalo berries, just nice little berries,
Spirit of the song.
Just nice little berries,
Spirit of the song.
Just nice little berries.

Tosa	Weyempih
White	Buffalo Berry

Totsa	weyempin,	totsa	weyempin
white	buffalo berry	white	buffalo berry

	tokkim	paampintsi,
	just right	little head

Totsa	weyempin,	totsa	weyempin
white	buffalo berry	white	buffalo berry

	tokkim	paampintsi,
	just right	little head

Hupia	mukuwa.
song's	spirit

Tokkim	paampintsi,
just right	little head

Hupia	mukuwa.
song's	spirit

Tokkim	paampintsi.
just right	little head

COMMENTS

This is a *nua hupia* 'round dance song'. *Weyempin* is the song form of *weyempih*. As in several songs before, *totsa* is the song form of *tosa"* 'white'. *Tokkim* is the song form of *tokai ~ tokwai* 'right, correct, perfect', *mukuwa* is the song form of *mukua* 'soul'. *Paampintsi* is the song form of *pampittsi* 'little head' but is metaphorically referring to the fact that the buffalo berries are just perfectly ripe little berries.

41

Tuuppantsuku 'Dark Mink'
Earl Crum

Tuuppantsuku

> Tuumpantsuku,
> Tuumpantsuku,
> Aaiya pantsahapiiyum mantu,
> Pui pantsahapi kwipipinna mantu,
> Paa tumante paapu natsantepikinna,
> Paa tumante paapu natsantepikinna.

> Tuumpantsuku,
> Tuumpantsuku,
> Aaiya pantsahapiiyum mantu,
> Pui pantsahapi kwipipinna mantu,
> Paa tumante paapu natsantepikinna,
> Paa tumante paapu natsantepikinna.

Dark Mink

> Dark mink,
> Dark mink
> Is swimming along somewhere,
> Swimming through the blue water frolicking along,
> Through the clear water paddling along,
> Through the clear water paddling along.

> Dark mink,
> Dark mink
> Is swimming along somewhere,
> Swimming through the blue water frolicking along,
> Through the clear water paddling along,
> Through the clear water paddling along.

Tuuppantsuku
Dark Mink

Tuumpantsuku,
dark mink

Tuumpantsuku,
dark mink

Aaiya	pantsahapiiyum	mantu,	
somewhere	be swimming	towards	

Pui	pantsahapi	kwipipinna	mantu,
blue	swim	shaking	towards

Paa	tumante	paapu	natsantepikinna,
water	through-towards	clear	self-paddle

Paa	tumante	paapu	natsantepikinna.
water	through-towards	clear	self-paddle

Tuumpantsuku,
dark mink

Tuumpantsuku,
dark mink

Aaiya	pantsahapiiyum	mantu,	
somewhere	be swimming	towards	

Pui	pantsahapi	kwipipinna	mantu,
blue	swim	shaking	towards

Paa	tumante	paapu	natsantepikinna,
water	through-towards	clear	self-paddle

Paa	tumanto	paapu	natsantepikinna.
water	through-towards	clear	self-paddle

COMMENTS

This is a *nua hupia* 'round dance song'. *Tuumpantsuku* is the song form of *tuuppantsuku* 'mink' from *tuu"* 'dark' plus *pantsuku* 'water mammal (= mink/otter)', literally 'old man of the water'. *Pantsahapi* is the song form of *pahapi* 'swim', and *kwipipi* is the song form of *kwippikke(n)* 'shake, shiver'. *Paapu* is the song form of *papun(pihten)* 'clear'.

Pia Wantsi 'Tall Grass'
Earl Crum

Pia Wantsi

> Pia wantsi toyatepannaa tenkam paa watontsi kwakkwapinna,
> Pia wantsi toyatepannaa tenkam paa watontsi kwakkwapinna,
> Maitim pee yekwiten naai paa wahnikinna,
> Maitim pee yekwiten naai paa wahnikinna.
>
> Pia wantsi toyatepannaa tenkam paa watontsi kwakkwapinna,
> Pia wantsi toyatepannaa tenkam paa watontsi kwakkwapinna,
> Maitim pee yekwiten naai paa wahnikinna,
> Maitim pee yekwiten naai paa wahnikinna.

Tall Grass

> Tall grasses covering the mountain side at the edge of the rocks,
> Tall grasses covering the mountain side at the edge of the rocks,
> Is what they're talking about sitting winnowing,
> Is what they're talking about sitting winnowing.
>
> Tall grasses covering the mountain side at the edge of the rocks,
> Tall grasses covering the mountain side at the edge of the rocks,
> Is what they're talking about sitting winnowing,
> Is what they're talking about sitting winnowing.

Pia   Wantsi
Tall Grass

Pia	wantsi	toyatepannaa	tenkam
tall	grass (type of)	mountain side	rock end
	paa	watontsi	kwakkwapinna,
	on	grass (type of)	lying (pl distrib)

Pia	wantsi		toyatepannaa	tenkam	
tall	grass (type of)		mountain side	rock end	
	paa	watontsi		kwakkwapinna,	
	on	grass (type of)		lying (pl distrib)	

Maitim	pee		yekwiten	naai	
quote-emph			themselves	sitting (pl)	from
	paa	wahnikinna,			
	about	winnowing			

Maitim	pee		yekwiten	naai	
quote-emph			themselves	sitting (pl)	from
	paa	wahnikinna.			
	about	winnowing			

Pia	wantsi		toyatepannaa	tenkam	
tall	grass (type of)		mountain side	rock end	
	paa	watontsi		kwakkwapinna,	
	on	grass (type of)		lying (pl distrib)	

Pia	wantsi		toyatepannaa	tenkam	
tall	grass (type of)		mountain side	rock end	
	paa	watontsi		kwakkwapinna,	
	on	grass (type of)		lying (pl distrib)	

Maitim	pee		yekwiten	naai	
quote-emph			themselves	sitting (pl)	from
	paa	wahnikinna,			
	about	winnowing			

Maitim	pee		yekwiten	naai	
quote-emph			themselves	sitting (pl)	from
	paa	wahnikinna.			
	about	winnowing			

COMMENTS

This is a *nua hupia* 'round dance song'. *Kwakkwapi* is the plural distributive form of *kwapi"* 'lie (pl)'. *Wahniki(n)* is the song form of *wettantani ~ wettaini* 'winnow', and *pee* is the song form of *pemma* 'themselves'.

Pantei Hupia 'Killdeer Song'
Beverly Crum

Pantei Hupia

> Paipaateeyonneh,
> Paipaateeyonneh,
> Paipaateeyonneh,
> Paipaateeyonneh
>
> Pam paan kematu
> Pam paa yetsekinna,
> Hainneh.
>
> Pam paan kematu
> Pam paa yetsekinna,
> Hainneh.

Killdeer Song

> Friend of the water,
> Friend of the water,
> Friend of the water,
> Friend of the water
>
> By the water, the water
> Flying along over the water,
> *Hainneh.*
>
> By the water, the water
> Flying along over the water,
> *Hainneh.*

Pantei
Water's Friend (= Killdeer)

Hupia
Song

Paipaateeyonneh,
water-over-friend

Paipaateeyonneh,
water-over-friend

Paipaateeyonneh,
water-over-friend

Paipaateeyonneh
water-over-friend

Pam	paan	kematu
water	water's	next to

Pam	paa	yetsekinna,
water	over	flying around

Hainneh.
rhythmical song word

Pam	paan	kematu
water	water's	next to

Pam	paa	yetsekinna,
water	over	flying around

Hainneh.
rhythmical song word

COMMENTS

This is a *nua hupia* 'round dance song'. *Paipaateeyonneh* is the song form of *pantei* 'killdeer', which literally means 'friend of the water'. *Paipaateeyonneh* is based on *paa (pai* obj) 'water', *pa'a* 'on, over', and *teeyonneh*, the song form of *tei* 'friend'.

AIPUNTU SONGS

Tukani Hupia 'Night Song'
Earl Crum

Tukani Hupia

> Tuka huuyaa tuu tu waantsi,
> Tuka huuyaa tuu tu waantsi,
> Tukumpe weyuu a̲itikinna,
> Tukumpe weyuu a̲itikinna.
>
> Tuka huuyaa tuu tu waantsi,
> Tuka huuyaa tuu tu waantsi,
> Tukumpe weyuu a̲itikinna,
> Tukumpe weyuu a̲itikinna.
>
> A̲ipuntu,
> A̲ipuntu,
> A̲ipuntu.

Night Song

> Wandering through the darkness of the night holding a bow,
> Wandering through the darkness of the night holding a bow,
> In the the sky holding it and taking aim,
> In the the sky holding it and taking aim.
>
> Wandering through the darkness of the night holding a bow,
> Wandering through the darkness of the night holding a bow,
> In the the sky holding it and taking aim,
> In the the sky holding it and taking aim.
>
> This way,
> This way,
> This way.

Tukani   Hupia
At Night   Song

Tuka	huuyaa	tuu	tu	waantsi,
night	bow-hold	darkness	through	wander

Tuka	huuyaa	tuu	tu	waantsi,
night	bow-hold	darkness	through	wander

Tukumpe	weyuu	aitikinna,
sky	hold	aim

Tukumpe	weyuu	aitikinna.
sky	hold	aim

Tuka	huuyaa	tuu	tu	waantsi,
night	bow-hold	darkness	through	wander

Tuka	huuyaa	tuu	tu	waantsi,
night	bow-hold	darkness	through	wander

Tukumpe	weyuu	aitikinna,
sky	hold	aim

Tukumpe	weyuu	aitikinna.
sky	hold	aim

Aipuntu,
this way

Aipuntu,
this way

Aipuntu.
this way

COMMENTS

This is an *aipuntu* song. It is about the constellation Orion as a warrior holding a bow and taking aim. *Weyuu* is the song form of *weyaah* 'hold, carry', and *waantsi* 'wander' is a song word, not in ordinary usage.

Hiim Patatsiinna 'Something Is Shining'
Earl Crum

Hiim Patatsiinna

> Tammen tukkananka waaka Wiintoya katete,
> Tammen tukkananka waaka Wiintoya katete,
> Hiim patatsiinna,
> Hiim patatsiinna.
> Hiim patatsiinna,
> Hiim patatsiinna.
>
> Tammen tukkananka waaka Wiintoya katete,
> Tammen tukkananka waaka Wiintoya katete,
> Hiim patatsiinna,
> Hiim patatsiinna.
> Hiim patatsiinna,
> Hiim patatsiinna.
>
> Aipuntu,
> Aipuntu,
> Aipuntu.

Something Is Shining

> To the south in the junipers on Smoky Mountain,
> To the south in the junipers on Smoky Mountain,
> Something is shining,
> Something is shining.
> Something is shining,
> Something is shining.
>
> To the south in the junipers on Smoky Mountain,
> To the south in the junipers on Smoky Mountain,
> Something is shining,
> Something is shining.
> Something is shining.
> Something is shining.

This way,
This way,
This way.

Hiim	Patatsiinna
Something	Shining

Tammen	tukkananka	waaka	Wiintoya	katete,
our (incl)	south-from	juniper-at	smoky mountain	sitting

Tammen	tukkananka	waaka	Wiintoya	katete,
our (incl)	south-from	juniper-at	smoky mountain	sitting

Hiim	patatsiinna,
something	shining

Hiim	patatsiinna.
something	shining

Tammen	tukkananka	waaka	Wiintoya	katete,
our (incl)	south-from	juniper-at	smoky mountain	sitting

Tammen	tukkananka	waaka	Wiintoya	katete,
our (incl)	south-from	juniper-at	smoky mountain	sitting

Hiim	patatsiinna,
something	shining

Hiim	patatsiinna.
something	shining

Aipuntu,
this way

Aipuntu,
this way

Aipuntu.
this way

COMMENTS

This is an *aipuntu* song. It is about enjoying nature and the scenery, taking it for what it is, sometimes puzzling but always exciting and mysterious. *Wiintoya* is the song form of *kwiittoya* 'smoky mountain', and *waaka* is the song form of *waakka(n)* 'at the juniper'. *Tukkananka* is the song form of *tukkanankwa* ~ *tukkananku* 'from below, underneath; from the south'.

Tammmem Piineen Temapaiappeh
'What Our Mothers Have Made'
Beverly Crum

Tammmem Piineen Temapaiappeh

> Tammmem pii'neen temapaia un kammante!
> Tammmem pii'neen temapaia un kammante!
> Mononoo patakwiintsi,
> Mononoo patakwiintsi.
>
> Aipuntu,
> Aipuntu,
> Aipuntu.
>
> Tammmem pii'neen temapaia un kammante!
> Tammmem pii'neen temapaia un kammante!
> Mononoo patakwiintsi,
> Mononoo patakwiintsi.

What Our Mothers Have Made

> What our mothers have made tastes so good!
> What our mothers have made tastes so good!
> We hold tender young greens in our mouth,
> We hold tender young greens in our mouth.
>
> This way,
> This way,
> This way.
>
> What our mothers have made tastes so good!
> What our mothers have made tastes so good!
> We hold tender young greens in our mouth,
> We hold tender young greens in our mouth.

Tammem	Piineen	Temapaiappeh
Our (incl)	Mothers	Having Made

Tammem	pii'neen	temapaia	un	kammante!
our (incl)	mothers'	having made	its	taste

Tammem	pii'neen	temapaia	un	kammante!
our (incl)	mothers'	having made	its	taste

Mononoo	patakwiintsi,
hold in mouth	tender young plant

Mononoo	patakwiintsi.
hold in mouth	tender young plant

Aipuntu,
this way

Aipuntu,
this way

Aipuntu.
this way

Tammem	pii'neen	temapaia	un	kammante!
our (incl)	mothers'	having made	its	taste

Tammem	pii'neen	temapaia	un	kammante!
our (incl)	mothers'	having made	its	taste

Mononoo	patakwiintsi,
hold in mouth	tender young plant

Mononoo	patakwiintsi.
hold in mouth	tender young plant

COMMENTS

This is an *aipuntu* song. It is about enjoying eating delicious, tender young plants prepared by one's mother. *Mononoo* is the song form of *monooh(kan)* 'hold/keep/carry in the mouth'. *Patakwiintsi* is the song form of *patekwittsi* 'tender young plants', which the Shoshoni used to eat, particularly in the spring and early summer (e.g., *kenka* 'wild onions'). *Pii'nee* is the song form of *piinnee* 'mothers'.

Nean Temapaiappeh 'What I Have Made'
Beverly Crum

Nean Temapaiappeh

Nean temapaia tetsimmuuka paa yamani,
Nean temapaia tetsimmuuka paa yamani,
Huumpi,
Huumpi.

Aipuntu,
Aipuntu.

Paa tu,
Paa tu
Paahapikinna.

What I Have Made

What I have made with a sharp point
From wood,
From wood,
Crosses the water.
What I have made with a sharp point
From wood,
From wood,
Crosses the water.

This way,
This way.

It floats along
Through the water,
Through the water.

Nean   Temapaiappeh
My   Having Made

Nean	temapaia	tetsimmuuka	paa	yamani,
my	having made	sharp point	water	cross over

Nean	temapaia	tetsimmuuka	paa	yamani,
my	having made	sharp point	water	cross over

Huumpi,
wood

Huumpi.
wood

Aipuntu,
this way

Aipuntu.
this way

Paa   tu,
water   through

Paa   tu
water   through

Paahapikinna.
float along

COMMENTS

This is an *aipuntu* song. It is about taking delight in fashioning a boat from wood and then putting it in water and watching it float along, especially in meandering mountain streams.

Tetsimmuuka is the song form of ordinary *tetsimmuka* 'sharp point(ed)', and *huumpi* is the song form of *huuppi(n)* 'wood, stick, log, tree'.

MEDICINE OR PRAYER SONGS

Hupia Waimpentsi 'Song Woman'
Beverly Crum

Hupia Waimpentsi

> Hupia Waimpentsi
> Hupia wentsituih,
> Hainna.
>
> Hupia Waimpentsi
> Hupia wentsituih,
> Hainna.
>
> Pennen napaa tuintsi
> Okwaitem mayente
> Hupia wentsituih, hainna.
> Hupia wentsituih, hainna.

Song Woman

> Song Woman
> Shaking the rhythm of her song.
> *Hainna.*
>
> Song Woman
> Shaking the rhythm of her song.
> *Hainna.*
>
> Next to the river,
> Her cousin, the water,
> Shaking the rhythm of her song, *hainna*.
> Shaking the rhythm of her song, *hainna*.

Hupia	Waimpentsi
Song	Woman

Hupia	Waimpentsi
song	woman

Hupia	wentsituih,
song	shake rhythmically to

Hainna.
rhythmical song word

Hupia	Waimpentsi
song	woman

Hupia	wentsituih,
song	shake rhythmically to

Hainna.
rhythmical song word

Pennen	napaa	tuintsi
her own	RFLX-water	cousin

Okwaitem	mayente
river	by

Hupia	wentsituih,	hainna.
song	shake rhythmically	rhythmical song word

Hupia	wentsituih,	hainna.
song	shake rhythmically	rhythmical song word

COMMENTS

This song is a *puha hupia* 'power song' or *nanisuntehai hupia* 'prayer song'. It is also sometimes sung as a *nua hupia* 'round dance song'. The song is about a *puha wa'ippe* 'power woman' or *puhakante* 'medicine person' or 'person with power', and it is also an ode to womanhood. *Waimpentsi* is the song form of *wa'ippe* 'woman'.

Tuun Nekentannan Tuattsi'an Nahupia
'Song of the Child of a Dark Goose'
Beverly Crum and Earl Crum

Tuun Nekentannan Tuattsi'an Nahupia   1st Version (Beverly Crum)

Tuun nekentannan tuantsi,
Tuun nekentannan tuantsi
Paseeweyaa,
Seeweyaa,
Paseeweyaa noote,
Paseeweyaa noote.

Tuun nekentannan tuantsi,
Tuun nekentannan tuantsi
Paseeweyaa,
Seeweyaa,
Paseeweyaa noote,
Paseeweyaa noote.

Song of the Child of a Dark Goose

Little dark gosling,
Little dark gosling in watery willows,
In a stand of willows,
Nestled in watery willows,
Nestled in a stand of watery willows.

Little dark gosling,
Little dark gosling in watery willows,
In a stand of willows,
Nestled in watery willows,
Nestled in a stand of watery willows.

Tuun	Nekentannan	Tuattsi'an	Nahupia	1st Version
Dark	Goose's	Young's	RFLX-Song	

Tuun	nekentannan	tuantsi,
dark	goose's	baby
= Canadian goose's		

Tuun	nekentannan	tuantsi
dark	goose's	baby

Paseeweyaa,
watery willow stand

Seeweyaa,
willow stand

Paseeweyaa	noote,
watery willow stand	nestled

Paseeweyaa	noote.
watery willow stand	nestled

Tuun	nekentannan	tuantsi,
dark	goose's	baby
= Canadian goose's		

Tuun	nekentannan	tuantsi
dark	goose's	baby

Paseeweyaa,
watery willow stand

Seeweyaa,
willow stand

Paseeweyaa	noote,
watery willow stand	nestled

Paseeweyaa	noote.
watery willow stand	nestled

Tuun Nekentannan Tuattsi'an Nahupia   2nd Version (Earl Crum)

Tuun nekentanna tuantsi,
Tuun nekentanna tuantsi,
Pennan tosən kasa tepanna,
Tosa, <u>ai</u>nka pan toyaa

Peteteinna.
Pennan tosan kasa tepanna,
Tosa, <u>ai</u>nka pan toyaa
Peteteinna.

Tuun nekentanna tuantsi,
Tuun nekentanna tuantsi,
Pennan tosan kasa tepanna,
Tosa, <u>ai</u>nka pan toyaa
Peteteinna.
Pennan tosan kasa tepanna,
Tosa, <u>ai</u>nka pan toyaa
Peteteinna.

Song of the Child of a Dark Goose

Little dark gosling,
Little dark gosling,
White wings at its side,
White, in the red water,
Fluttering.
White wings at its side,
White, in the red water,
Fluttering.

Little dark gosling,
Little dark gosling,
White wings at its side,
White, in the red water,
Fluttering.
White wings at its side,
White, in the red water,
Fluttering.

Tuun	Nekentannan	Tuattsi'an	Nahupia	2nd Version
Dark	Goose's	Young's	RFLX-Song	
Tuun	nekentanna	tuantsi,		
dark	goose's	baby		
Tuun	nekentanna	tuantsi,		
dark	goose's	baby		

Pennan	tosan	kasa	tepanna,
its own	white	wing	on side

Tosa,	ainka	pan toyaa	
white	red	water carry along	

Peteteinna.
fluttering

Pennan	tosan	kasa	tepanna,
its own	white	wing	on side

Tosa,	ainka	pan toyaa	
white	red	water carry along	

Peteteinna.
fluttering

COMMENTS

This song is a *puha hupia* 'power song' or *nanisuntehai hupia* 'prayer song', in two different versions. Earl Crum says, "This song is about a Canadian goose." *Tuun nekenta(n)* literally means 'dark goose' but specifically means 'Canadian goose'. However, baby Canadian geese are not dark, rather light gray with white wings.

Nanisuntehai Hupia 'Prayer Song'
Earl Crum

Nanisuntehai Hupia

Haainna,
En nemmi manemenaippehkantenti.
Een tosa wayapputunkih naannu,
H<u>a</u>inneh.

En nemmi manemenaippehkantenti.
Een tosa wayapputunkih naannu,
H<u>a</u>inneh.

Prayer Song

Behold,
You are the one who created us.
You have become a white butterfly,
Behold!

You are the one who created us.
You have become a white butterfly,
Behold!

Nanisuntehai	Hupia
Prayer	Song

Haainna,
rhythmical song word

En	nemmi	manemenaippehkantenti.	
you	us (excl)	by hand-people-make-remote past-o	

Een	tosa	wayapputunkih	naannu,
you	white	butterfly	became

Hainneh.
rhythmical song word

En	nemmi	manemenaippehkantenti.	
you	us (excl)	by hand-people-make-remote past-o	

Een	tosa	wayapputunkih	naannu,
you	white	butterfly	became

Hainneh.
rhythmical song word

COMMENTS

This song is a *puha hupia* 'power song' or *nanisuntehai hupia* 'prayer song'.

Tuukkwi'naa'an Nahupia 'Song of the Golden Eagle'

Beverly Crum

Tuukkwi'naa'an Nahupia

> Haainna,
> Tuukkwi'naa'an kwasiintsi
> Tempim ma namattsiwenenemmi
> Haainna,
> Tuukkwi'naa'an kwasiintsi
> Tempim ma namattsiwenenemmi
> Hainah.
>
> Haainna,
> Tuukkwi'naa'an kwasiintsi
> Tempim ma namattsiwenenemmi
> Haainna,
> Tuukkwi'naa'an kwasiintsi
> Tempim ma namattsiwenenemmi
> Hainah.

Song of the Golden Eagle

> Behold,
> The tail feather of a golden eagle
> Stands there alive on a rock,
> Behold!
> The tail feather of a golden eagle
> Stands there alive on a rock,
> Behold!
>
> Behold,
> The tail feather of a golden eagle
> Stands there alive on a rock,
> Behold!
> The tail feather of a golden eagle
> Stands there alive on a rock,
> Behold!

Tuukkwi'naa'an	Nahupia
Golden Eagle's	RFLX-Song

Haainna,
rhythmical song word

Tuukkwi'naa'an	kwasiintsi	
golden eagle's	tail feather-affectionate	

Tempim	ma	namattsiwenenemmi
rock	on	self-point-stand-living

Haainna,
rhythmical song word

Tuukkwi'naa'an	kwasiintsi	
golden eagle's	tail feather-affectionate	

Tempim	ma	namattsiwenenemmi
rock	on	self-point-stand-living

Hainah.
rhythmical song word

COMMENTS

This song is a *nanisuntehai hupia* 'prayer song' or *puha hupia* 'power song'. Eagle feathers were used by traditional Shoshoni healers, called *puhakante(n)*, to purify and cure in healing and other ceremonies. See Earl Crum's discussion of *puhakante(n)* and the use of eagle feathers in Crum and Dayley 1997 (77–78, 85–86). As he states there: *Tease ama kwi'naa'an kwasi ma utii wemmapuisi'iyu* . . . 'Also, they (*puhakante*) would purify patients with the tail feather of an eagle . . .'

Beverly Crum's late mother, Anna Premo, was raised by her aunt *Tuuppampi* 'Black Hair', who was a *puhakante(n)*. When asked about *um paha'am puha* 'her aunt's healing power', Beverly's mother replied: *Osen kwa'i nattahsu'um puhakante* 'She was one who was a medicine doctor'. Her aunt used different birds as spirit helpers when treating sick people who came to her for help. Of the eagle, Beverly's mother said: *Pia kwi'naa osen kwa'i te'oi tsaam meete* 'Thus, the eagle is one who cures sickness'.

BEAR DANCE SONG

Tamme Yampa Sateettsi 'Our Wild Carrot Pet'
Beverly Crum

Tamme Yampa Sateettsi

> Tamme yampa sateettsii,
> Okwai manti puiwennekkinna.
> Yampa t<u>aai</u>,
> Yampa t<u>aai</u>,
> Yampa t<u>aai</u>.
>
> Yampa t<u>aai</u>,
> Yampa t<u>aai</u>,
> Yampa t<u>aai</u>.

Our Wild Carrot Pet

> Our wild carrot pet,
> Standing looking around toward the river.
> Friend of the wild carrots,
> Friend of the wild carrots,
> Friend of the wild carrots.
>
> Friend of the wild carrots,
> Friend of the wild carrots,
> Friend of the wild carrots.

Tamme	Yampa	Sateettsi
Our (incl)	Wild Carrot	Pet-diminutive
Tamme	yampa	sateettsii,
our (incl)	wild carrot	pet
Okwai	manti	puiwennekkinna.
flow = river	towards	see-stand around

Yampa	t<u>aa</u>i,
Wild carrot	friend

Yampa	t<u>aa</u>i,
Wild carrot	friend

Yampa	t<u>aa</u>i.
Wild carrot	friend

Yampa	t<u>aa</u>i,
Wild carrot	friend

Yampa	taai,
Wild carrot	friend

Yampa	t<u>aa</u>i.
Wild carrot	friend

COMMENTS

This is *wehe'neki hupia* 'rasping song', or what is called in English a bear dance song. *Satee* means 'dog' but in its diminutive affectionate form *sateettsi*, it may be used generically and affectionately for 'pet'. The animal wasn't necessarily someone's actual pet, but was probably so named because it hung around in or near the fields of wild carrots where people used to gather food. In this song the singer is expressing the Shoshoni view that human beings share their space and environment with *sokopittan nanewenee* 'the creatures of the earth' (or literally: 'earth's relatives'). *T<u>aa</u>i* is the song form of *tei* 'friend', but *t<u>aa</u>i* also evokes the sense of *tai*, the short form of *tami* 'younger brother'. As mentioned earlier, *yampa* 'wild carrots' were an important and relished food source for the Shoshoni.

CONTEMPORARY SONGS

Nattahsu'u Hupia 'Medicine Song'
Earl Crum

Nattahsu'u Hupia

Tap<u>ai</u> to'innaa n<u>aai</u> yanna ho,
Tap<u>ai</u> to'innaa n<u>aai</u> yanna ho,
Tap<u>ai</u> to'innaa n<u>aai</u> yanna ho.
Wanna h<u>ai</u> yanna,
H<u>ainai</u> noowaineh.

Piyottittsi yanna ho,
Piyottittsi yanna ho,
Wanna h<u>ai</u> yanna,
H<u>ainai</u> noowaineh.
Piyottittsi yanna ho,
Piyottittsi yanna ho,
Piyottittsi yanna ho,
Wanna h<u>ai</u> yanna,
H<u>ainai</u> noowaineh.

Tsitsaseh tai kimmayu,
Tsitsaseh tai kimmayu,
Wanna h<u>ai</u> yanna,
H<u>ainai</u> noowaineh.
Tsitsaseh tai kimmayu,
Tsitsaseh tai kimmayu,
Tsitsaseh tai kimmayu,
Wanna h<u>ai</u> yanna,
H<u>ainai</u> noowaineh.

Tosa Isa tai suntehaikkinna,
Tosa Isa tai suntehaikkinna,
Wanna h<u>ai</u> yanna,
H<u>ainai</u> noowaineh.
Tosa Isa tai suntehaikkinna,
Tosa Isa tai suntehaikkinna,

Tosa Isa tai suntehaikkinna,
Wanna h<u>ai</u> yanna,
H<u>ainai</u> noowaineh.

Medicine Song

The sun has risen, behold!
The sun has risen, behold!
The sun has risen, behold!
Behold,
Behold!

Blessed peyote, behold,
Blessed peyote, behold,
Behold,
Behold!
Blessed peyote, behold,
Blessed peyote, behold,
Blessed peyote, behold,
Behold,
Behold!

Jesus is coming to us,
Jesus is coming to us,
Behold,
Behold!
Jesus is coming to us,
Jesus is coming to us,
Jesus is coming to us,
Behold,
Behold!

White Wolf blesses us,
White Wolf blesses us,
Behold,
Behold!
White Wolf blesses us,
White Wolf blesses us,
White Wolf blesses us,
Behold,
Behold!

Nattahsu'u Hupia
Medicine Song

Tapai	to'innaa	naai	yanna ho,
sun	rise	rhythmical song words	

Tapai	to'innaa	naai	yanna ho,
sun	rise	rhythmical song words	

Tapai	to'innaa	naai	yanna ho.
sun	rise	rhythmical song words	

Wanna hai yanna,
rhythmical song words

Hainai noowaineh.
rhythmical song words

Piyottittsi	yanna ho,
peyote-blessed	behold

Piyottittsi	yanna ho,
peyote-blessed	behold

Wanna hai yanna,
rhythmical song words

Hainai noowaineh.
rhythmical song words

Piyottittsi	yanna ho,
peyote-blessed	behold

Piyottittsi	yanna ho,
peyote-blessed	behold

Piyottittsi	yanna ho,
peyote-blessed	behold

Wanna hai yanna,
rhythmical song words

Hainai noowaineh.
rhythmical song words

Tsitsaseh	tai	kimmayu,
Jesus	us (incl)	be coming

Tsitsaseh	tai	kimmayu,
Jesus	us (incl)	be coming

Wanna h<u>ai</u> yanna,
rhythmical song words

H<u>ainai</u> noowaineh.
rhythmical song words

Tsitsaseh	tai	kimmayu,
Jesus	us (incl)	be coming

Tsitsaseh	tai	kimmayu,
Jesus	us (incl)	be coming

Tsitsaseh	tai	kimmayu,
Jesus	us (incl)	be comeing

Wanna h<u>ai</u> yanna,
rhythmical song words

H<u>ainai</u> noowaineh.
rhythmical song words

Tosa	Isa	tai	suntehaikkinna,
White	Wolf	us (incl)	bless-hither

Tosa	Isa	tai	suntehaikkinna,
White	Wolf	us (incl)	bless-hither

Wanna h<u>ai</u> yanna,
rhythmical song words

H<u>ainai</u> noowaineh.
rhythmical song words

Tosa	Isa	tai	suntehaikkinna,
White	Wolf	us (incl)	bless-hither

Tosa	Isa	tai	suntehaikkinna,
White	Wolf	us (incl)	bless-hither

Tosa	Isa	tai	suntehaikkinna,
White	Wolf	us (incl)	bless-hither

Wanna h<u>ai</u> yanna,
rhythmical song words

H<u>ainai</u> noowaineh.
rhythmical song words

Comments

This is a modern or contemporay *nanisuntehai hupia* 'prayer song' or
puha hupia 'power song', but with a very traditional rhythm. It and songs
like it are sung in Native American Church services. The Native American
Church religious movement began among the Comanche and Kiowa in
southeastern Oklahoma in the 1890s and then spread to most other North
American Indian tribes by the early part of the twentieth century. The
church was formally incorporated in 1918 by members from a number of
different tribes. The movement first came to the Duck Valley Reservation
in 1916 but didn't become popular until the 1930s. The Native American
Church combines a number of Native American beliefs, moral principles,
and practices with some elements of Christian belief. For example, as in the
song presented here, Jesus is equated with White Wolf. Peyote is considered
a sacred substance and is taken as sacrament in part of the church ritual.

Natsiwenne Hupia 'Flag Song'
Beverly Crum

Natsiwenne Hupia

> Taattsewi ainka wooppite,
> Naahpaihten tosa wooppite,
> Oyo sokopa'an tammen napitenka
> Tetsiwenne pentsi.
> Un tatsinompittsi
> Pui tatawennekkumpa
> Yeyekwite,
> Hainna.

> Taattsewi ainka wooppite,
> Naahpaihten tosa wooppite,
> Oyo sokopa'an tammen napitenka
> Tetsiwenne pentsi.
> Un tatsinompittsi
> Pui tatawennekkumpa
> Yeyekwite,
> Hainna.

Flag Song

> Seven red stripes,
> Six white stripes,
> It stands on every land
> Where we have fought.
> Its stars sit scattered about
> Inside the blue,
> *Hainna.*

Seven red stripes,
Six white stripes,
It stands on every land
Where we have fought.
Its stars sit scattered about
Inside the blue,
Hainna.

Natsiwenne	Hupia
Be Stood Up (dur)	Song

Taattsewi	ainka	wooppite,	
seven	red	stripe	

Naahpaihten	tosa	wooppite,	
six	white	stripe	

Oyo	sokopa'an	tammen	napitenka
all	land-on	we	fight

Tetsiwenne		pentsi.	
by point-stand (dur)		self	

Un	tatsinompittsi
its	star

Pui	tatawennekkumpa
blue	scattered about (dur)-inside

Yeyekwite,
sit (pl distributive)

Hainna.
rhythmical song word

COMMENTS

This is a contemporary song. It is one of the songs sung during the opening ceremony at pow-wows.

Music

Kenneth Kuchler, music director and conductor of the Wasatch Community Symphony Orchestra, transcribed the following songs from tapes and set the text to music. Roger Wangerin, associate conductor of the Wasatch Community Symphony Orchestra, set the manuscripts in a format for publication.

Track 4

SAI PAA HUPIA 'BOAT AND WATER SONG'
Beverly Crum

Beverly Crum's Version

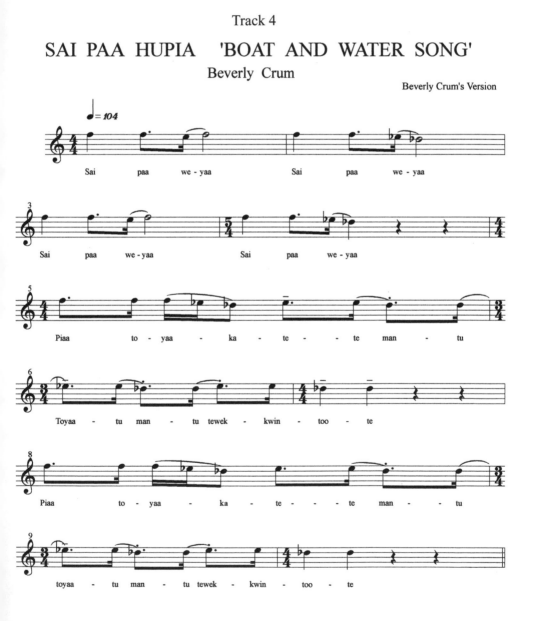

This is an additional version, by Earl Crum, of *Sai Paa Hupia*. It is not included on the compact disc.

SAI PAA HUPIA 'BOAT AND WATER SONG'
Beverly Crum

Earl Crum's Version

HOAKKANTENNA NAHUPIA 'Song of the Warrior'

Beverly Crum   (Beverly Crum"s version)

This is an additional version, by Earl Crum, of *Hoakkantenna Nahupia*. It is not included on the compact disc.

HOAKKANTENNA NAHUPIA 'Song of the Warrior'

Beverly Crum (Earl Crum's version)

Track 17
TUITTSI'AN NAHUPIA 'Song of the Young Man'
Earl Crum (Earl Crum's version)

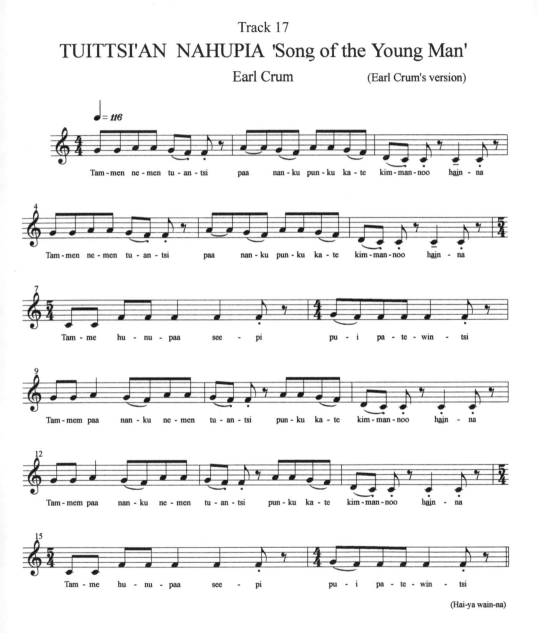

Tam-men ne-men tu-an-tsi paa nan-ku pun-ku ka-te kim-man-noo hain-na

Tam-men ne-men tu-an-tsi paa nan-ku pun-ku ka-te kim-man-noo hain - na

Tam - me hu - nu - paa see - pi pu - i pa - te - win - tsi

Tam - mem paa nan - ku ne-men tu - an - tsi pun - ku ka - te kim - man - noo hain - na

Tam - mem paa nan - ku ne - men tu - an - tsi pun - ku ka - te kim - man - noo hain - na

Tam - me hu - nu - paa see - pi pu - i pa - te - win - tsi

(Hai-ya wain-na)

Glossary

INTRODUCTION

The alphabetical order of Shoshoni words in the glossary is as follows:

a ai ch e h i k kw m n o p s t ts u w y '

It should be noted that no words begin in glottal stop ', since it only occurs in the middle of words. Furthermore, in alphabetizing words in the glossary, the glottal stop is largely ignored because in rapid speech it may be omitted and almost always is in poetry songs. Also, a number of entries ending in final -n are entered in two places in alphabetical order, both with and without the final -n, if the entries would occur far apart in the glossary (e.g., e(n) ~ en 'you, your'). This is to help readers find forms ending in -n even when it is dropped, for example, when the words are said in isolation or at the end of a phrase or sentence, and before certain other sounds (i.e., before s, w, y, and all vowels).

All of the lexical entries in the glossary contain at least the following three kinds of basic information: (1) the primary entry in bold letters; (2) an abbreviation of the grammatical class or part of speech of the primary entry; and (3) one or more translations of the entry. Some of the lexical entries also contain other kinds of information. For example, after some primary entries alternate forms are given following the varying sign ~. In some cases the primary entry is followed by a special combining form enclosed in parentheses; the combining form is typically used in making compounds with other words. In addition, after the abbreviation of the grammatical class, before the translations, principal grammatical forms of the primary entry are enclosed in brackets. Thus, a lexical entry with all of these kinds of information might look like:

principal entry ~ variant form (combining form) abbreviation of grammatical class
    [principal grammatical forms] translations

Not all entries have all of the kinds of information above, but the different kinds always occur in the same relative order as indicated above. Note that throughout the glossary, Shoshoni forms are written in boldface type, while English text occurs in regular typeface.

The reader should be aware that the principal entries for some kinds of words would not be spoken alone as such by a native Shoshoni speaker. For example, verbs in the glossary are nearly always given in their bare stem form, but normally they require at least one suffix such as a final tense or aspect suffix. In addition, transitive verbs in Shoshoni (e.g., hannih 'do, make', yaa" 'carry, take') must always occur with an object pronoun, noun, or noun phrase (unless they are made intransitive with the prefix te-). So, for a native Shoshoni speaker, a transitive verb alone without its object sounds like it is missing something. Similarly, postpositions (e.g., ka 'at', ni 'like') must always occur in a phrase with their objects; they are virtually never said alone by themselves. So, for a native Shoshoni speaker they will definitely sound like they are missing something, or may not even be recognizable when not in a postpositional phrase.

SHOSHONI TO ENGLISH

A

a- DEM/LOC BASE [sa-] that, there yonder; *see* ate(n), ateweh, atee(n), a'ana, akkuh, ama(n), anni, ap<u>ai</u>, ap<u>ai</u>ka(nten), api, apuhni, ase(n), attu(n), awa'ih

aa(n) N [-na] horn, antler

a'ahwai TV pl [ahwai sg] miss (a shot in hunting); dig

a'akkuh LOC there yonder somewhere

a'akkuse(n) ADV way back then, long ago

Aamutsa TOP 'Pale Point' = valley of North Fork, NV

aa(n) N [-na] horn, antler

a'ana DEM-LOC [sa'ana] that place; there somewhere yonder

Aanoo N [-a] Cree

aantsi'i N [-'a] termite

aan kuha ~ aan kuhma N [aan kuantsi song form] buck deer, stag

aapihte(n) (aa-) ADJ pale, whitish

a'ate(n) ADV somewhere

aato'ih IV turn pale, fade

aato'ihtaippeh faded, turned pale

aattoko N [-'a] potato bug

aattuse(n) ADV from way back (in time), way back then; in time

a'ayente(n) DEM-LOC somewhere

ahnatukka N underarm, armpit

ahtahpeh N [-a] jaw

ahwai ~ ahwi ~ awi TV [a'ahwai pl] miss (a shot or target), miss aim; dig

akai N salmon

Akai Tekka'a N [-a] Salmon Eaters (Shoshoni on Snake River)

ake" IV open up (of pinecones)

akka DEM obj [ate(n) subj, akka(n) poss] that yonder

akke(n) N [-na] sunflower

akkuh LOC there yonder

akwate'i" IV [akwate'ikki dur] burp

akwisi" IV sneeze

ama(n) DEM-P [sama(n)] with that

ama'ai DEM-DEM-P [sama'ai] with that (person)

amattampeh N [-a] rib

Amputih NAME Hombre

[1]ana P here or there somewhere; *see* haka.ana, sa'ana, s<u>ai</u>'ana, si'ana, so'ana, su'ana

[2]ana N top of (hill, mountain); *see* toya'ana

a'ni(n) N [-na] ant, black ant (especially with red head)

a'nii N [-'a] beaver

a'nimuih N [-'a] fly

A'nimuiham Pampi TOP Fly('s) Head

a'ni(n) N [-na] black ant, pissant

anni DEM-ADV that way, like that over there

annih IV [kwampi ~ yuma pl] fall down

annita(n) N [-na] black ant (song word); *see* a'ni(n)

anta" ADJ, ADV different, strange, separate; easy; easily

Anta Katete(n) TOP 'Sitting Alone' = Lone Mountain

antakku ADV separately

antananku ADV separately, different(ly); out of place, wrong way

antannewe N stranger; NAME (woman's)

antapittseh N, ADJ [-a] stranger, foreigner; strange, foreign

antapittseh kwana N [-'a] monkey flower (medicinal plant)

antappu(n) ~ antappuse(n) ADV, P different(ly), else; elsewhere, away from

antappunte(n) (anta", antappu(n)) ADJ
[-ti] different, strange

antappuyu(n) IV be different or strange

antase(n) ADV away; just

antsi TV search, look for

apai DEM-LOC around there yonder;
back then

apaika(nten) ~ apika(nten) DEM that
much, that amount (yonder)

apai mannaise(n) ~ apai mannise(n) ADV
since way back in time, from back
then until now

apaise(n) DEM ADV long ago, that time
long ago, back then

api DEM-LOC around there yonder,
thereabouts

apika(nten) ~ apaika(nten) ADV that
much, that amount (yonder)

appe N [-'a] father; sun (ritually)

appe ma'ai pii PHRASE [no appe ma'al nil
pii 'my . . .'] father and mother, parents

appo(n) N [-na] apple

apuhni ~ apu(n) DEM-LOC [apunte(n)]
over that way yonder

apuse(n) ADV at that time back then

ase(n) DEM that yonder (is the) one

ata N [-'a] uncle, mother's brother;
nephew/niece of a man

ataa INTRJCT ouch!

Atakkuh TOP Elko, NV

atamuh N [-a] car, automobile

atantohi N [ø] sister-in-law of woman
[also of a man by some]

atattsi N [-a] father-in-law

ate(n) DEM [akka obj, akka(n) poss] that
yonder

atee(n) DEM [atii obj, atee(n) poss] those
yonder

ateweh DEM [atehi obj, atehe(n) poss]
those two yonder

attankih N [-a] grasshopper

attu(n) DEM-LOC over that way yonder,
here and there; throughout, all over

atsa napuite(n) ~ atsa napunnite(n) ADJ
ugly

atsa bad, nasty, mean, evil

awa'ih ADV like that yonder

awe ~ awo N dish, cup

awi ~ ahwi ~ ahwai TV miss (a shot or
target), miss aim (in hunting); dig

AI

ai- DEM/LOC BASE [sai-] this here
nearby; *see* aite(n), aitee(n), aiteweh,
aikkih, aima(n), ainni, aipai, aipaika(n),
aii, aipuhni, aise(n), aittu(n), aiwa'ih

ai'ana DEM-LOC [sai'ana] this place;
here somewhere nearby

aihko(n) N [-na] pinecone hook

aiitte(n) DEM [aiitti obj] this (special)
kind nearby

aikka DEM obj [aite(n) subj, aikka(n) poss]
this

aikkappeh (aikka-) N [-a] frost

aikkapo'antuah IV become covered
with frost

aikkawekkatuah IV pile up with frost

aikkih DEM-LOC here, near here

aiko(n) N [-na] tongue

aikopi(n) N [-tta] thorn, cactus; quill

aikotooweneh IV (for steam to) rise,
steam

aikotooweneh(pui)te(n) N steam

aikkwimpihte(n) [aikkwin-] ADJ purple,
smokey colored

aima(n) DEM-DEM-P with this (instrument)

aimeah IV be disoriented; get drunk

aimeahka(n) IV be drunk

aimeattsi ~ ai'meattsi N [-a] retarded
person, simpleminded person

ainkapihte(n) (ainka"-) ADJ red

ainkappata N [-'a] orangish red currants in mountains

ainkappawia N [-'a] dock plant
(Rumex crispus)

ainni DEM-ADV this way, like this nearby

aipai DEM-LOC near here somewhere

aipaika(nten) DEM-DEM-P this amount,
this much

aipi DEM-LOC near here somewhere,
hereabouts

aipika(nten) ~ aipaika(nten) DEM-DEM-P
this amount, this much

aipi(n) N [-tta] white chalky clay, chalk

aippo'intsiappeh N, ADJ mildew, moldy

aipuhni ~ aipu(n) LOC over this way
nearby

-'aipui ~ -'aipunni INSTR V destroy; *see*
ma'aipui, ni'aipui ~ ni'aipunni

aipuipihte(n) (aipui"-) ADJ whitish gray,
bluish white

aipu(n) ~ aipuhni DEM-LOC over this way
nearby

aise(n) DEM this (is the one)

aise! (aise!) PHRASE thank you.

aisem ma'i tsa'i PHRASE This is good. =
Thank you.

aisemmunih N [-a] silver money

aisempihte(n) (aisen-) ADJ gray,
silverish

aise(n) DEM this (is the one)

aite N [-i] gun, bow

aite(n) DEM [aikka obj, aikka(n) poss]
this near here

aitee(n) DEM [aitii obj, aitee(n) poss]
these near here

aiteweh DEM [aitehi obj, aitehe(n) poss]
these two

aiti N [ø] gun, bow; *see* huu'aiti

aiti kuttih TV shoot at

aitiki(n) V [-na] aim, take aim; use a bow

aitte(n) DEM [aitti obj] that (special)
kind

aittu(n) DEM-LOC over this way nearby

aiwa'ih ADV like this

aiyoo rhythmical song word

CH

Chikko NAME Chico

cho'appeh N [-a] rascal, scoundrel,
rogue, hateful person

E

e(n) PRO you, your

E aise hakate?
You are who? = Who are you?
= What lineage are you from?
= Who's your family?
= What's your parent's name?
— **Ne ma'i aise . . . ham paite/tu'a.**
— I am . . . 's daughter/son.

E aisen ne tei/haintseh.
You are my friend.

E ha newe taikwante?
Do you speak Shoshoni?
— **Haa'a, ne newe taikwa
   sumpana'inna.**
— Yes, I know how to speak
   Shoshoni.

E ha taipo taikwante?
Do you speak English?
— **Haa'a, ne taipo taikwa
   sumpana'inna.**
— Yes, I know how to speak English.

E ha u nankasumpaatuhka?
Do you understand (it)?
— **Haa'a, ne u nankasumpana'inna.**
— Yes, I understand (it).
— **Kai, ne kai u nankasumpana'inna.**
— No, I don't understand (it).

E witsa saimanti ne suntehai.
Could you please give me some of
   this? = Please.

e'apekka(n) IV have a wound or sore

e'attsih N [-a] sore, wound, injury

e'attsihpa'i(n) INCORP V have a sore,
wound or injury

e'atua IV develop or get a sore or
wound, have a sore or wound, be
injured

eei(ttsi) ADV long time

e'eki ADV recently, newly

eenee INTRJCT scary! watch out!

eese(n) RFLX PRO yourself

ehe N blanket

eitsee INTRJCT brrh (in response to
cold)

eitse'i" ADJ, N cold

eitse'i(h) V be cold

eitse'inte(n) N [-ti obj] cold

Eitse'ippaa ~ Eitse'ihpaa TOP Cold
Springs

eke ADJ, ADV new, young, fresh; newly,
just

ekepittseh N [ekepittsehnee pl] young
person, youth

eki" ADV now, at this time

ekittapaima ~ ekittapaini ADV nowadays

ekise(n) ADV pretty soon, still

ekittsi ADV right now, today

ekkoih IV pl [eppeih sg] sleep, fall
asleep

ekkoihka(n) IV pl [eppeihka(n) sg] be
asleep

ekwi" TV [ekkwi dur] smell

ekkwikki(n) V sniff (around)

em puinnuhi ~ Ne noohimpai em
puinnuhi GREETING [me(mm)i
puinnuhi pl; mehi puinnuhi dl] I'll see
you sometime. = Goodbye.

ema" ~ pa'emah IV rain

emappatompittseh N rainbow

emate(n) ~ pa'emate(n) N [-ti] rain

emmese(n) RFLX PRO yourself

emmi ~ e(n) PRO obj you

e(n) PRO you, your

enee ADJ scary, frightful

ene'e N spirit (being); something scary

enkinaa(n) NO first

enne ~ e(n) PRO [emmi ~ e(n) obj, e(n) ~
emme(n) ~ enne(n) poss] you, your

enuhi ADJ exhausted, pooped out

eppeih IV [ekkoih pl] sleep, fall asleep

eppeihka(n) IV [ekkoihkan pl] be
asleep, be sleeping

eppeikki(n) IV doze off, fall asleep

eppeipekkah(kan) IV get sleepy, be sleepy

ese(n) ~ eese(n) RFLX PRO yourself

etei(n) IV be hot

eteinte(n) N, ADJ [-ti] heat, hot

e witsa . . . ne suntehai PHRASE You
might bless me with . . . = Please.

H

ha INTER yes/no question particle

ha INTRJCT hem

ha tukuh ADV all right, so be it

haa('a) AFFIRMATIVE yes, sure, right

haaiyuh rhythmical song word

haappai N [-'a] wild parsnip (eaten
raw, cooked or dried)

haka'ana INTER where; somewhere,
anywhere, wherever

hakakka INTER where (at)

hakannai INTER where from; from
somewhere

hakannanku INTER which direction,
which side

hakanni INTER how, what (way), (like)
what, why; however, anyhow, somehow

Hakanni e? GREETING How are you?
— Ne ma'i tsa'i.
— I'm fine.
— Ne kaitsaan neesunkanna.
— I'm not feeling well.

hakanni kia noo(n) ADV uncertain, really
don't know

hakannikku INTER how so, why; way,
anyway, whatever way, for some reason

hakanniyun(ten) ~ hakanniu(ten) INTER
why; for whatever reason

hakapai INTER what time; whatever
time, anytime

hakappu(n) INTER where to; somewhere, anywhere

hakate(n) INTER [hakkai" ~ hakki" obj,
hakka(n) poss] who; someone, some-
body, anyone, anybody, whoever
E aise hakate?
You are who! = Who are you?
[asked to find out one's parent's name]
— Ne ma'i aise . . . ham paite/tu'a.
— I am . . . 's daughter/son.

hakattu(n) INTER where; through
wherever

hakai INTER how, what; somehow,
anyhow
Hakai en nanihanna ~ Hakai en
nanihante?
What's your name? = What are you
called?
— Ne . . . mai nanihante.
— My name is . . . = I'm called . . .
— Ne ma'i aise . . . mai nanihante.
— My name is . . .
Hakai en neesunkanna?
How do you feel? = How are you?
— Ne tsaan neesunkanna.
— I feel well. = I'm OK.
— Ne ma'i tsa'i.
— I'm fine.
— Ne kaitsaan neesunkanna.
— I don't feel well.

hakkai" ~ hakki" INTER obj [hakate(n) subj] whom; someone, anyone; whomever

hakaitte(n) INTER [hakaitti obj] what kind of, whatever kind, some kind, any kind; somehow weird

hakka(n) INTER [hakate(n) subj] whose; someone's, anyone's

hannih TV do, make, use, fix, prepare; hunt; gather, get; put; take; hold

hanninka(n) ~ hanninke(n) TV do for, make for; give, provide

hannippeh ADJ done, made

hapi" IV [happi dur; kwapi" pl] lie (down); float

hapikku IV fall down, fall over; land

hapinka(n) ~ hapinke(n) TV lay down; have (someone) lie down

hapinaite(n) N [-na] lazy

hapinnemmi IV lie around, rest

hapittaippeh ADJ, N layed up, invalid

hattai N poison parsnip, water hemlock

hattu(n) INTER question particle

hawo ADJ hollow, empty

hawo'ih IV be hollow, be hollowed out

hawo'ihkante(n) ADJ hollowed out

haainna(h) ~ haaiyaanna ~ haina(h) ~ hainna(h) ~ hainai(h) meaningless rhythmical song words

haih N [-a] raven, large crow; uncle, father's brother; man's nephew/niece

Haihan Nokahni TOP Raven Nest

haikku IV, TV choke (on)

haikwi N spleen

haina(h) ~ hainna(h) ~ haainna(h) ~ hainai(h) meaningless rhythmical song word

haintseh N [-a] friend; boyfriend, girl-friend; see **nahaintsehneweh**
    E aisen ne haintseh.
    You are my boyfriend/girlfriend.

haiwi ~ haaiwi N [-'a] dove

haiya ADV very, really

haiya wainna rhythmical song words used to bless songs

haiyaho meaningless rhythmical song word

haiyani P more than

haiyo(n) meaningless rhythmical song word

hea" TV trap, set a trap, catch

he'eh(ten) QUANT, ADV a few, few, several, some; a few times, several times

he'e hapikkante(n) ADV after a few days

heehni N [-'a] barn owl

he'ehte(n) QUANT, ADV [he'eh] a few, few, several, some; a few times, several times

he'ehtettsi QUANT very few

heette(n) INTER [heetti obj] how many, how much

heettenka INTER what time
    Heettenka en tapai (nahayu)?
    What time is it? = What time do you have?

heheiku ADV a little bit

heite(n) N, QUANT [-ti] small amount

hekankah ~ hekanke(n) TV cool down

heki N shade, shadow

hekikahni N [ø] shade house

henapi(n) N [-tta] bitterbrush

henapittseh N [-a] bat

hepinkeppeh N [-a] flower

hepitsoo(ttsi) N [-'a; heheppittsiannee(n) ~ heeppittsianee(n) ~ hepitsoonee(n) ~ hehepitsoonee(n) pl] old lady, old woman

hepittsipekka V INCORP become an old lady

hettsippeh N [-a] spit, saliva

hii(n) ~ hinni INTER [hinna obj, hinna(n) poss] what; something, anything, thing(s), some, any

hiinnee(n) INTER pl [hii(n) sg subj, hiinnii obj] what; somethings, things

hiinneweh INTER dl [hii(n) sg subj, hiinnihi obj] what, something, anything

hiintuah IV become (something)

hiittoo(n) N [-na] meadowlark

hima" TV pl [yaa" sg] carry, take

himakka(n) TV pl [yaakka(n) sg] hold, keep, carry

himakki(n) TV [yaakki(n) sg] bring

himih TV pl [uttuh sg] give

himp**ai** INTER when; sometime, anytime; somewhere, anywhere

himp**ai**ka'i V be how much, be so much

himp**ai**kan(ten) INTER [-i] how many, how much; much, many, any amount

himpaise(n) ADV long ago

himpeh QUANT, N [himpeha obj] some, (some)thing; stuff, possessions, property; place

hinna ~ hinnattsi'a INTER obj [hii(n) subj, hiinnii pl] what; something, anything, thing(s), some, any
Hinna e suwainna?
What do you want?
—Ne k**ai** hinna suwainna.
—I don't want anything.

hinni ~ hii(n) INTER [hinna obj, hiinnee(n) pl] what; something, anything

hipi" TV [hippi dui] drink

hipikka(n) IV be drunk

hipinka(n) ~ hipinke(n) TV water, make drink

hipite(n) N [-ti] drinker, drunk

hipittaippeh ADJ completely drunk up

hipittsuku N [-a] drunkard

hittsaah IV be left up to

ho meaningless rhythmical song word

hoa" ~ hua" N bow

hoa'aiti ~ hua'aiti N bow and arrow

hoakkante(n) ~ huakkante(n) N [-i] archer, bowman, warrior

hoami'a ~ hoamahaih ~ huamahaih TV stalk

hoawoppih ~ huawoppih N [-a] protector, sentinel, guard, scout, lookout, stalker, warrior

hoi P [hoiten, hoiti] around; see mahoi, uhoi

hoinkeh ~ hoinkih N hog

homokaite(n) N powdery stuff

hopi'i V shed fur or hair; (for hair to) fall out

hopittseh N flour

hotah TV dig

hotappeh ADJ, N [-a] dug out; hole

hua" N bow

hua'aiti ~ hoa'aiti N bow and arrow

huakkante(n) ~ hoakkante(n) N [-i] archer, bowman, warrior

huamahai ~ huami'a ~ hoami'a TV stalk

huawoppih ~ hoawoppih N [-a] protector, sentinel, gaurd, scout, lookout, warrior, stalker

huittsaa(n) N [-na; huintsaantsi song form] sage hen

huittsi IV spurt, ejaculate

huittsuu N sparrow; small bird

hukkumpeh N [-a] dust

huna(n) N [-na] badger

hu'nita(n) ~ hunnita(n) N [-na] red ant

hunna kahni N moon house, menstrual house

hunna peeppi(n) N [-tta] menstrual flow

hunnapekkayu(n) V menstruate, have a period

hunni N menstruation, menses, menstrual blood

hunnito'ih ~ hunnitu'ih IV menstruate, have a period

hunupi(n) N [-tta] ditch, arroyo, ravine, narrow canyon

hupa N [-i] broth, juice

hupia ~ nahupia N [-i] song

Hupia Waimpentsi NAME Song Woman

hupiakante(n) N [-ti] singer, composer of songs

hupianai V make music, sing

huttsi N [-'a] paternal grandmother, grandchild of a woman

huttsimpia [-'a] daughter-in-law

huu'aiti N bow and arrow; see aiti

huukkuna" ~ huukuna N quiver, holster

Huukwitsa Patetsoppih TOP Huukwitsa Spring, NV

huukwitsappeh N a kind of tree

huummutsi N, TOP [-a] end of a wooded place; Woods End, NV

huuppaka(n) N [-na] stick arrow

huuppi(n) (huu"-) N [-tta] stick, wood, log, tree, stand of trees

I

i- DEM/LOC BASE [si-] this right here; iten, ikkih, inni, ip**ai**, ip**ai**ka(nten), ipaika(nten) ipuhni, ise(n), ittu(n), iwa'ih

i'ana DEM-LOC [si'ana] this place; right here somewhere

i'ana hattu(n) ADV so long ago

i'imaa N, ADV [imaa] (in the) mornings

iitte(n) DEM [iitti obj] this (special) kind right here

ikka DEM obj [ite(n) subj, ikka(n) poss] this right here

ikkih DEM-LOC right here

imaa N, ADV [i'imaa dist] (in the) morning, tomorrow, the next day

imaase(n) ADV early in the morning

imaayu(n) IV become morning

imante(n) DEM-DEM-P [imanti obj] some of this, part of this, member of this (family)

ina P less than, shorter than, smaller than

ina DEM-LOC this side

ina" ~ inna" TV hang (meat) out to dry, jerk (meat)

inanka(n) ~ innanke(n) TV hang (meat) out to dry for

inappeh ~ innappeh N [-a] jerky

inni DEM-ADV this way, like this right here

ipai ~ ipi DEM-LOC around here, here somewhere

ipaika(nten) DEM this amount, this much

ipi ~ ipai DEM-LOC around here, here somewhere

ipika(nten) ADV this much, this amount

ipuhni ~ ipu(n) DEM-LOC over this way

isa ~ pia isa N wolf

isampeh N [-a] liar

isa(n) N lie, trick

isannai IV lie, tell a lie

isannainka(n) ~ isannainke(n) TV lie to, tell a lie to, trick

isannainna N lying, lie

ise(n) DEM this right here (is the one)

ite(n) DEM [ikka obj, ikka(n) poss] this right here

itee(n) DEM [itii obj, itee(n) poss] these right here

iteweh DEM [itehi obj, itehe(n) poss] these two right here

ittu(n) DEM-LOC through this area

itsa (itsappe) N coyote

itsanahayu IV be dishonest

Itsapehe NAME Coyote Fur

itsapaikkah TV fool, trick

itsappe (itsa) N [-a] coyote

Itsataipo NAME Coyote White Man

itsawene(kku) IV [itsawenne dur] have a cramp, have cramps

iwa'ih ADV like this right here

iyampeh ADJ aware, alert; wild

iya'ih V watch, be alert

iya'ihka(n) TV watch over

K

ka" P [kai, kakku, kattu(n), katte(n), katti, kayente(n))] at, to, toward; about (a topic); see penka

ka'ah IV, INSTR V [ponka'ih pl] break (of a flex obj); see kekka'ah, kukka'ah, pikka'ah, sekka'ah, takka'ah, tsakka'ah, tsikka'ah, wekka'ah

kaa(n) N [-na] rat

Kaan kwasi kwai'ahku! the end (e.g., of a story)

kaan tetahain naappeh N rat urine powder medicine

kaha(n) N [-na] blue grouse

kahni N [∅] house, home, building

kahnikante(n) ADJ have a house; dwell, live

kahninai V build a house

kahnipa'i(n) V have a house; dwell

ka'i N forehead

kaku N [-a] maternal grandmother, grandchild of a woman

kakku P [ka", kai, kattu(n), katte(n), katti] at, to, toward; about (a topic)

kammawaihkwai(n) IV for pain or soreness to go away

kammahpuinna N pain, ache, soreness

kamma(n) ~ kammah IV hurt, ache, be sore, suffer, be in pain; taste

kammanka(n) ~ kammanke(n) TV hurt for, feel for, suffer for

kammanna N suffering, pain, hurt

kammawaih IV for pain to diminish or go away

kammu ~ kamme [**kammuntsi** song form] N [-i] jackrabbit, black tailed jackrabbit

kammuyenka(ten) N, ADV [-ti] (at the) door; (in) front of the house

kana(n) N [-na] bitterroot

-kante(n) N, ADJ suffix having, be characterized by; there is

kanokkoh TV roast in cones

kanokkohka N roast-in-cones method of preparing pinenuts

kantih N [-a] candy

kapa(n) P [**kapai(ten)**, **kapanku**, **kapantu(n)**, **kapante(n)**, **kapanti**] among, between, through(out); *see* **nanakkapa(n)**

kappai N [ø] bed

kappaikoitsoih V clean the house, scrub the floor

kappainnanku ADV behind the house

kappaipusia N [-i] bedbug

kappaisoni N bedding, bedroll

kappeh N [-a] pinecone; seed pod

kasa N [-i] wing

kate" IV [**katte** dur; **yekwi"** pl] sit (down), stay, remain; land

katekka(n) IV sit, stay

katemi'a V ride away

katenooh V ride around

katenkahka(n) TV set aside; heat up

katennompeh N [-a] chair

kateppui IV sit still, stay

katete(n) N hill

katettai(n) IV sit around, stay around; be disabled

katettaippeh ADJ, N invalid, disabled; one confined to a wheelchair

katte(n) P [**ka"**, **kai**, **kakku**, **kattu(n)**, **katti**] at, to, toward; about (a topic)

katsu(n) N [-na] end, tip, edge

katsunka ADV at the end

ka'wi P more than, taller than, bigger than

ka'wi IV gather together

ka'wimpite IV gather together, come together

kayattsih ~ kaiyattsih N [-a] pine jay

kai NEG no, not, don't, doesn't, didn't

kai P [**ka"**, **kakku**, **kattu(n)**, **katte(n)**, **katti**] at, to, toward; about (a topic)

kai himpai ADV not ever, never; not there

kai (kia) naketsa ADV surely not

kai natekkate(n) N [-na] inedible, poisonous

kai nittapu'i V express lack of confidence in or low opinion of

kai puite(n) ADJ [-i] blind

kai sampai ADV not even; likely not

kai tapu'i V not do well, do poorly, be poorly, get worse; afraid of

kai tapu'inna naakka V not do well

kai tepuihtapu'i V be hardly able to see

kai tepuihtapuinte(n) ADJ hardly able to see

kai tokaiyu ADV not enough

kaihaiwa(n) ADV no more, nothing, all gone

kaihaiwan naammi'a IV be dying, pass away

kahaiwayu(n) IV be no more

kaikkaitsaa(n) ADJ not good, wrong, really bad

kaippai(ttsi) ADV in a little while; in a hurry

kaise(n) ADV not yet, before

kaisuante(n) ADJ thoughtless, dumb, retarded

kaital'kwa'a N mute

kaite(n) ~ kaiti NEG never, not

kaitsaan napuite(n) ADJ ugly, looking bad

kaitsaan(ten) ADJ [**kaitsaayente(n)**] bad, no good, not well

kaitsaan neesunkanna PHRASE feel bad, feel not well

   Ne kaitsaan neesunkanna.
   I don't feel well.

kaitsaanku ADV bad(ly)

kaiyattsih ~ kayattsih N [-a] pine jay

kaiyu(n) ADV late

ke"- INSTR PRFX with the mouth or
  teeth

kea N [-i] locust

kea" IV pl [to'ih sg, toto'ih dl] emerge,
  come out, go out

keempai N [ø] ground squirrel, prairie
  dog

kekka'ah TV [kepponka'ih pl] bite in
  two; break with teeth

kekkate" TV bite (like snake)

kekkentuse(n) ADV day before yesterday

kekkepetaa ADJ tall

kekkopah TV [kekkopai'ih pl] bite in
  two; break with teeth

kekkwanah TV (for breath to) smell of

kemah N [-a] edge, sharp edge

kemaka ~ kemahka ~ kematu ADV, P
  next to, close to, by, (by the) side of

kemappeh ADJ sharp-edged

kematu ~ kemaka ADV, P next to, close
  to, side of

kemmai ADJ, N [-a; kekkemmai pl] different (one), foreigner

kenah [kenna song form] INSTR V
  cover; see makenah, pakenah, pikkenah, takkenah, tsakkenah, wekkenah

kenka N [-a] wild onion

kennaawai TV do with the mouth, snap
  at

kenno'ai TV graze

kentu(n) ADV yesterday

kenu N [-a] paternal grandfather,
  grandchild of a man

kepetaa(nten) ADJ long, tall

kepetaa wenete(n) ADJ tall

kepetaaante(n) ADJ long, tall

kepi aiti N pistol

kepi wenete(n) ADJ short

kepihte(n) (kepih) ADJ short

keppatantsih N [-a] chin

keppeah V let go with mouth; stop
  drinking

keppeittseiki(n) V [keppeittseittseiki(n)
  dur] chew or chomp making noise

keppikko'o(n) N [-na] chin

kepponka'ih TV pl [kekka'ah sg] bite
  (flex obj) in pieces

kesaa(pah) V open mouth

kesaapappeh ADJ opened mouth

kesi'wah TV tear or rip with mouth or
  teeth

keso'ih TV bite many times

keti(h) N [-a] cat

ketian tua" N kitty, kitten

kettaa(n) ADV hard; fast; really

kettaan(ten) ADJ hard; fast

kettaanku ADV really, very

Kettaa Okwai" TOP 'Fast Flowing Water'
  = Miller Creek

Kettaa See TOP 'Hard Willow' = Miller
  Creek NV

kettemmaih TV make sick eating

kettokwai TV kill with mouth or teeth

ketsokkwaih TV chew

kettsi'ah TV bite once

kettsu'ah ~ kettsumah TV eat up,
  consume

kettsu'appeh ~ kettsumappeh ADJ
  eaten up, drunk up, all gone (of food)

kettsumah ~ kettsu'ah TV eat up, consume

keyaah(kan) TV carry in mouth

kia ~ ki'a ADV maybe, perhaps; wonder;
  myth marker

kia noo(n) ADV probably

kiippeh N [-a] elbow

Kiiki N NAME (woman's)

kikimma IV dl [kimma" sg/pl] come

kimma" IV [kikimma dl] come

kimmanke(n) ~ kimmanka(n) TV chase
  (down), come after

kinii N [-'a] hawk, falcon

-kkuh ~ -kkih LOC here/there; see
  sakkuh, saikkih, sikkih, sokkuh,
  sukkuh

koa INSTR V pile up; see takkoa, tsikkoa,
  wekkoa

koanta N [-'a] sandhill crane

Koanta Paa TOP 'Sandhill Crane
  Spring' = Summit Creek

Koanta Paa Hunupi(n) TOP 'Sandhill
  Crane Ravine' = Fawn Creek

koappeh N [-a] corral; antelope surround

kohai ~ kohi N intestines, guts

kohipekka(n) IV have diarrhea

kohno(n) N [-na] cradleboard, cradle basket

ko'i N hill, knoll, peak, tiptop, point

koi" IV pl [tiyaih sg] die

ko'ih IV [koko'ih dl] return, come back, go back, go home; *see* tsakko'inka(n)

ko'inii IV go and return

koippeh ADJ pl, N pl [-a; tiyaippeh sg] dead, deceased; bodies

koitsoih ~ koitsohi TV wash, bathe

koitsoippeh ADJ washed

kokko(n) ~ pasikkokko(n) N [-na] bull snake

kokooniyenka IV dl [kooni sg, kooniyenka pl] come and go

kono'ih IV be hollow

kono'ihkante(n) (konoki) ADJ hollow

kooni IV [kokooniyenka dl, kooniyenka pl] come and go

kopa" ~ kwana" TV carry in arms, lug

kopakka(n) ~ kwapakka(n) TV hold in arms

kopah IV, INSTR V [kopi'ih ~ -kopai'ih pl] break (rigid obj); *see* kekkopah, kukkopah, mukopah, pikkopah, sekkopah, takkopah, tsakkopah, tsikkopah, wekkopah

kopai N [ø] face

kopakko'ih TV carry back (home)

koppooh ~ kuppooh TV brand

koppih ~ koppii N [-a] coffee

kosopi(n) N [-tta] fire drill

kotokki [-'a] necklace

kottooh TV light a fire, make a fire, set on fire, burn

kottoohka(n) TV have a fire burning

kottoonka(n) ~ kottoonke(n) TV make fire for, build a fire to keep (someone) warm

kottoonnompeh N [-a] stove

kottooppeh N [-a] fire

kottsaah ~ kuttsaah ~ kwattsaah TV make pudding, gravy or gruel

kottsaappeh ~ kuttsaappeh ~ kwattsaappeh N pudding, gravy, gruel

ku"- INSTR PRFX with or by heat or fire

kuha ~ kuhma N male; gelding

kuhannih TV cook

kuhappe ~ kuhmappe N [-a] husband

kuhatiyainkappeh N [-a] widow

kuhatu IV marry, get married (of a woman)

kuhawatte(n) ADJ husbandless, single mother, old maid, woman who has never married

kuhnai" IV (start to) run, run off; *see* namakuhnai", takkuhnai", wekkuhnai"

kuhuyah(kan) V peek

kuittseh ~ kuittsih N [-a] throat

kuittseh kamma(n) N + IV have a sore throat

kuittseh kammanna N a sore throat

kuittsehpekka(n) IV have a sore throat

kuittsu(n) N [-na] cow

kukka'ah IV [kupponka'ih pl] break from heat (flex obj)

kukki TV gather firewood

kukkuin IV pl [kuttiyaih sg] die from heat

kukkopah IV [kukkopai'ih pl] break from heat (rigid obj)

kukkwase IV be done cooking (of food); be ripe (of fruit)

kukkwaseppeh ADJ done, cooked

kukkwiikkih IV smolder

kuna" N firewood, fire

-kunaih INSTR V rub; *see* makunaih, pikunaih, takunaih

kunukippeh N [-a] elderberry

kupisi N brain

kuppa(n) P [kuppai(ten), kuppanku, kuppantu(n), kuppante(n), kuppanti] inside, within, in; *see* penkuppa(n), makuppa(n), sukuppa(n)

kuppasa IV dry up from heat

kuppe'appeh ADJ cooked

kuppeittseittseiki(n) IV crackle and sputter (in a fire), sizzle

kuppihto TV light a match

kupponka'ih IV pl [kukka'ah sg] break from heat (flex obj)

kuppooh ~ koppooh TV brand

kuppunnunnukki(n) IV spin around

kusa N [-i] pants

kusaakakakai" IV sizzle, boil sizzling

kusiakke(n) N [-na] small sunflower with gray-green leaves

kusippeh [kotsim song form] N, ADJ [-a] dust, ashes; dusty

Kusiyuttah N [-a] Gosiute Shoshoni

kusuai V be very hot, feel very hot

kusuainna N [ø] heat wave

kutaha ~ kutiha N corral; fenced in place

kutahanaih V INCORP build a corral

kuttapaitua(n) IV become light, get light

kuttento'i(n) IV boil up

kuttento'inka(n) ~ kuttento'inke(n) TV boil

kuttih ~ kwettih TV shoot

kutiha ~ kutaha N corral

kuttiyaih IV [kukkoih pl] die from heat

kuttuhsippeh N [-a] ashes

kuttumpittseh ~ putumpittsi N woodpecker

kuttsaah ~ kottsaah ~ kwattsaah TV make pudding, gravy or gruel

kuttsaappeh ~ kottsaappeh ~ kwattsaappeh N pudding, gravy, gruel

kuttsawene TV [kuttsawenne dur] fry

kuttseni TV heat up

kuttsihanni N [-'a] fire starter

kuttsihtunah TV light up (a fire)

kuttsippeh [kotsimpoo song form] N [-a] coals, hot embers

kuu" TV bury; dive

kuuhkinka TV lasso, rope (an animal)

kuuta(n) N coat

kuwii N [-'a] sandpiper

kuyu'ainka(n) ~ kuyu'ainke(n) TV warm up

KW

kwahaimpeh N [-a] back

kwahain kupisi N spinal cord

kwahaintsuhni N spine, backbone

kwahate(n) N [-na] antelope

kwa'i ADV so, thus, therefore, that is

kwa'i kia ADV uncertain (about whatever it is)

kwa'i witsa ADV for example

kwakkuhu(n) ~ kwakkwaha(n) TV win, beat

kwakkuhuppeh ~ kwakkwahappeh N [-a] winnings

kwakkwappi IV pl distr [kwappi dur; hapi" sg] lie (down); go to sleep

kwana" IV [kwanna dur] smell

kwapa" ~ kopa" TV hug

kwapakka(n) ~ kopakka(n) TV hold in arms

kwapi" IV pl [kwappi dur, kwakkwapi distr; hapi" sg] lie (down); go to sleep

kwase" IV ripen; roast, cook

kwasenka(n) ~ kwasenke(n) TV roast, ripen

kwaseppeh ADJ ripe; cooked, done

kwasi N tail, tail feather

kwasi appe N [-a] devil

kwasi taipo N monkey

kwasintsi N [song form] tail, tail feather; see kwasi

kwasu'u(n) N [-na] dress

kwasu'uhka(n) IV be dressed

kwasu'unke(n) ~ kwasu'unka(n) TV dress, get (someone) dressed

kwattsaah ~ kuttsaah ~ kottsaah V make pudding, gravy, or gruel

kwattsaappeh ~ kuttsaappeh ~ kottsaappeh N [-a] pudding, gravy, gruel

kwayu'i IV shed, molt

kwai'ah IV break off, come off

kwaitu'a V shed, take off

kwee" ~ kwehe" N [-i] wife

kweekkante(n) ~ kwehekkante(n) ADJ married (of a man), having a wife

kweeppa'i(n) V INCORP have a wife

kweettu ~ kwehettu V marry, get married (of a man)

kwehe" ~ kwee" N [-i] wife

kwehekkante(n) ~ kweekkante(n) ADJ married (of a man), having a wife

kweheppa'i(n) V INCORP have a wife

kwehetiyainkappeh N [-a] widower

kwehettu ~ kweettu V marry, get married (of a man)

kwettih ~ kuttih TV shoot

kwi'ampeh ~ kwi'yampeh ADJ [kwikkwi'ampehnee(n) pl] lazy

kwi'ankante(n) ~ kwi'yankante(n) ADJ lazy

kwiippeh N [-a] smoke

kwi'naa N bird

kwi'naattsi N [-a] pet bird

kwiippeh N [-a] smoke

kwiiweneh IV be smokey, smolder

kwikkwiya'wente(n) ADJ frightened, scared

kwikkwihtu(n) IV distrib defecate, shit (*vulgar*)

kwinahainaih(ten) ADV from the north

kwinahainankuhte(n) ADV north

kwinahaippaitu(n) ADV northward, toward the north

kwini" TV lick; eat pudding-like food

kwininnompeh N [-a] spoon

-kwintuih INSTR V stir; *see* tsikkwintuih, wekkwintuih

kwinuhi IV turn around, twist around

kwippikka(n) IV shiver

kwipuntah(kan) IV bend, be/get crooked

kwipuntahkante(n) ADJ, N crooked, bent; hunchbacked

kwipuntsih N [-a] scorpion

kwisi" V weave; be tangled, ensnared

kwisinka(n) ~ kwisinke(n) TV trap, catch, ensnare, net, entangle

kwita" IV [kwitta dur, kwikkwihtu(n) distrib] defecate, poop, shit (*vulgar*)

kwita" N [-i] butt, behind

kwitakkahni N toilet, outhouse

kwitakkwana N [-'a] lupine

kwitappeh N [-a] feces, excrement, dung, stool, poop, shit (*vulgar*)

kwitatlaina N anus

kwitattemi V be constipated

kwitattsi N [-a] rectum

kwitawoyampeh N [-a] snakeweed

kwitawoyo(n) N [-na] magpie

kwitsunaih IV survive

kwiya'a V be surprised, be startled, be frightened

kwiyampeh ~ kwi'ampeh ADJ [kwikkwi'ampehnee(n) pl] lazy

kwiyankante(n) ~ kwi'ankante(n) ADJ lazy

M

ma PRO obj it, him, her

ma- DEM/LOC BASE this; *see* mate(n), mateweh, matee(n), mase(n), matukka(n), mawakka(n)

ma- INSTR PRFX with the hand

ma" ~ ma(n) P [mante(n), manku] with (an instrument); by means of; *see* sima ~ simma, suma ~ summa

ma(n) P [mannai, manku, mantu(n), mante(n), mayente(n)] on (the surface of); about; *see* sima(n), soma(n), suma(n)

maanankwah ~ manakkwah ADV far away; distant

maananku ~ mananku ADV, P far away; on other side

maayunte(n) CONJ because of it/that

ma'ai ~ mai ~ ma'i P [ma'aihku, ma'aise(n)] with (accompaniment); and; *see* nanamma'ai, nahma'ai, naneema'ai, pemma'ai, sama'ai sima'ai, suma'ai

ma'aipui TV destroy

mahai ~ mai IV INCORP go get, go after, hunt, gather; *see* temahai", tepammahai

ma'aise(n) CONJ with, and

mahoi DEM-LOC around it, around this

mahoihta TV hurt, injure

mahoi(n) TV sneak up on

mahyani ~ mayani P more than

ma'i ADV emphatic; that is, therefore, thus

maka" TV [makka dur] feed, give (especially food)

makappeh ADJ given

makenah TV cover with hand, hold down with hand

makateh(kan) TV set (keep) hand on

makia(han) TV stop, cease

makitsa'a TV (s)mash with hand

makka DEM obj [mate(n) subj, makka(n) poss] that, him, her

makunaih TV rub with hand

makuppa(n) P more than, taller than, bigger than

makwantupi TV roll up

makwantupinke(n) ~ makwantupinka(n) TV roll up for

makwisunai TV save

makwiya'a TV scare with hands, frighten, startle, spook

mamakkoi ~ ta wehe'neki nekkanna N
bear dance

mammapaiku ADV little bit at a time

ma(n) P [mannai, manku, mantu(n),
mante(n), mayente(n)] on (the surface
of); about; *see* sima(n), soma(n),
suma(n)

ma(n) PRO poss its, his, her

ma(n) ~ ma" P [mante(n), manku] with
(an instrument); by means of; *see*
pemma(n), (s)ama(n), (s)aima(n),
(s)ima(n), (s)oma(n), (s)uma(n)

ma'nahna TV raise, rear

ma'nahayetse IV rear up (like a horse),
raise up

manakki(n) TV copy, mimic, imitate

manakkwah ~ maanakkwah ADV far
away, far off; distant, on the other
side

mananku ~ maananku ~ manakwa ADV,
P, ADJ [manankuhte(n), manankuhti,
manankuhtu(n)] far away, far off; distant; (on) the other side

manapuih ~ manapunnih TV take care
of, look after, treat; let be seen

manayaha TV hurt, injure

manekihte(n) (maneki-) ~ manaikihte(n)
(manaiki-) NO five

manaikimaahte(n) (manaikimah-) NO
[manaikimaayente(n)] fifty

maneki pia seemaahte(n) ~ manaiki pia
seemaahte(n) NO five hundred

Manekin Nawookkah N Friday

maneesunka'ah ~ maneesunkanna TV
make feel

maneettsikkwa IV suffer, be in (emotional) pain

manemenai TV create (people)

mani(yun) IV cross (over/through a
body of water), ford

ma'nii N [-'a] short-legged dog

ma'nika'a N ring

maniyu(n) IV be naked

maniyunte(n) ADJ naked

manku P [ma(n)] from; for; about; *see*
sumanku, susumanku

mankuse(n) P according to, depending
on

mannai P [ma(n)] from

mante(n) P, N [-ti] some of, part of,
member of (family); *see* simante(n),
sumante(n)

mante(n) P [ma(n)] to, towards; about;
with, among

mantu(n) P [ma(n)] to, towards,
through; *see* sumantu(n)

mantsih N [-a] matches

mapa'a(n) DEM-DEM-P on it, on this

mapahai" IV (for the hand to) drop
down or fall off

mapana'ai(n) ~ mapana'aih(kan) TV
know how to do

mapanatuh TV know how to do by
hand

mapataatsi TV make shine

mapaiah TV do, make, build, create,
prepare, take care of

mapaianka(n) ~ mapaianke(n) TV do for,
make for, build for, create for

mapaiappeh ADJ made, done, created,
prepared

mapaitettsi QUANT, N, ADV [-a] small
amount, little bit

mapiku(sen) ADV a little bit

mapitenka(n) ~ mapitenke(n) TV care
for, take care of

mapitsi'a TV prepare; strengthen; put a
priority on doing

mappana N palm

mapuih V try, attempt

mapuisi" TV cleanse, purify

mase(n) DEM, ADV thus

maseanka(n) ~ maseanke(n) TV plant,
sow

maseki N finger

masetto'o(n) N glove(s)

masitoo(n) N [-na] fingernail

masunai" ~ ma'sunai" TV bother, annoy

masunka'ah ~ masunka'a" TV feel with
hand

matakki ~ mattakki TV slap

matakihka TV slap around

mate(n) DEM [makka obj, makka(n) poss]
this, he, she

matee(n) DEM [matii obj, matee(n) poss]
these, they, their

matekih TV put, place with hand

matemah TV put away, keep, close up, cover

matenkah TV finish, complete

matenkappeh ADJ finished, completed

mateweh DEM dl [matehi obj, matehe(n), poss] these two, they

mattakki ~ matakki TV slap

mattepiha N middle finger

mattepiha nankuhte(n) N [-ti] ring finger

mattoko N thumb

mattua N little finger

mattutua V stretch out arms

matukka(n) DEM-LOC under it, under this

matsaka TV knock out with hand

matsappaki TV stick (on)

matsu'ah TV empty; try

matsuhinka(n) ~ matsuhinke(n) ~ matsuh-ninka(n) ~ matsuhninke(n) TV overcome, strong-arm, bully

mattsankih N [-a] horned toad

mattsinko'no N wrist

mattsuhnippeh ADJ strong-armed

mawai TV feel in (e.g., pocket)

mawa'ih ADV like this/that

mawakka(n) DEM to, towards, with someone

mawaihyanke(n) TV start a fire, start to burn; burn one's hand

mawehtiah TV spill

mawenenka(n) ~ mawenenke(n) TV stop, make stop with hand

mawiih(tain) TV push away, cast away; see nimmawiih

mawiih(tai)nka(n) TV cast away for

mawintsa N wrist

mayaah TV mix (together), combine (together)

mayahnai(n) TV make laugh with actions

mayani ~ mahyani P more than

mayanuhi IV hurry up!

mayekwi TV do, prepare, take care of, care for

mayente(n) P [ma(n), mannai, manku, mantu(n), mante(n)] on (the surface of), by; about

mayunaih TV winnow

maaikkuh ADV okay, all right, well, affirmative; now then

-mai ~ -mahai TV INCORP go get, go after, hunt, gather, harvest; see tepammai, yahammai

mai QUOTE [maiti] say(s), said; it is said, they say; call, name

mai ~ ma'ai P [ma'aihku, ma'aise(n)] with (accompaniment), in company with; and

maiso(n) N [-na] Mormon cricket

mai'ukka ADV now, at this time, today

maittenkah(ten) ADV, N [-ti] outside, outdoors

mea N moon, month

mee" ~ mehe(n) TV do, make, gather; put; use; go get rations or commodities

meeldla(n) TV keep

mee(n) ~ memme(n) PRO 2nd pl subj, poss you all, your

meenka(n) ~ meenke(n) TV do for, make for

meeppeh N, ADJ [-a] rations, commodities; done, gathered

mehe(n) PRO 2nd dl poss your

mehe(n) ~ mee" TV do, gather; put; go get rations or commodities

mehenka(n) ~ mehenke(n) TV do for, gather for

mehese(n) RFLX PRO yourselves

mehi PRO 2nd dl obj you two

mei ~ memmi PRO 2nd pl obj you all

meih ~ menih TV, AUX V be unable to do; can't, fail to

memme(n) ~ mee(n) PRO 2nd pl subj, poss you all, your

memmese(n) RFLX PRO yourselves

memmi ~ mei PRO 2nd pl obj you all

menih ~ meih TV, AUX V be unable to do; can't, fail to

metekki TV turn

meweh PRO 2nd dl subj [mehi obj, mehe(n) poss] you two

mi'ah ~ miah IV [mimi'ah dl] go, walk, leave

mi'ahtai(n) IV leave, go away

mi'ahtaippeh ADJ left, gone away

mi'aki(n) IV go along, walk along

mi'akwa(n) IV leave, go away

mianka(n) ~ mianke(n) TV chase

miannooh IV walk along, go along

mi'appeh ADJ gone, left

mii(sen) ADV near, close by

mimi'ah IV dl [mi'ah sg/pl] go, walk, leave

mittaa ~ mitteha N [-'a] woodtick

mo- ~ mu- INSTR PRFX with the nose or face

mo'o N [-i] hand

mokottsih N [-a] bag, sack

monoo N candy jawbreakers

monooh(kan) TV [mononoo song form] carry in mouth, keep in the mouth, hold in the mouth

mooppo N [-'a] mosquito

mosotto'ih TV snort out, blow out (of nose)

motsom painkwi N [ø] catfish

motso(n) N [-na] whiskers, beard

mu- ~ mo- INSTR PRFX with the nose or face

muha N, ADJ [-i] onion; bitter

muha kamman(na) IV taste bitter or of onion

muhumpittseh ~ muumpittseh N [-a] great horned owl

Muittsaittseh NAME (man's) Muchacho

mukate N [-'a] sucker fish

mukopah V [mukkopai'ih pl] break (one's own) nose

mukua(pin) N spirit, soul

mukwantuah IV roll or turn over on face

munappe N [-a] son-in-law

munkih N monkey

munnai P ahead of, in front of, before

munnanku ADV last year

mupi(n) ~ muupi(n) N [-tta] nose

mupisippeh N [-a] snot, mucus

mupitsi TV suck out

mutehai(n) V to kiss

mutekih TV touch with nose; place mouth on

muto'ih V come out the nose; spit out

muttehappi ADV lying on one's stomach (face down)

mutsa N point (topographical)

mutsikante(n) ADJ sharp-pointed

mutsipi(n) N [-tta] point

mutsippeh ADJ sharp-pointed

muumpittseh ~ muhumpittseh N [-a] great horned owl

muunih N [-a] money

muupi(n) ~ mupi(n) N [-tta] nose

muuta N [-'a] mule

mu'yahnaisuah IV smile

muyakainka(n) ~ muyakainke(n) TV play a horned instrument

N

naa" LINK V [naah AUX] be, become, get, happen; do

naahpai pia seemaahte(n) NO six hundred

naahpaihte(n) (naahpai-) NO six

naahpaimaahte(n) (naahpaimaah-) NO [naahpaimaayente(n)] sixty

Naahpain Nawookkah N Saturday

na'ahpu(nten) N, ADV half; in half, halfway

na'akka N, ADV (in the) middle

naakka(n) IV stay; live, exist; be, become, remain

naakkante(n) N [naakkantee(n) pl] being

naakki(n) IV get, become; get to (someplace)

naakkwai(n) IV come to be, get, become

naappeh(kanten) ADJ former, has/had been; late (deceased)

na'antappu(n) ADV separately, apart

na'appunte(n) ADV in all directions

naha" V do, make, act; get; be, become, happen (to)

Heettenka en tapai nahayu? What time is it? = What time do you have?

nahanke(n) TV do for, make for

nahannih IV be done, be made, be fixed, be used, be prepared

nahapite IV come to be

nahappeh ADJ, N (having) done, made, fixed, used, prepared; doings

nahawatekih IV be lacking or missing; *see* watekih

nahaintsehneweh N dl [(na)nahaintsehnee(n) pl] boyfriend and girlfriend (relationship); friend relationship; *see* haintseh

nahimihtai(n) IV pl be given away

nahimihtaippeh ADJ given away

nahipittaippeh ADJ completely drunk up

nahma(ten) ADV [nahmantu(n)] together

nahma'ai ADV dl [nanamma'ai pl] with each other, together

nahna" IV grow (of humans and animals only)

nahnammi'a IV grow up

nahnapite IV grow older

nahnappeh ADJ, N [-a] grown; grown up, adult

nahpa'a(n) ADV dl [nanappa'a(n) pl] on top of each other

nahpaikanku ADV in equal amounts, in half

nahupia N [-i] song of; *see* hupia

nakaha ADJ youngest (of offspring), last born; lesser

Nakaha Payuppuka TOP 'Lesser Bog' = Willis Meadows, NV

Nakaha Tettsohpai TOP Little Canyon, NV

na'kamma'a N delicacy, favorite food

nakea" IV pl [to'ih sg, toto'ih dl] emerge, come out; become visible

nakenneemai TV be tired of eating

nakettemmaih IV be made sick eating, get sick eating

naketsa ADV surely, really

naketsa hattu(n) ADV perhaps not

naketsa natia(n) ADV really too, terribly, extremely

nakettsu'ah ~ nakettsumah V consume

nakettsu'appeh ~ nakettsumappeh ADJ consumed, eaten up, all gone (of food)

nakoitsoih ~ nakuitsoih IV bathe, wash self

nakoppooh(kan) ~ nakuppooh(kan) IV be branded

nakoppooppeh ~ nakuppooppeh ADJ branded

nakuuppeh ADJ, N [-a] buried; grave

na'kwana'a N perfume

nakweekkante(n) ~ nakwehekkante(n) ADJ, N married; marriage

na'kweettu V marry each other

nakwehe V wrestle

na'ma'ai ADV with each other

nama'atiyaihku IV pretend to be dead

namahannih TV dress, get dressed, put clothes on

namahannihka(n) IV be dressed

namahannihkappeh N [-a] clothes

namahanninke(n) TV dress (someone)

namahoita IV be hurt, be injured

namakah(tain) IV, TV (for food to) be given away; give (away) food; feed

namakappeh ADJ given (especially food)

namakuhnai" TV run away from

namanapuih(kan) IV take care of self

namante(n) P [namantu(n)] with each other

namanukkih IV run away

namapataatsiki IV make self shine

namapatekki IV be anointed, anoint oneself

namapaiah IV be made, be done, be built, be prepared, be created; take care of self, prepare oneself

namapaiappeh ADJ made, done, created, prepared

namapuisi" V purify oneself, cleanse oneself, make a motion with hand pushing one's prayers towards higher being

namasohi IV hurry

namasuah TV dress, get dressed

namasuahka IV be dressed

namasuappeh N [-a] clothes

namatenkah IV be finished; be prepared

namatenkappeh ADJ finished, prepared

namatsawai(kin) IV feel one's way down

namattsiwene IV stand by self on end (e.g., feather, stick)

namawene IV run off

namayekwi v take care of self, prepare oneself for

nameeh IV be done, be made, be gathered; be used

nameeppeh ADJ done, gathered

namiante(n) ADJ both

nammi N [-a] younger sister, close female cousin

nampai N [ø] foot

nampatu'ih IV [song word] wade by foot; *see* pato'ih

nampeh N [-a] shoe

nampuih TV track (down)

namukua N one's own spirit

nana" ADV together, each other

nana appeneweh N dl father and son (relationship)

nana nammineweh N dl sisters (relationship)

nana paitenneweh N dl mother and daughter (relationship)

nana papineweh N dl [nana papi(ttsi)nee(n) pl] brothers (relationship)

nanaah IV be, become; do

nanaahka(n) IV live

nana'ahpu(n) ADV in pieces; in different directions

nana'anta(hku) ADV each separately; away from each other

nana'antappu(n) ADV separately or differently from each other; in different directions

nanah ADV just, only

nanah hinna ADV whatever, just anything

nanahaitah(kan) LINK V, IV be, become, get; live; be scattered

nanahoi ADV in equal amounts

nanahoih TV divide up, share

nanahteppeh ADJ worthless

nana'imaa ADV every day, every morning

nanakai ~ nanaki v mate (of animals), copulate (of animals)

nanakkapa(n) ADV sometimes, intermingled

nanakwaha(n) IV lose, be beaten

nanakwahappeh N [-a] what is lost in a game

nanakweenneweh ~ nanakwehenneweh N dl married couple, husband and wife

nanakweettu ~ na'kweettu v marry each other

nanamannippahai(kkan) v argue

nanamma'ai ~ nanama'ai ADV pl [nahma'ai dl] (all) together, with each other

nananewenee N pl [nanewe sg] relatives, relations

nananisummaha(n) v joke together

nananisummaate(n) [-a] jokes

nananittehu'i(n) v fuss about, scold each other

nananka" IV be heard, sound, make noise, echo

nanankasuanka(n) ~ nanankasuanke(n) TV sound like, make noise like

nanappa'a(n) ADV [nahpa'a(n) dl] on top of each other

nanappaikante(n) ADV in the same amount

nanappaiyekwi ADV next to each other, sitting in a row

nanappinnai ADV behind each other

nanappittuse(n) ADV back and forth

nanapuih v pl [napuih ~ napunih sg] look, appear, seem, be seen, be visible

nanapuisunka'a(n) v look, appear (instilling feeling); be recognizable; be obvious (that)

nanasamunneweh N dl siblings of opposite sex

nanasumma(nten) ADJ, PRO [-ti] different (things), other things

nanasuwekai(n) IV be wonderful, be amazing, be awesome

nanasuwekainte(n) ADJ, N [-na] awesome (one, things), amazing (one, things)

nanatea N cousin, relative

nanatea TV accept as relative, count as relative

na'natea IV race (in a footrace)

nanateate TV count (as) relations

nanate'eya(n) IV be dangerous

nanate'eyante(n) ADJ dangerous

nanatei N friends (with one another), friendship

nanatemu'i ~ nanateme'i V [nananate-mu'i pl] tell each other, discuss with each other

nanatemmuneweh N dl opponents

nanatetteha(n) N, ADJ grievous; pitiful, awful, sorrowful

nanatettehase(n) ADV grievously; piti-fully, sorrowfully

nanattahsu'a IV be treated, (to) doctor oneself

nanawase" V pl [napaikkah sg] kill selves, commit suicide

nanawaikia recip V meet each other or together

nanewe ~ naneme N [-i; nananewenee(n) pl] relative(s), rela-tion(s); *see* newetuhi

nanewettsi N [nanewettsinnee(n) pl] blessed relative

naniha(n) IV, N be named, be called; name

Hakai en nanihanna? = Hakai en nanihante?

What's your name? = What are you called?

Ne . . . mai nanihante.

My name is . . .

Ne ma'i aise . . . mai nanihante.

My name is . . .

nanihanna N [ø] name

nanikkimma TV mention

nanikkoi IV pl [nanittiyaih sg] laugh uproariously

naninnakkih ~ naninnahki" IV be valued, be held in high regard

naninnewetuah IV (for a spirit to) change itself into a person (with words)

nanippitenka(n) V argue back and forth

nanippunuhaki V express exuberance; *see* punuhaki

nanisuntehai N praying, prayer, religion

nanisuntehai(n) IV pray

nanisuntehai hupia N prayer song

nanisuntehai kahni N house of prayer, church

nanisuntehainka(n) ~ nanisuntehainke(n) TV pray for

nanisuntehaippeh N [-a] religion

nanisuntehaite(n) N [-ti] person who prays

nanisuntsaa ~ ninnasuntsaa TV make fun of, abuse verbally, disparage

nanittematsai TV ask to help

nanittiyaih IV [nanikkoi pl] laugh uproariously

nanittsawaih(kan) TV beseech, appeal to/for, supplicate for

nanittsawainka(n) ~ nanittsawainke(n) TV beseech (someone) for, appeal to (someone) for, supplicate (someone) for

naniwaiki'a TV answer (back to); sass; explain

naniwatsi" IV deny

nankah TV hear, listen; sound, echo, make noise

nankakwiya'a V become afraid from hearing something

nankappeh ADJ heard

nankapitsia(n) TV [nankapittsia(n) dur] believe

nankasua(n) V hear with feeling, feel hearing

nankasuanka(n) ~ nankasuanke(n) TV listen carefully, pay attention, listen thinking about, wonder about, think about

nankasumpana'i TV understand

Kai, ne kai u nankasumpana'inna.

No, I don't understand (it).

Haa'a, ne u nankasumpana'ite.

Yes, I do understand (it).

nankasumpaatu(n/h) TV understand

E ha u nankasumpaatuhka?

Do you understand (it)?

nankih ~ nainkih N [-a] ear

nankih kamma(n) IV have an earache

nankih kammanna N [ø] earache

nanku ~ nankwa P, N on the side of, beside; towards; side; *see* antananku, hakannanku, kappainnanku, kwinahainankuhte(n), maananku, ohinnanku(hten), pinnanku,

sainankuh, senkwinanku,
tapaito'inankuh(ten), tematahain
nankuh(ten), yu'ainankuh(ten)

nanokkoppeh ADJ roasted, baked

nanoote'aikka IV be stored, be packed,
be stashed

napaa N [napaai obj] juice

napaka(n) N [-na] arrowhead, bullet

napatottsema IV sponge oneself off

napaikkah IV [nanawase" pl] kill oneself, commit suicide

napaisai ~ napisai ADV later on, after a
while, in a little while

napeaittempeh N [-a;
napeaittempehnee(n) pl] elderly
relative

napi'ai(yun) IV be in heat (of a female
animal); mate (of a female animal)

napisah(ka) IV have or put rouge or red
face paint on

napisai ~ napaisi ADV later on, after
while, in a little while

napisappeh ADJ made up (with face
paint or makeup)

napitenkah ~ napitenkeh V fight

na'piyaa N fifteen cents

napooppeh N [-a] picture, photo,
drawing, inscription, piece of
writing

nappiasi(n) ~ nappiaseh N money

nappihtuh ~ napittuh TV trade

napuha N [puha] supernatural power;
(healing) ceremony

napuhakante(n) N treatment, cure; one's
own doctor

napuhanai IV be cured, be healed, be
treated (for an illness); for a healing
ceremony to be held, hold a healing
ceremony

napuhanainna N doctoring, curing,
healing; curing service or ceremony

napuih ~ napunih IV [nanapui pl] look,
appear, seem, be seen, be visible, be
light

napuihtai(n) ~ napuittai(n) V divorce,
separate (of a couple)

napuihtaippeh ~ napuittaippeh ADJ
divorced, separated

napuikka(n) IV be light, be visible, be
seen

napuikki(n) ~ napuimpite V become
(day)light

napuinna N appearance, looks

napuippeh ADJ, N seen; appearance

napuippehkante(n) ADJ having (a certain) appearance

napuisunaih V dream

napuite(n) ADJ looking, appearing

napuittai(n) ~ na'puittai(n) ~ napuihtai(n)
IV divorce; separate (of a couple)

napuittaippeh ~ napuihtaippeh ADJ
divorced, separated

napuinna N appearance

napuippeh N, ADJ appearance; seen,
visible

napunih ~ napuih IV [nanapuni pl] look,
appear, seem, be seen, be visible, be
light

Nasanti" ~ Nasuntih ~ Taattsewin
Nawookkah N Sunday

nasuntamah(kan) TV remember

Nasuntih ~ Nasanti" ~ Taattsewin
Nawookkah N Sunday

nasuntiyaih IV die giving up on life

nasuntsaa TV abuse, torment, pick on

nasuntsaappeh ADJ abused, tormented

nasuwatsih TV forget

nasuyakai TV covet, desire

nasuyekwi" ~ nasu'yekwi" TV pretend;
think of oneself as; be arrogant, be
conceited, be obnoxious, be a smart
aleck

nasu'yekwite(n) N, ADJ arrogant, conceited, obnoxious, smart aleck

natainna(n) N one's man (said by a
woman); husband

natainnappettsi N (dear) husband [wife
speaking]

natakkoa IV (for rocks to) be piled up

Natakkoa TOP Elko, NV

natayaa IV pl walk in ritual procession
(praying or singing) before round
dance; parade

natea TV ask for; accept

nate'ahwaikka(n) IV tell; be told, be
explained

nate'ahwaikkante(n) ADJ foretold

natekih(ka) IV be placed, be located, be put; be buried

natekkate(n) N [-ti] edible food, good to eat

natekotah TV spread out

natekwina V tell a story, narrate

natekwinanka(n) ~ natekwinanke(n) TV tell a story to, narrate to

natekwinappeh N [-a; nanatekwinappeh pl] story, myth, folktale; rascal, naughty person

natemaka TV sell

natemakanke(n) ~ natemakanka(n) TV sell to

natemakappeh ADJ sold

natemakate(n) N [-ti] merchant, seller

natemeeh IV be bought, be paid for, cost

natempai N voice, mouth

natemu'i ~ nateme'i TV tell, narrate

natemu'inka(n) ~ natemu'inke(n) ~ nateme'inke(n) TV tell to, narrate to

natenoo N [-'a] saddle

natenoo punku N [-i] saddle horse

natenoo'am pampi N saddle horn

natenootekih TV saddle, put a saddle on

natepaha(n) TV be bet, be wagered

natepahappeh N [-a] bet, wager; payment

natia(n) ADV, ADJ very, really, terribly, too, highly; extreme, great, powerful, strong, difficult, hard, terrible; enter-prising; lots, much

natianku ADV, ADJ forceful(ly), strong(ly), extreme(ly), rigorous(ly); fearfully, distressfully

natia suante(n) ADJ smart, intelligent

natoppaikkah IV be piled up

natottsema IV wipe or sponge oneself off

nattahsu'a TV treat, (to) doctor

nattahsu'u(n) N [-na] medicine

nattahsu'unkahni N hospital

nattahsu'unkante(n) N [-ti] one who has medicine; doctor

natukku N [-i] (one's own) body

natusuppeh ADJ ground up

natsaasuanka(n) ~ natsaasuanke(n) V like each other

natsammayaappeh ADJ mixed up, mixed together

natsasunaih IV scratch oneself

natsattamahkante(n) ADJ tied up

natsattamappeh ADJ [natsattami'ippeh pl] tied up

natsattawaih ~ natsattawih N [-'a] gate, opening, door

natsattawaih ~ natsattawih IV be open

natsattekih(kan) IV be placed (with hand), put, located; lie in state (of a deceased)

natsattekihkante(n) ADJ placed, located; lying in state (of a deceased)

natsattema N door, gate

natsattemah IV be closed

na'tsawaini ~ wanatsawaini N [-'a] oriole

natsittoo V walk with a cane

natsuku N [-a] stepfather

na'uttuppeh ADJ given

na'uttuhtaippeh ADJ given away

na'wa'i ADV dl [na'wa'iten] like each other, similar to each other

nawasettaippeh ADJ pl killed

nawate'inte(n) ADJ lacking, missing

nawatsinkappeh ~ nawatsinkeppeh ADJ lost

nawaih IV climb (down), descend, incline

nawaihyanka(n) ~ nawaihyanke(n) ~ nawaihanke(n) IV get burned, be burned

nawaihyankappeh ~ nawaihankeppeh ADJ burned

nawaiti IV purify oneself with smoke, smoke oneself

nawekkoappeh ADJ enclosed

nawoih IV pl [yakai"] cry

nawookkah N day of week

nayaa TV track (down)

nayaanka(n) ~ nayaanke(n) TV have taken away from

na'yahnai IV pl [yahnai" sg] laugh

nayekwin/h IV pl [nemi sg] move about, travel, wander; gather, hunt for

naaiyawi V play handgame (stickgame)

nai P [naiten] for, to, from (this/that) direction

nai P from; *see* sanai, s<u>a</u>inai, sinai,
sonai, sunai

nai meaningless rhythmical song word

-nai V INCORP make, build, create; *see*
hupianai, isannai, kahninai, manememe-
nai, ohaanai, pipihnai, tuannai,
puhanai, tepannai

-nainka(n) ~ -nainke(n) V INCORP make
for, have (someone) make

n<u>a</u>inkih ~ nankih N [-a] ear

n<u>a</u>inkiwatte(n) ~ nankiwatte(n) ADJ
earless

naipi(n) N [-tta; nai'yannee(n) pl]
teenage girl, young lady

nai'pi(n) N [-tta] little girl

naippeh ADJ made, built, created

na'isape ADJ horny, sexually aroused

Nai'yan Tekkoi TOP Young Ladies' Rock
Peak

nai'yannee(n) N pl [naipi(n) sg] teenage
girl, young lady

ne PRO I, my

neai" IV blow

neaippeh N [-a] wind

neaippi(n) N [-tta] wind

neaite(n) N [-ti] wind

nea(n) PRO my

nease(n) PRO my own

neekki'ah IV nick oneself

neekkwantupihkanna N [ø] bundle; *see*
wekkwantupi

neekkwintsunah IV [neekkwintsuni'ih pl]
curl up, coil up

neemapatekki(n) IV wet oneself, anoint
oneself, be anointed

neemai TV be tired of

neemeennooh IV carry oneself around

neempeattai(n) ~ neempuihtai(n) V leave
a mate or spouse, separate from,
divorce

neennooh(kan) TV carry a cradle board

neeppa'ih IV be spanked

neeppahih IV be thrown off (a horse)

neeppatah [neeppati'ih pl] IV spread out

neeppatekki(n) IV wet oneself, anoint
oneself, be anointed

neeppuinuinuh IV spin around

neesipi IV shave (oneself)

neesunka'ah ~ neesunkan(na) TV feel
Hakai en neesunkanna?
How do you feel?
—Ne tsaan neesunkanna.
—I feel good.
—Ne k<u>a</u>itsaan neesunkanna.
—I don't feel well.

neettemah IV be locke up

neettemahkante(n) N [-ti] inmate, prisoner

neettemappeh ADJ locked

neettiah IV spill

neettutua ~ neettutai" IV stretch oneself

neettunaittseh IV pull away

neewainihka(n) IV be hanging

neewihtuhappeh ADJ worn out

neeyekwimmi'a(kwain) IV carry oneself
around

nehe(n) PRO 1st dl excl poss our

nehese(n) RFLX PRO dl excl ourselves

nehi PRO 1st dl excl obj us two

nei PRO me

nekenta(n) N [-na] goose; *see* tuun
nekenta(n)

nekkah IV dance

nekkakwai ~ nekkanemi IV dance around

nekkamaih IV 'go dancing', pass on,
pass away, die

nekkatenka N, P dance place

nekkatenkappai'i NP dance time

nekkawoppih N [-a] dancer

nekki N [ø] belt

neme ~ newe [-i; nemenee(n) pl] person, people, Indian, Shoshoni; *see*
manemenai

nemi IV [nemmi dur, yeyenkah dl, yenka
pl] travel, wander, roam; live

Nemi Manemenaippehkante(n) N Maker
of People

nemikka(n) IV sg live

neminemmi IV travel around, wander
around, roam

nemme(n) PRO 1st pl excl subj, poss we,
our

nemmese(n) RFLX PRO 1st excl ourselves

nemmi PRO 1st pl excl us

nempitsinka(n) ~ nempitsinke(n) TV (for
a mother to) nurse

nenkappeh ~ nennappeh N [-a] chest

nenneema'ai ADV along with other people

nese(n) RFLX PRO myself

newe ~ neme [-i; newenee(n) pl] person, people, Indian, Shoshoni

newe natekwinappeh N [-a] Shoshoni story, folktale

newe pahu(n) N [-na] Indian tobacco, wild tobacco

newe taikwa" V speak Shoshoni
E ha newe taikwante?
Do you speak Shoshoni?
— **Haa'a, ne newe taikwa sumpana'inna.**
— Yes, I know how to speak Shoshoni.

Newe Tekkoi TOP Indian Rock Hill

newe tepooh V write Shoshoni

neweh PRO 1st dl excl [nehi obj, noho(n) poss] we two

newe(n) ~ neme(n) N [-na, -'a] liver

Newen Topo'ih TOP 'Standing People' = Horseshoe Bend, NV

newetuhi N [newetuhinee(n) pl] relative, relation; *see* nanewe

Newi Manemenaippehkante N Maker or Creator of People

ni P [-nni] like, similar to, as, (this/that) way; *see* sanni, sainni, sinni, sonni, sunni

ni"- INSTR PRFX with words or by talking

nia" ~ niha TV call, name

niakka(n) ~ nihakka(n) V call, name; be called, be named

ni'aipui ~ ni'aipunni TV destroy with words, make fun of

niha ~ nihya N name

niha ~ nia TV call, name

nihakka(n) ~ niakka(n) V call, name; be called, be named

nihannih TV [nimmee pl] talk about, discuss; decide, judge

nihannippeh ADJ discussed

nihya ~ niha N name

niikwi" TV say (to), tell, mean, mention; remind

nikkawi TV ask to gather together

nikkwitah IV scream

nikkwiya'a TV scare with words, startle

nikkwisinka(n) ~ nikkwisinke(n) TV trap with words

nimmawiih TV tell to go away

nimma'anka(n) ~ nimma'anke(n) ~ nimma'oonka(n) TV calm someone upset by talking to

nimma'i(n) ~ nimma'ikki TV call, say to, speak to; calm (someone who is upset); persuade

nimmapitsi'a TV strengthen with words

nimmawiih(tain) TV send away, tell to go away

nimmakwittsi TV criticize, scorn

nimmapana'ai(n) TV know how to say

nimmatenkah TV finish talking

nimmatsuhinka(n) ~ nimmatsuhinke(n) TV overpower with words

nimmeeh TV pl [nihannih sg] talk, refer to, decide, judge

nimmuya'i TV reject

ninnaah ~ ninnaha TV speak up for, stick up for, defend

ninnakkih ~ ninnahki" TV value, give value to, hold in high regard

ninnapunni ~ ninnapui V explain, discuss; call, say, tell, mean

ninnasuntsaa ~ nanisuntsaa TV make fun of, abuse verbally, disparage

ninnatawi'i(n) TV warn against

nippahai" V argue

ni(sen) P [-nni(sen)] like, similar to, as, (this/that) way; *see* sannise(n), sainnise(n), sinnise(n), sonnise(n), sunnise(n)

nisua" TV express, say, sound

nisu'nai TV bother with words, annoy by talking

nisummaa TV joke, tease

nisummampeh N humorous person, joker

nisummaappeh ADJ, N (something) funny or humorous

nisunka'ah TV discuss, feel out with words

(kai) nittapu'i V express a lack of confidence in or low opinion of; not express confidence in nitteah TV curse

nitteappeh ADJ cursed

nittehai TV speak tenderly or kindly to

nittehu'i(n) ~ nittuhu'i(n) TV scold, chide, fuss about

nittepui TV wake up

nitto'i(n) TV sing (a song)

nitto'inka(n) TV sing (a song) for

nittuhu'i(n) ~ nittehu'i(n) TV scold, chide, fuss about

nittunaitseh IV insist, be insistent or vehement; persist

nittsu'ah TV finish talking

niwaih TV ask for, beg for

niwatsi" TV deny

niweneh TV pl [taikwa" sg, yekwi" sg] speak, talk, say

niwenenka(n) ~ niwenenke(n) TV ask to stand, have (someone) stand

niwiih(tain) TV cast away mentally or spiritually

niyahnai(n) TV make laugh with words, joke

niyekwi TV tell, instruct

niyokottsi N [-a] comic, joker

no'akante(n) ADJ pregnant

noha ADV used to

noha ~ nuha ADV just

noha kia ADV doubtfully, could be, might be

noha kwa'i ADV used to

nohappi V dur be setting (of a chicken)

no'ipeh N [-a] womb, uterus

noitsai ADJ, ADV [nointsai song form] sticky (as feet in mud); stickily

noittsi'i IV squirt, ejaculate

noittsi'ippeh ~ noittso'i(ppeh) N [-a] semen, sperm

nokahni N (laying) nest

nokateh IV stay at home

nokatenka(n) ~ nokatenke(n) TV care for, take care of, babysit

nokko(n) ~ nokkoh TV roast, bake

nokkoppeh ADJ, N [-a] roasted; roast; loaf of bread

noo PRO any, some

noo ADV even though; indefinitely; maybe, perhaps; must, might

noo" TV carry on back, bring, take; carry in truck, haul

noo(n) ADV, CONJ awhile, for some time, duratively; while, though, although

noo(n) ADV just, only

noo sampai ADV maybe so

noo sunninte sampai ADV even so, just the same

nooh AUX V move about

noohakai PRO however, whatever; somehow, anyhow

noohakaitte(n) PRO [noohakaitti obj] any kind, some kind, whatever kind; somehow weird

noohakanni(kku) PRO anyway, someway, whatever way, however, somehow; somehow weird

noohakate(n) PRO [noohakkai obj] anyone, anybody, someone, somebody, whoever

noohakattu(n) LOC anywhere, somewhere, wherever

noohakka LOC anywhere, somewhere, wherever

noohakkai PRO obj [noohakate(n) subj] anyone, anybody, someone, somebody, whoever

noohihiintsinee(n) pl PRO anyone else, anybody else, whoever else

noohii(n) PRO [noohinna ~ noohinnattsi'a obj] something, anything, whatever, thing(s)

noohimpai ADV anytime, sometime, whenever

noohimpaika ADV anywhere, somewhere, wherever

nookatete(n) N [-na] hill

nookka(n) TV pack, carry

nookki(n) TV carry hither

noomi'a(taih) IV move (away)

noomi'ataippeh ADJ moved away

noomi'ate(n) N [-ti] mover, person who moves

noommi'a TV carry, move

noo(n) ADV, CONJ awhile, for some time, duratively; while, though, although

noo(n) ADV just, only

noon (kwa'i) kia ADV not certain, not
  sure

noon tea CONJ, ADV or, or else; even

noon tea . . . noon tea CONJ either . . .
  or (else)

noonnii TV go get

no'opi(n) (noa-) N [-tta] hill

noopite ~ nooppite TV bring back, take
  back; make camp; arrive at

noose(n) ADV in addition

noote'aikah TV stash, pack

noote(n) V [song form] nest(le), make a
  nest

nopontah IV bend over

nopontahkante(n) ADJ hunchbacked,
  hunched

nottsoni N nest

nottsoninai IV make a nest

noyo N [-i] egg; testicle

noyopunku N [i] stallion

nua ~ nuwa IV move

nuha ~ noha ADV just

nuhi(n) ~ nui(n) V play

nukki IV [nunukki dl, nutaa(n) pl] run

nukkikki(nna) IV run along slowly,
  travel

nukkimi'a IV run fast

nukkinka(n) ~ nukkinke(n) TV make run,
  make function

nukkinooh IV run along, jog

nunukki IV dl [nukki sg, nutaa(n) pl] run

nutaa(n) IV pl [nukki sg, nunukki dl] run

nuwa ~ nua IV move

nuyuah IV crawl

O

o- DEM/LOC BASE [so-] that, there; *see*
  ote(n), oteweh, otee(n), okkuh, onni,
  opi, opuhni, ose(n), ottu(n), owa'ih

o'ana DEM-LOC [so'ana] that place;
  there somewhere

ohaa(ttsi) N [-'a] baby, infant

ohaanai V INCORP have a baby, bear a
  child

ohahuittsuu N small yellow bird

ohainnankuh ~ ohinnankuh ADV (on
  the) left side, leftward

ohainnankuhte(n) N left side

ohakamma(n) V INCORP taste salty

ohamunih ~ ohamoonih N [-a] gold
  money

ohapi(n) N [-tta] salt

ohappihte(n) (oha"-) ADJ yellow,
  golden

Ohattewene" TOP 'Yellow Rockface' =
  Hundred Mile Post, NV

ohi" IV cough

ohinnankuh ~ ohainnankuh ADV (on
  the) left side, leftward

ohipekka(n) V have a cold, get a cold

ohippeh N [-a] a cold

ohpi N mesquite beans

oitte(n) DEM [oitti obj] that (special)
  kind

okia ~ osen kia ADV probably, maybe

okka DEM obj [ote(n) subj, okka(n) poss]
  that

okkuh DEM-LOC there

okkwaikki(nnemmi) IV meander (e.g.,
  stream)

okwai" IV flow

okwaite(n) N, ADJ [-na] stream, creek;
  flood; flowing, flooding

onni DEM-ADV that way, like that

ontempaa N whiskey

ontempihte(n) (onten-) ADJ brown

oo(n) N [-na] leg

ooki V gather together

oompi(n) (oon-) N [-tta] lava rock

oo(n) N [-na] leg

Oon Natsippata TOP Spread Out Lava
  Rock Hill

oosaante(n) N rust

Oosaanten Kate(n) TOP 'Rusty Place' =
  Merrit Mountain northeast of
  Mountain City, NV

oosaanto'ih IV rust, get rusty

oosaanto'ippeh ADJ rusted, rusty

oowatte(n) ADJ legless

ooyoku(sen) ~ oyoku(sen) ~
  ooyote(sen) ADV, QUANT always;
  all, every; whole

opai DEM-LOC around there

opaika(nten) ~ opika(nten) DEM-DEM-P
  that amount, that much

opi DEM-LOC around there, thereabouts

opika(nten) ~ op<u>a</u>ika(nten) DEM-DEM-P [-na/-i] that much, that amount

opuhni ~ opu(n) DEM-LOC over that way

osa ~ pa'osa N [-i] water jug, water basket, bottle

ose(n) DEM that (is the one)

ose ha kia naketsa? ADV Is that really so?

osen kia ~ okia ADV probably, maybe

ote(n) DEM [okka obj, okka(n) poss] that

otee(n) DEM [otii obj, otee(n) poss] those

oteweh DEM [otehi, otehen poss] those

oto'oto INTRJCT ouch!

ottappeh N [-a] fine dust

ottu(n) DEM-LOC over that way

owa'ih ADV like that

oyo(n) ~ oyose(n) ADV, QUANT always, every time; all, every

oyointe(n) (oyon) QUANT all

oyoku(sen) ~ ooyoku(sen) ~ ooyote(sen) ADV, QUANT always; all, every; whole

oyonte(n) ~ oyontettsi N [-ti ~ -na] stuff, possessions, belongings, property, things, clothing

oyontempa'i(n) V INCORP have property

oyose(n) (oyon) ADV, QUANT always, every time; all, every

P

paa (pa-, pappa distrib) N, ADJ [-i] water, drink, liquid, liquor; juicy, liquidy

paakkappeh N [-a] ice

Paam Pasa TOP Dry Spring, NV

pa'a(n) P, ADV [pa'ai, pa'anku, pa'antu(n), pa'ante(n), pa'anti] on (top of), above, over; high, up; after; more than; see nahpa'a(n), nanappa'a(n), pempa'a(n), supa'a(n)

pa'annaih P, ADV from above

pa'ante(n) P, ADV, ADJ [pa'a(n), pa'ai, pa'anku, pa'antu(n), pa'anti] on (top of), above, over; up; high

pa'atai ~ pa'ataihku ADV on one's back

paatekkappeh N [-a] watermelon

pa'attsi ADJ high

paatua(mpite) IV (for water to) accumulate, spring forth

pa'ai P, ADV [pa'a(n), pa'anku, pa'antu(n), pa'ante(n), pa'anti] on (top of), above, over; high, up; after; for; more than

pa'<u>ai</u>meah(kan) IV get drunk, be drunk

pa'<u>ai</u>meahkante(n) ADJ drunk

pa'emah ~ pa'emeah ~ ema" IV rain

pa'emate(n) ~ pa'emeate(n) ~ emate(n) N [-ti] rain

paha N [-'a] aunt, father's sister; nephew/niece of a woman

pahampia N [-'a] sister-in-law of a man

pahapi IV swim, float

pahapite(n) N [-ti] bather, swimmer

pahattsi N [-a] mother-in-law

pah<u>ai</u>" ~ pahi" IV [papahi dl, sawe'i pl] fall off, drop down; see mapahai", nippahai, tsappah<u>ai</u>"

pahai pia seemaahte(n) NO three hundred

pahaimaahte(n) (pahaimaah-) NO [pahaimaayente(n)] thirty

Pahain Nawookkah N Wednesday

pahaitte(n) (pahai-) NO three

pahki ~ pakki N canvas

pahkiwanappeh N [-a] canvas

paho ~ pahu N hunger

pahoko'ih IV pl [pahotiyaih sg] starve, be hungry

pahopekka(n) ~ pahonapekka(n) ~ pahupekka(n) IV be hungry

pahotiyaih IV [pahoko'ih pl] starve, be very hungry

pahukoih ~ pahunakoih IV pl [pahutiyaih sg] starve, be hungry

pahu ~ paho N hunger

pahu'i V smoke (tobacco)

pahu(n) N [-na] tobacco, cigarette; ceremony

pahunapekka(n) ~ pahupekka(n) IV be hungry

pahunkahni N ceremonial house

pahunkahninai INCORP V make a ceremonial house

pahunkwitsa(n) N [-na] angle worm

pahupekka(n) ~ pahunapekka(n) ~
pahopekka(n) IV be hungry

pahupekkante(n) N [-ti obj] hunger

pahutiyaih IV [pahukoih pl] starve, be
very hungry

-pa'ih INSTR V pl [-tekwah sg] hit; *see*
tappa'ih, toppa'ih, weppa'ih

-pa'i(n) V INCORP have; there is, there
are

pakahni N bar

paka(n) N [-na] arrowhead, arrow, bullet; penis

Pakannapoo N [-a] Cheyenne Indian

pakantutuh N [-a] dragonfly

pakantsukkih N [-a] blackbird

pakateh ~ pakate(n) IV be a body of still
water, lake or pool

pakatete(n) N, ADJ pool or body of
water; still (of water)

pakenaih(kan) IV get blurry, get foggy

pakenappeh [pakenna ~ pakenaa song
forms] N [-a] fog

pakenapuih(kan) IV have blurry eyes

pakkatuuh ~ pakkiata N buckaroo,
cowboy

pakki ~ pahki N canvas

pakkiata ~ pakkatuuh N [-a] buckaroo,
cowboy

pakku P ways

pakuyu'ai(n) IV cool down/off

pa'kwana N mint

paakkwitahawo ~ pankwitahawo N [-'a]
raccoon

pakwinompi(n) N [-tta] large sagebrush

pakwittsu'ih IV splash

pamaka TV water, give drink to

pammuhi N [-'a] mole

pammuuse TV hurry!

pampi N [ø] head, hair

pampi kamma'a N [-a] orange-red currant in mountains

pampi kamma(n) V have a headache

pampi kammanna N [ø] headache

pampi pusi'a N [-i] head lice

pampitsikka'ah TV cut hair

Pampittsimminna N Sioux

pampo'naih N [-a] mole

pampunua IV swirl around, twirl around

pampunuaniite(n) N whirlpool, swirling
water

Pamuseh NAME (man's)

panai ADV up, upwards

-pana'in/h ~ -pana'ai(n) V know how to;
see mapana'ai(n), nimmapana'ai(n),
puisumpana'ih, sumpana'ih

panapui N [-'a] window

paninkah(tain) ~ panittainka(n) ~ panit-
tainke(n) TV leave for; drop off for;
deliver for

panipite TV bring back

panippu(n) ADV upwards

panittaih ~ panittai(n) TV leave; drop
off, deliver

panittainka(n) ~ panittainke(n) ~
paninkah(tain) TV leave for; drop off
for; deliver to

pankwitahawo ~ pakkwitahawo N [-'a]
raccoon

Pannaihte(n) N [-na] Bannock

pantei N [-'a] killdeer

pantoyaah TV for water, to carry
off/along

pantsuku N [-'a] otter

pa'ohaa N [-'a] water baby (mythological being)

Pa'ohaa'an Kappai TOP Water Baby's
Bed

pa'osa ~ osa N [-i] water jug, water
basket, bottle

papi N [-a] older brother, close older
male cousin

papitsii N [-'a] weasel

Papiyotsa ~ Paiyuti ~ Payuti N [-'a]
Northern Paiute

Pappatappisi N Italian

papuih(ka) IV be teary-eyed

papumpihte(n) (papun) ADJ clear,
transparent; pale

pasa" IV dry up

pasaattointsi N watery foam; *see* saattointsi

pasakkwinapa'i ADJ muddy

pasakwinappeh N [-a] mud

pasampeh ADJ skinny, thin

pasampettsi N [-a] skinny one

pasanka(n) ~ pasanke(n) TV dry

pasankappeh ~ pasankeppeh ADJ, N [-a]
dried things

pasappeh ADJ dry, dried

pasattaippeh ADJ dried up

pasattukku N [-i] "dry flesh" =
tuberculosis

paseepi(n) N [-tta] water willow

paseeweyaa N water willow stand or
place

pasekkittah N [-a] basket

Pasekkoh N Basque

pasikkokko(n) ~ kokko(n) N [-na] bull
snake

pasikoo N [-'a] camas

pasiwakkatete(n) [patsiwankaten song
form] N sand dune; see katete(n)

pasiwampi(n) ~ pasiwompi(n) N [-tta]
sand

Pasiwa Wia TOP Sand Pass near
Horseshoe Bend, NV

pasokompii N [-'a] swallow

Pasokompii'a Hunupi(n) TOP 'Swallow
Canyon' = Barn Swallow Canyon

pasokwai N [-'a] sweet cicely, sweet
root

pasu'attsih N [-a] water spider (that
runs on top of water)

pata N butter

-patah INSTR V [-pati'ih pl] spread out;
see keppatantsih, neeppatah,
tsappatah, tsippatah, weppatah

patasikaih IV sparkle

patatsi(ki) IV shine; see mapataatsi,
namapataatsi, tatsiki

pateheya N [-'a] elk

patehwi ~ patuhi IV melt

patekkih TV soak, wet; see weppatekkih,
neeppatekki(n), neemapatekki(n),
namapatekki(n)

patekwinappeh N [-a] clay

patemeenka(n) ~ patemeenke(n) TV buy
drinks for

patetsoppih ~ patetsoppeh N [-a]
spring, spring water

patewintsi N willow shoots

patokoa N [-i] water snake

pato'ih ~ patu'ih IV wade; see nampatu'ih

patontsia N [-'a] yarrow

patottsema TV sponge off

patuhi ~ patehwi IV melt

patu'ih ~ pato'ih IV wade

patuntsi [patewaantsi song form] N a
large grass seed

patsawenneh(kan) TV soak; put water
out (for an animal) in a container

patsawennenka(n) TV soak

patsi N [-'a] older sister, close female
cousin

patsittempi(n) N waterworn cobblestone

patso'i IV be wet

patso'ippeh ADJ wet

patsokki IV drip

pattsokki(kin) IV drip repetitively

pawaaka N [-'a] columbine

pawikkah ~ pawikkih IV (for) water (to
break away/loose, as in a flash flood)

payakwahni ~ yakwahni N [-'a] frog

payampa N juicy wild carrots

payuppuka N bog

Payuti ~ Paiyuti N [-'a] Northern
Paiute

Payuttsi ~ Paiyuttsi N Southern Paiute

¹pai N artery, blood vessel

²pai N, P [paite(n)] time; see sipai,
saipai, sopai, sapai, supai

³pai P around here/there; see sipai,
saipai, sopai, sapai, supai

paihai N [ø] seed

paihapinna N blood vessel

paika'i V be the height of

paika(nten) ~ pika(nten) N, P [paikanti
obj] amount; (this/that) much, size;
see sapaika(n), saipaika(n), sipaika(n),
sopaika(n), supaika(n)

paikkah TV [wase" pl] kill

paikkanke(n) ~ paikkanka(n) TV kill for

paikko'ah ~ paikoah V [paiko'ih pl]
split open

paikwakkwapih ~ peekkwakwapih N
[-pihti obj] blood vein(s)

paikwi" IV swell

paikwikante(n) N [-ti] swollen part or
area

paikwikka(n) IV be swollen

paikwippeh ADJ swollen

paikwiwainkah TV stop the swelling

paina(n) N [-na] yellow jacket, wasp, hornet

painampekka(n) IV have canker sores in mouth

painke(n) N [-na] nettles

painkwi N [ø] fish

painkwihea TV fish, catch fish, trap fish

paite" N [-i] daughter

paite(n) (pai) N, P time; *see* sapai, saipai, sopai, supai

paiteppe N [-a] young daughter (pre-puberty)

paiti" TV pl [tawiih ~ tahwii sg] throw, scatter; sow, plant

paitittai(n) ~ paittai(n) TV pl [wiittai(n) sg] throw away

paitse" TV [paittse dur] holler, call (out to), invite

paitse" TV [paittse dur] go get (a person), take (a person)

paitsenkakki TV holler after, call to

paitseppite TV bring (a person)

paiwekka'ah TV let blood; cut a blood vessel

paiyekwi P next to

Paiyuti ~ Payuti N [-'a] Northern Paiute

Paiyuttsi ~ Payuttsi N Southern Paiute

pe EMPH emphatic particle

pe(n) RFLX PRO its own, his own, her own

pea" TV leave

peattai(n) ~ peaittai(n) ~ puittai(n) TV leave, stop, cease

peattenkah ADV outside

peai ADV, ADJ long ago, a long time ago; old

peai taka ADV that's all

peaise(n) ADV already; all over; completely

peaittaih ~ peattai(n) ~ puittai(n) V stop, cease

peaittempeh ~ peaite(n) (peai) ADJ, N [pepeaittempehnee(n) ~ pepeaitte(n) pl] old (person)

peehapi" IV (for a bloodline to) flow or lie

peehapinna N bloodline

peekkih IV bleed

paikwakkwapih ~ peekkwakwapih N [-pihti obj] blood vein(s)

peentsi N, ADJ [-a] fine fur, down; furry; *see* peesi

peeppi(n) (pee"-) N [-tta] blood

peesi [peentsi song form] N, ADJ [-a] fine fur, down; furry

pehai(ten) ADJ, ADV lightly, light footed(ly), graceful(ly); lively, active(ly)

pehe N [pehi obj] fur, hide, outer covering

pehe(n) RFLX PRO dl their own

pehi RFLX PRO obj dl themselves

pehnah/n CONJ because, for

pehyø(n) ~ peye(n) N [-na] duck, mallard duck

pei RFLX PRO obj it, him, her

-peittseiki(n) INSTR V [-peittseittseiki(n) dur] make noise; *see* koppeittseiki(n), keppeittseittseiki(n), kuppeittseittseiki(n)

-pekka(n) V INCORP be afflicted with, suffer from

pemma" ~ pemma(n) REL PRO with which

pemma'ai REL PRO with whom

pemma(n) REL PRO on which; with which

pemmanku REL PRO from which, from whom

pemmayente(n) REL PRO from whom, from which

pemme(n) RFLX PRO their own

pemmese(n) RFLX PRO themselves, their own

pemmi RFLX PRO them

pempa'a(n) REL PRO on which, where; about which

pempai REL PRO when, during

pe(n) RFLX PRO its own, his own, her own

pen taka(sen) RFLX PRO itself, himself, herself

penka REL PRO [penkayente(n)] where, at which

Penka Tan Tapaitekka'inna TOP 'Place Where One Eats Lunch' = Dinner Station or Twenty-Five Mile Station penkahtu(n) REL PRO through which

penkuppa(n) REL PRO [penkuppai(ten), penkuppayente(n)] in which

pennaih IV be only one

pennaihka(n) IV remain

pennaipih N only one

penne(n) ~ penna(n) ~ pennese(n) ~ pennase(n) RFLX PRO itself, himself, herself

pentukka(n) REL PRO under which

pentsi RFLX PRO [song form] its own, his own, her own; self; see pe(n)

pentu(n) REL PRO, ADV through which; through there

pese(n) RFLX PRO itself, himself, herself

pesu'a N self, oneself, himself, herself

peta N [-i] arm

petawatte(n) ADJ armless

petette(kin) IV scurry, flutter (poetic); see weppetette(kin)

pettente(n) ADJ heavy

petteeyu(n) IV be heavy

pettitah ~ tetesih N [-a] potato

peweh(sen) RFLX PRO 3rd dl itself, himself, herself

peye(n) ~ pehye(n) N [-na] duck, mallard duck

pi"- INSTR PRFX with the back, behind, or butt

pia ~ pii N mother

pia ADJ [pipia pl; piya song form] big, large, tall, grand, great

Pia Hunupi(n) ~ Pia Sennahunupi(n) TOP 'Big (Aspen) Canyon' = Indian Meadows, NV

pia isa ~ isa N [-i] wolf

Pia Neaippittan Kahni TOP Home of the Big Wind

Pia Payuppuka TOP 'Big Bog' = Indian Hay Meadows, NV

Pia Pohopi Hunupi(n) TOP 'Big Sagebrush Canyon' = Taylor Canyon, NV

pia seemaahte(n) NO one hundred

Pia Sennahunupi(n) ~ Pia Hunupi(n) TOP 'Big (Aspen) Canyon' = Indian Meadows, NV

pia tekkah V feast, have a big meal

Pia Tettsohpai TOP Pleasant Valley Canyon

piaittsi N big one, fat one

piakammu N [-i] white tailed jackrabbit; snowshoe rabbit

pi'ake(n) N [-na] caterpillar

piakuittsu(n) N [-na] buffalo

piakwi'naa N [-'a] large bird, eagle

Pianampai NAME Big Foot

pianku ADV openly

piante(n) ADJ [pianti, pipiante(n) pl] big, large, tall

piapaa N sea, ocean

piapeh N female, animal mother, mare; coward, sissy

piapoko N [-i] medicinal plant (large leaves, white flowers)

piappehte(n) ADJ [pipiappete(n) pl] big, large, tall

Piappehtem Po'in Nawainnna TOP 'Big Trail Going Down' = Highway 51, Big Hill south of Little Valley, ID

Pia Sennahunupi(n) TOP [-tta] Indian Meadows

piasonippeh N [-a] bunchgrass, tall rye grass

piatetsii N [-a] wild rice (now extinct)

piattsi N [-a] aunt, mother's sister; nephew/niece of a woman

piawaako ~ waako N bull frog

piawaikite(n) ADJ wide

piawaiku N wide area

piawoppih N [-a] the biggest one

piayu IV be large

pihaa ~ pihnaa ~ pihyaa N, ADJ sugar, honey; sweet

pihatukku ~ pihyatukku N [-i] sugar diabetes

pihetsih N [-a] meat

pihianneweh dl, pihiannee(n) pl N [tuineppe sg] boys

pihittsaah TV lift behind up

pihnaa ~ pihyaa ~ pihaa N, ADJ [pihya-] honey, sugar; sweet

pihuittsi V defecate loosely and quickly

pihuitsittsiki V defecate extremely loosely and continuously

pihyakih IV [pihyakkih dur] itch

pihyaa ~ pihnaa ~ pihaa N, ADJ honey, sugar; sweet

pihyaa te'oikante(n) ADJ having sugar diabetes

pihyaa kamman(na) IV taste sweet

pihyaamua N [-'a] honeybee

pihyatukku ~ pihatukku N [-i] sugar diabetes

pihye(n) N [-na] heart

pii ~ pia N [-'a] mother, mom

piisi N [-'a] hummingbird

piiya N beer

pikan(ten) ~ paikan(ten) N, P [pikanti obj] amount; (this/that) much; *see* sapika(n), saipika(n), sipika(n), sopika(n), supika(n)

pikappeh N [-a] buckskin

pikase(n) P, ADV the same as

pikih N [-a] pig

pikka'ah TV [pipponka'ih sg] break (flex obj) with behind

pikkenah TV sit on top of

pikkopah TV [pikkopai'ih pl] break (rigid obj) with behind

pikkitsa'a TV smash by sitting on

pikkontatah N [-a] big dollar

pikunaih TV rub butt against

pikkwaitu'ah TV take off (e.g., pants, skirt)

pimmaa N, ADJ [song form] cow, bovine

pimmito'ih ~ pimpito'ih IV back out

pimmokottsih N [-a] pocket

pimpippu(n) ADV backwards

pimpito'ih ~ pimmito'ih IV back out

pinna ADJ, ADV [-i] previous, preceding, latter; again

pinnah CONJ but

pinnaih P behind, in back of

pinnaih(ka) V be left over

pinnaippeh ADJ left over

pinnanku ADV last, behind; next time

Pinnanku tease em puinnuhi GREETING See you again next time. = Goodbye.

pinnoo(n/h) TV carry on the back

pintsai CONJ but (song word); *see* pinnah

pintsih TV [song form] suck, suckle; *see* pitsih

pipih N [-a] baby

pipihnai V INCORP have a baby

pi'pihta N [-'a] horsefly

pippite IV dl [pite sg/pl] arrive, come back

pipponka'ih TV pl [pikka'ah sg] break (flex objs) with behind

pippupuah(kan) IV bend over; raise up the behind (bending over)

pipuntu IV go back (song word)

pipusi N [-'a] stinkbug

pisa" TV paint, put face paint on

pisappi(n) N [-tta] red ocher, red face paint

pisenteki N [-'a] pacer horse

pisi" IV rot, become rotten; be infected, become infected

pisikkamman(na) IV taste rotten

pisikkwanah IV smell rotten

pisippeh ADJ, N [-a] rotten; pus

pisoni N diaper

pisunaih TV rub butt against

pisuuh V fart slowly

pisuuppeh N [-a] intestinal gas, fart (*vulgar*)

pite IV, AUX [pippite dl] arrive, come back, return;

pittakkai IV fall on behind

pittataah V stoop over with legs spread apart

pittekih TV touch with behind

pittsoka N waist

pittehku ~ pittuhku N buttocks, hindquarters, rump, behind

pittuse(n) ADV back

pitturaittseh TV push down or out from within the butt

pitsa N milk

pitsa kuittsu(n) N [-na] milk cow

pitsakka'a IV choke

pitsi N breast

Pitsi Ko'i TOP Breast Hill

pitsi ko'i N nipple

pitsih TV [pintsi song form] suck, suckle

pitsinka(n) ~ pitsinke(n) TV nurse, breastfeed

pitsite puhippeh N [-a] milkweed

pittsi" v (for a baby to) suckle

pi'utua N [-'a] foxtail plant

piwea v have diarrhea

piwo'sa N hip

piwonua v stoop over, stick up behind (e.g., like a stinkbug)

piya ADJ [song form] big, large, grand, great; *see* pia

piyaah TV carry on the behind or on the tail or in back

piyuppuki(n) IV walk wiggling the behind

piyuttsa TV break down by sitting on

po'a katenoa N small lone hill in valley

po'a(n) N [-na] skin, bark, outer covering

po'appasanka(n) ~ po'appasanke(n) TV dry with wind

po'ayaah IV blow away

pohni'attsih N [-a] skunk

Pohoko'i N Sagebrush Butte near Fort Hall

Pohoko'ikkate(n) N [-i; Pohoko'ikkatee pl] person from Fort Hall, ID

pohonte(n) ~ pohontante(n) ADJ thick

pohopi(n) N [-tta] sagebrush

po'i" N road, path, trail

pokkoo N [-'a] burrowing owl

pokoitsi N [-'a] lizard

pokompih N [-a] currant; berry

poma TV pick

pommi'a IV migrate (of birds)

po'naih N [-a] mouse

ponka'ih IV pl [ka'ah sg] break (of a flex obj)

pono~poono N sphere,

pono'ih IV be spherical, round

ponopihte(n) ADJ spherical, round

pono'ihkante(n) ADJ short, stocky-shaped, chubby

pooh TV write, inscribe, draw; *see* kuppooh ~ kappooh

pookkuse ~ pookkusih N box

poono ~ pono N sphere

poopitsih N half dollar

poppin ~ poppih v hop, jump

poppontsanite(n) ADJ [-ti] round

poseke(n) ~ posika(n) N [-na] bridge

posia(ttsi) ~ pusia(ttsi) N [-i (-a)] louse, lice

posika(n) ~ poseke(n) N [-na] bridge

poto(n) N [-na] staff, cane, digging stick

pottainnanankah IV make a popping sound

potto(n) N [-na; potoompin song form] grinding stone

pottsa'ni (weneten) ADJ short and stocky

pottsi IV hop, jump

poyoha IV jog, lope, go along

poyokka IV trot

puha N [-i] supernatural power, (powerful) spiritual medicine; healing power

puha naakkante(n) N [puha naakkantee(n) pl] power being

Puha Wa'ippe N Medicine Woman

puha yaami'a v go on a vision quest; go to seek supernatural power for oneself

puhai(n) TV look for, search for

puhakahni N ceremonial house

puhakante(n) N [-ti; puppuhakantee(n) pl] doctor; healer, medicine person, shaman

puhanai TV (to) doctor, treat (a sick person), heal

puhiam paikwasi N [-a] end of a green place

puhikaih IV be blue, be green

Puhi Paa Hunupi(n) TOP 'Blue Spring Canyon' = Spring Creek

puhipihte(n) ~ puhipihte(n) (puhi- ~ pui-combine) ADJ, N blue, green; greenery

puhippeh ~ puippeh N [-a; puih- combine] green grass

puhitapai(n) N [-na] meadow

puhitenka(n) ~ puitenka(n) N green place

puhitte(n) ~ puitte(n) (puhi- ~ pui-) ADJ, N green, greenery

puhiwoo N [-'a] small native fish with green stripes

puhni ~ pu(n) P (this/that) way; *see* sipuhni, s<u>ai</u>puhni, sopuhni, sapuhni, supuhni

puhwih N [-a] money

pui" ~ punni" TV see, look (at); deliver a child

Em puinnuhi. ~ Ne noohimpai em puinnuhi. I'll see you sometime. = Goodbye.

Ne noohimpai mehi puinnuhi. I'll see you (dl) sometime. = Goodbye.

Ne noohimpai me(mm)i puinnuhi. I'll see you (pl) sometime. = Goodbye.

pui aipi(n tempin) N bluish chalk, bluish chalky rock

pui'awatsi TV spy on (song word); *see* **watsippuih**

puih N [-a] eye

pu'ih N [-a] gall bladder

puihpekka(n) IV have an eye infection or disease

puihpekkate(n) N [-ti] person afflicted with an eye infection or disease

puihtamah ~ puitamah TV guard, watch closely

puihwatte(n) ADJ eyeless, blind

puikai(yun) IV be green

puikka(n) TV watch, look at

puinui ADJ round, circular

puinuinuh IV spin

puipaawoo N [song form of puiwoo] little fish with green stripes

puipihte(n) ~ puhipihte(n) (pui- ~ puhi- combine) ADJ, N blue, green; greenery

puippeh ~ puhippeh N [-a; puih- combine] green grass

puisenna N green aspen (leafing in the spring)

puisih N [-a] eyebrow

puisippeh N [-a] eyelash

puisumpana'ih TV recognize

puisunkanna TV see (with feeling), feel seeing; look at (with feeling)

puitamah ~ puihtamah TV watch closely, guard

puittai(n) ~ peattai(n) ~ peaittai(n) TV leave; stop, cease

puitte(n) ~ puhitte(n) ADJ, N green, greenery

puitenka(n) ~ puhitenka(n) N green place

puiwa(n) N [song form] green grass; *see* **puippeh**

puiwoo ~ puhiwoo [puipaawoo song form] N little fish with green stripes

pukkiih V pass wind, fart (*vulgar*)

pu(n) ~ puhni P (this/that) way; *see* **sipu(n), saipu(n), sopu(n), sapu(n), supu(n)**

punku N [-i] horse

punku kate" V ride a horse

punku katekki(n) V ride a horse hither

punku katemi'a V ride a horse away

punku katenooh V ride along on a horse

punkukahni N barn

punkukante(n) N [-i] horse owner, horseman

punkum piapeh N [-a] mare

punkum tua N [-'a] colt

punkuttsi N [-'a] pet; little horse

punni" ~ pui" TV look (at), see

punnunkaite(n) ADJ spherical, perfectly round

punu N navel

punuhaki V spin around; *see* **nanippunuhaki**

pusia(ttsi) ~ posia(ttsi) N [-i (-a)] louse, lice

putumpittsi ~ kuttumpittseh N woodpecker

putusippeh N [-a] eyebrow

puuteh N [-a] bull

S

sa- DEM/LOC BASE [a-] that, there yonder; *see* **sate(n), sateweh, satee(n); saitte(n), sakkuh, sama(n), sanni, sapai, sapalka(n), sapi, sapuhni, sattu(n), sawa'ih**

saa" TV boil

saampunku N [-i] devil

sa'ana DEM-LOC that place; there somewhere yonder

saampittseh ADJ raw

saannompeh N [-a] boiling pot, cooking pot

saappeh ADJ, N [-a] boiled; boiled meat or food, soup

saattointsi N, ADJ foam, foamy; *see* **pasaattointsi**

saawittu'a N [-i] boiling pot

sakappi(n) ~ wakappi(n) N [-tta] type of willow

sakka DEM obj [sate(n) subj, sakka(n) poss] that yonder

sakkuh DEM-LOC [sakkuhte(n), sakkuhti obj] there yonder; about that

sama(n) DEM-DEM-P with that (instrument)

sama'ai DEM-DEM-P with that (person)

samappe ~ samuppe N [-a] man's sister, woman's brother; sibling; close cousin of same age (of opposite sex)

sampai ADV even so

sampai noo(n) ADV uncertainly, wonder about

samuppe ~ samappe N [-a] man's sister, woman's brother; sibling; close cousin of same age (of opposite sex)

sanai DEM-LOC from that direction, from thereabouts

sanakkante(n) ~ sanankante(n) ADJ sticky

sanakkoo N gum, rubber, elastic

sanakkoo aiti N slingshot

sanakwi'naa N [-'a] golden eagle

sanappa'i(n) V INCORP be sticky

sanappi(n) N [-tta] pitch

sanawaappi(n) N [-tta] cedar

sanni DEM ADV that way, like that over there

sapai DEM ADV then, that time

sapai DEM-LOC around there yonder

sapaika(n) DEM-DEM-P that amount, that much (yonder)

sapi DEM-LOC around there yonder, thereabouts

sappeh N [-a, sasappeh pl] stomach, belly

sapuhni ~ sapu(n) DEM-LOC over that way yonder

sate(n) DEM [sakka obj, sakka(n) poss] that yonder

satee N [-'a] dog

Satee Tekka'a N [-a] Dog Eaters (Plains tribe)

satee'an tuattsi N puppy

sateekante(n) N [-ti] dog owner

satee(n) DEM [satii obj, satee(n) poss] those yonder

sateettsi N [-a] pet; little dog

sateweh DEM [satehi obj, satehe(n) poss] those two yonder

sattu(n) DEM-LOC over that way yonder

sawa'ih DEM ADV like that yonder

saya(n) ~ saiya(n) N [-na] mudhen

sai N boat

sai ~ saippeh N tule

sai- DEM/LOC BASE [ai-] this nearby; saite(n), saiteweh, saitee(n), saiitte(n), saikih, saima(n), sainai, sainankuh, sainni, saipai, saipaika(n), saipi, saipuhni, saittu(n), saiwa'ih

sai'ana DEM-LOC this place; here somewhere nearby

saikka DEM obj [saite(n) subj, saikka(n) poss] this

saikkih DEM-LOC here, near here

saima(n) DEM-DEM-P with this (instrument)

sainankuh DEM-DEM-P [sainankuhten] this side

sainankuhte(n) N [-ti, -teen pl] one from here

sainai DEM-LOC from this direction, from hereabouts

sainni DEM ADV this way, like this nearby

saipakantsukkih (saaipakantsunkii song word) N [-a] tule blackbird, red-winged blackbird

saipai ~ saipi DEM-LOC near here somewhere

saipai DEM-ADV then, this time

saipaika(n) DEM-DEM-P this amount, this much

saipi ~ saipai DEM-LOC near here somewhere, hereabouts

saippeh ~ sai N [-a] tule, bulrush

saipuhni ~ saipu(n) DEM-LOC over this way nearby

saite(n) DEM [saikka obj, saikka(n) poss] this

saitee(n) DEM [saitii obj, saiteen poss] these

saitetsoih N [-a] straw hat, tule hat

saiteweh DEM [saitehi obj, saitehe(n) poss] these two

saitte(n) DEM [saitti obj] that (special) kind yonder

saitte(n) DEM [saitti obj] this (special) kind nearby

saittu(n) DEM-LOC over this way nearby

saiwa'ih ADV like this

saiya(n) ~ saya(n) N [-na] mudhen

se"- INSTR PRFX with or by cold

sea" V grow

seakkante(n) N [-ti] plant

seemaahte(n) (seemaah-,) NO [seemaayente(n)] ten

seemayentem manekihtemman to'inkanna NO fifteen

seemayenten naahpaihtemman to'inkanna NO sixteen

seemayentem pahaittemman to'inkanna NO thirteen

seemayente semmeman to'inkanna NO eleven

seemayente seewemmihamman to'inkanna NO nineteen

seemayenten taattsewihtemman to'inkanna NO seventeen

seemayente wahattemman to'inkanna NO twelve

seemayente wattsewihtemman to'inkanna NO fourteen

seemayente wooswihtemman to'inkanna NO eighteen

seepa ADV maybe, perhaps, possibly

seepa kia ADV perhaps, maybe

seepatte(n) ADJ certain (other), other, another (one)

seepi(n) ~ sehepi(n) N [-tta] willow

seeppaite(n) ADJ smooth, level

seewemmiha pia seemaahte(n) NO nine hundred

seewemmihammaahte(n) (seewemmi-hammaah-) NO [seewemmiham-maayente(n)] ninety

seewemmihante(n) (seewemmihan-) NO nine

seeweyaa N willow stand, willow place

sehepi(n) ~ seepi(n) N [-tta] willow

seken kamman(na) IV taste sour

seki N [0] leaf

sekituah IV leaf, sprout leaves

sekka'ah IV [sepponka'ih pl] break from cold (flex obj)

sekkoih IV pl [settiyaih sg] die from cold

sekkopah IV [sekkopai'ih pl] break from cold (rigid obj)

sekkuttih ~ sekkwettih TV (for a human to) kick

sekkwipippiki(n) IV shiver furiously from cold

sekkwippiki(n) IV shiver from cold

seme ~ sewe ~ semme NO, ADV [-'a] one; once; continuously; completely, once and for all

semese(n) ~ sewese(n) ADV at once, completely; all alone

semmai ADV, PRO thus, that (which is said), what is said

semme ~ seme ~ sewe NO [-'a] one

Semme Nawookkah N Monday

semmettsi N [-'a] only one

semmewa'i(se) ADV like one

senkwi N side, one side

senkwinanku ADV on one side

senkwippu(n) ADV to one side, on one's side, sideways

sennapi(n) N [-tta] quaking aspen; tree

sepponka'ih IV pl [sekka'ah sg] break from cold (flex objs)

sesema QUANT [sesema'a obj] some

sesemanikku ~ sesema ADV one at a time

sese'ni IV be numb

sese'ninka(n) ~ sese'ninkeh TV make numb

sesewekka ~ semekka ADV some(times), once in a while

settiyaih IV [sekkoih pl] die from cold, freeze to death

Settoya TOP Independence Mountain Range

sewaiha ~ sewaihya IV be frostbitten or burned

sewe ~ seme NO, ADV [semme] once; continuously; completely, once and for all

sewese(n) ~ semese(n) ADV at once,
completely; all alone

si- DEM/LOC BASE [i-] this right here;
see site(n), siteweh, sitee(n), sitte(n),
sikkih, sima'ai, sima(n), simante(n),
sumantu(n), sinai, sinni, sipai,
sipaika(n), sipi, sipuhni, sittu(n),
siwa'ih

si'ana DEM-LOC this place; right here
somewhere

si'apai DEM ADV about this time

siapi(n) ~ siappi(n) N [-tta] feather

sihu(n) ~ sihuh N [-na] tall grass whose
seeds were harvested (now extinct)

sii" IV [sisiiwen pl distrib] urinate, pee,
piss (*vulgar*)

siiawo N urinal

siimmokottsih N [-a] bladder

siippeh N [-a] urine, pee, piss (*vulgar*)

sitte(n) DEM [sitti obj] this special kind
right here

siittemi V be unable to urinate

sikka DEM obj [site(n) subj, sikka(n)
poss] this right here

sikki ADJ, ADV slanted; sideways

Sikkikate(n) TOP Slanted Mountain

sikkih DEM-LOC right here

sikkumpeh N [-a] shoulder blade

sikoo N [-'a] sego lily

siku N [-i] umbilical cord

sima'ai DEM-DEM-P with this (one), and
this (one)

sima(n) DEM-DEM-P on this

sima(n) ~ simma(n) DEM-DEM-P
[simanku] with this, for this (reason); about this

simante(n) DEM-DEM-P [simanti obj]
some of this, part of this, member of
this (family)

sinai DEM-DEM-P from this direction,
from hereabouts

sinni DEM ADV this way, like this right
here

sipai DEM ADV then, this time exactly

sipai DEM-LOC around here, here somewhere

sipaika(n) DEM-DEM-P this amount, this
much

sipappi(n) N [-tta] rabbit brush

sipi DEM-LOC around here, here somewhere

sippeh N [-a] sheep

sippehan tua N [-'a] lamb

sippunneh N [-a] spoon

sipuhni ~ sipu(n) DEM-LOC over this way

si'si'we(n) ~ sisiiwe(n) IV distrib [sii" sg]
urinate frequently, pee frequently

sitee(n) DEM [sitii obj, sitee(n) poss]
these right here

site(n) DEM [sikka obj, sikka(n) poss]
this right here

siteweh DEM [sitehi obj, sitehe(n) poss]
these two right here

sittu(n) DEM-LOC through this area

-situ'ih INSTR V scratch; *see* tsasitu'ih,
wesitu'ih

siwah ~ si'wah TV tear, rip; *see*
kesi'wah, tsasiwah

siwa'ih DEM-ADV like this right here

so- DEM/LOC BASE [o-] that, there; *see*
sote(n), soteweh, sotee(n), soitte(n),
sokkuh, soma(n), sonai, sonni, sopai,
sopaika(n), sopi, sopuhni, sottu(n),
sowa'ih

so'ana DEM-LOC that place; there somewhere

-so'ih ~ sonih INSTR V *see* keso'ih,
tsaso'ih, weso'ih

so'o N cheek

sohopi(n) N [-tta] cottonwood, native
poplar

soitte(n) DEM [soitti obj] that (special)
kind

sokka DEM obj [sote(n) subj, sokka(n)
poss] that

sokkuh DEM-LOC there

sokopehye(n) N [-na] small reddish duck

sokopi(n) N [-tta] land, earth, ground

sokopittan nanewe N [sokopittan
nanewenee pl,-i] creature, animal

sokoppeh N [-a] soil, ground, dirt,
earth

sokoteheyampehe N [-a] Oregon
grape, bearberry

soma(n) DEM-DEM-P with that
(instrument)

sonai DEM-DEM-P from that direction, from thereabouts

soni(ppeh) N [-a] mature grass, hay, alfalfa

sonikuna" N [-i] matches

sonitsikka'ah V INCORP cut grass

soniwekka'ah V INCORP mow, hay

sonko ~ sonno N lung

sonni DEM-ADV that way, like that

sonno ~ sonko N lung

soo(n) QUANT, ADV a lot, lots, much, many

soonkahni N city, Salt Lake City

soonte(n) (soon) ADJ [sooyente(n)] many, much, a lot, lots

soose(n) ADV lots, a lot

soosi ADJ foamy

sooyu(n) IV be lots of, be a lot of

sopai DEM-ADV then, that time

sopai DEM-LOC around there

sopaika(n) DEM-DEM-P that amount, that much

sopi DEM-LOC around there, there-abouts

sopuhni ~ sopu(n) DEM-LOC over that way

sosipaa N carbonated water; beer

Sosoni N [-i] Shoshoni

sosoni taikwa" N, TV speak Shoshoni

sotee(n) DEM [sotii obj, sotee(n) poss] those

sote(n) DEM [sokka obj, sokka(n) poss] that

soteweh DEM [sotehi obj, sotehe(n) poss] those two

sottu(n) DEM-LOC over that way

sowa'ih DEM-ADV like that

su- DEM/LOC BASE [susu- pl, u-] that, there (not visible); see sute(n), suteweh, sutee(n), suitte(n), sukkuh, su'ana sukuppa(n), suma(n), sumanku(n), summa(n), sumante(n), sumantu(n), sunai, sunni, supa'a(n), supai, supaika(n), supi, supuhni, suttu(n), sutukka(n), suwa'ih, suwaka(n)

sua N mute

sua" TV [suan AUX] think, want, need, feel; breathe; seem

suakikki IV breathe repeatedely

suakki IV breathe hard

suakkimmaah IV stop breathing, die

suakkwaiyah IV unable to catch the breath, run out of breath

su'ana DEM-LOC [su'ahte(n), su'ahti obj, su'anahtu(n)] that place; there somewhere not visible

su'ana nahate(n) ADV by and by, at some point (in time)

suanka(n) ~ suanke(n) V think about, think of

Ne en tepitsi tsaa suankanna.
I love you very much.

suanna N thought(s), thinking

suante(n) ADJ thinking

suapitai(n) V awaken, come to, regain consciousness; revive, bring to consciousness

suappeh N [-a] breath; mind

su'aipui TV think negatively of

suhannih TV think

suhi N pubic hair

suikkokko(n) N [-na] robin

sulkkuh ADV that (particular) way

suitte(n) DEM [suitti ~ suittenna obj, suittee(n) pl] that (special) kind out of sight

sukka DEM obj [sute(n) subj, sukka(n) poss, susukka pl] that out of sight

sukkuh DEM-LOC [sukkuhte(n), sukkuhtu(n), sukkuhyente(n), sukkuhse(n)] there out of sight

sukkuhte(n) DEM [sukkuhti obj] therein, about that; something there

sukuppa(n) DEM-DEM-P [sukuppayenten] inside that

suma'ai DEM-DEM-P [suma'aihku] with that (one), and that (one)

suma(n) ~ summa(n) DEM-DEM-P [sumanku, sumayente(n)] with that, for that (reason), because of that; about that

suma(n) DEM-DEM-P on that

sumanku DEM-DEM-P, ADV [suma, susumanku pl] from that; for that (reason), because of that; about that

sumante(n) DEM-DEM-P [**sumanti** obj]
some of that, part of that, member of
that (family)

sumantu(n) DEM-DEM-P [**man**] to that,
towards that, through that

summa(n) ~ suma(n) DEM-DEM-P
[**sumanku, sumayente(n)**] with that;
for that (reason), because of that;
about that

summatsuhninka(n) ~ summatsuhninke(n)
TV overpower with the mind

summeeh(kan) TV think of/about

sumpaatu(n) TV know (how to)

(kai) sumpaitsappih ~ (kai) sumpitsappih
TV not like, not love

sumpana'ih(kan) TV know (how to)

sumpana'ihki(n) TV (come to) understand; (come to) know

sumpana'aipite TV come to know (how
to)

(kai) sumpitsappih ~ (kai) sumpaitsappih
TV dislike, not like, not love

sun- INSTR PRFX with the mind, by
thinking

sunai DEM-DEM-P from that direction,
from thereabouts out of sight

-sunka'a(n) ~ -sunka'ah INSTR V feel;
see **masunka'ah, nanapuisunka'a(n),
neesunka'ah, nisunka'ah, tasunka'ah,
tsisunka'ah, wesunka'ah ~
wesunka'ah**

sunkwitanka(n) TV like, love, desire

sunni DEM-ADV [**sunnikku, sunniunte(n);
susunni** pl] that way, like that (not
seen); for that reason, why

sunni taka ADV finally, that was it

sunni kia ADV maybe so, could be

sunniyu(n) IV be that way, be like that

suntehai TV bless (with); ask; see
nanisuntehai(n)

suntehainka(n) TV bless (with); ask
someone for
E witsa saimanti ne suntehainka.
Could you please give me some of this?

supa'a(n) DEM-DEM-P [**supa'ante(n)**] on
that; about that

supai DEM-ADV then, that time

supai DEM-LOC around there out of sight

supaika(n) DEM-DEM-P that amount,
that much (out of sight)

supaika'i IV be that much, be that
amount

supaise(n) ADV right away

supi DEM-LOC [**supitte(n)**] around there
out of sight, thereabouts

supuhni ~ supu(n) DEM-LOC over that
way out of sight

susu- DEM/LOC BASE pl [**su-** sg, **u-**]
those, there (not visible); see
susumanku

susu'a ADV poorly, any old way

sute(n) DEM [**sukka** obj, **sukka(n)** poss]
that out of sight

sutee(n) DEM [**sutii** obj, **sutee(n)** poss]
those out of sight

suteweh DEM [**sutehi** obj, **sutehe(n)**
poss] those two out of sight

suttu(n) DEM-LOC over that way out of
sight, through there; for that,
through that

sutukka(n) DEM-DEM-P under that

suwa'ih DEM-ADV [**suwa'iten, suwa'ihku,
suwa'ihkuten, suwa'isen,
suwa'ihyenten**] like that out of sight

suwatsi" TV conceal

suwai TV want, think
Hinna e suwainna?
What do you want?
—Ne kai hinna suwainna.
—I don't want anything.

suwaka(n) DEM-LOC [**suwakanten**] to
him or her, towards him or her

suwiih(taih) TV disregard, ignore, dismiss, cast out of the mind

suyekwi TV think

T

ta PRO sub subj [**ta(n)** poss] one, someone, somebody, something

ta"- INSTR PRFX with the feet

ta"- INSTR PRFX with a hard or rock-
like object

taattsewi pia seemaahte(n) NO seven
hundred

taattsewihte(n) (taattsewi-) NO seven

taattsewimaahte(n) ([taattsewimaah-)
NO [taattsewimaayenten] seventy

Taattsewin Nawookkah ~ Nasuntih N
Sunday

taha(n) PRO 1st dl incl poss [taweh subj]
our

tahase(n) RFLX PRO dl incl ourselves

tahi PRO 1st dl incl obj [taweh subj] us
two

tahiipa TV flatten or smash with foot

tahippa N [-'a] tapaderos on saddle

tahittsaah TV lift feet up

tahma N, ADJ spring; renewed

tahma isampeh N buttercup (flower)

tahma puhatuah PHRASE renew spiritual
power

tahmani N, ADV spring, in the springtime

tahmato'ih IV be(come) spring

tahna" TV pl [teki" sg] put, place,
locate, store, bury

tahnakka(n) TV pl [tekikka(n) sg] put
away, keep, store

tahwi ~ tawi TV [tappaitih ~ paiti" pl]
throw

ta'i" N vagina, vulva

taka N [-i] partner, pal, mate, cousin,
twin

taka(n) ADV only, just, alone; self

takapoo N ball, sphere

takattsi N only one

takipoo N kidney

takka'ah TV [tapponka'ih ~ tappunka'ih
pl] break (flex obj) with hard object;
chop; separate from

takkahuittsuu N [-'a] snowbird

takkamah TV encounter, meet face to
face; round up (animals)

takka(n) N semen, sperm

takkapi(n) N [-tta] snow

takkatuah IV snow, for snow to
accumulate

takkaweai" IV snow

takkenah TV cover with rock

takkinahkan(ten) ADJ flat

takkintsai" ~ takkintsaih TV smash with
foot, flatten with foot

takkitsa'ah TV smash with foot, crush
with foot

takkoa TV pile up with rock

takkooni TV detain; round up; drive
together

takkooninke(n) TV detain for; round up
for; drive together for

takkopah TV [takkopai'ih pl] chop with
rock

takkuhnai" TV throw

takkumpa TV kill with feet

taku" N thirst

takukkoih IV pl [takuttiyaih sg] die of
thirst, be very thirsty

takunaih TV iron

takuppekka(n) IV be thirsty

takusippeh N sweat

takusito'ih IV sweat

takusito'ihtaippeh(ttsi) ADJ sweaty

takuttiyaih IV [takukkoih pl] die of
thirst, be very thirsty

takwittsih IV wilt; be thirsty

takkwaitu'ah TV take off of feet

takkwitihku V slip on slippery surface

Tam Puittsuhtaippai'i N Fourth of July

tam pia tekkanna N feast

-tamah INSTR V [-tami'ih pl] secure, tie;
see nasuntamah(kan), puihtamah,
tsattamah, wettamah

tama(n) N [-na] tooth

taman kamman N + v have a toothache

taman kammanna N toothache

tami N [-a] younger brother, close male
cousin

tammahka TV drive on foot

tamme(n) PRO 1st pl incl we, our

tammese(n) RFLX PRO 1st incl ourselves

tammetekki TV turn over with foot

tammi ~ tai PRO 1st pl incl us

tamminkuttih ~ tamminkwettih TV (for a
horse to) kick

tammu N sinew, tendon; thread

tammuhka N shoestring

tammuhkah TV lace up, tie shoes

ta(n) PRO sub subj one('s), someone('s),
somebody('s), something('s)

ta weyakainkanna ~ ta weyakainkenna N
violin, stringed instrument

tan naaiyawinna N handgame

tan napaiwekka'anna N bloodletting

tan natayaanna N ritual done before round dance

tan newe nekkanna N Indian dance

tan tase'yekwinna N moving the feet (dance), war dance

tan tekkanna N food

tan tetsayakainkanna ~ tan tetsayakainkenna N piano

tanihku N seed beater

tankappeh ~ tannappeh N [-a] knee

tankwisi TV braid

tannahottoo IV kneel down

tannappeh ~ tankappeh N [-a] knee

tannehki TV trample in

tantantak(k)i(n) IV for a drum to be beating

ta'oo(n) ADJ rancid

ta'oon kammanna taste rancid

ta'oon kwana" smell rancid

tapai N sun, day, daytime; clock, watch, timepiece

tapai hapi" IV [tapai happi dur] rest in the daytime

tapai patompittseh N [-a] rainbow

Tapai Pui NAME [-'a] (man's) Sees the Sun

tapaima ADV in the daytime; today

tapaini ADV noon, at noon, (in the) daytime

tapaitekkanna N lunch

tapaito'inaihte(n) ADV from the east

tapaito'inankuhte(n) ADV east

tapaito'ippaitu(n) ADV eastward, towards the east

tapaituah IV (for sun to) shine, (for sun to) come up

tapaiyuanaihte(n) ADV from the west

tapaiyuanankuhte(n) ADV west

tapaiyuappaitu(n) ADV westward, towards the west

tappa'ih TV pl [tattekwah sg] hit with a hard object

tappaitih TV pl [tawiih sg] throw aside or down

tappaitihtai(n) TV pl [tawiihtai(n) sg] throw away

tappana N sole of foot

tappiha(a) ~ tappihyaa N [-'a] sock, stocking

tappihah TV [tappiyuih pl] break, shatter

tappihyaa ~ tappihaa N [-'a] sock, stocking

tappikko'o(n) N [-na] heel

tappiyuih TV pl [tappihah sg] break, shatter

tapponka'ih ~ tappunka'ih TV pl [takka'ah sg] break (with rock); separate from

tappuinuinuh TV spin around with foot

(kai) tapu'i V not do well; be poorly; not be strong

tapu(n) ~ taputtsi N [-na ~ -a] cottontail rabbit

tasaa V open legs apart, spread legs apart

taseki N toe

tase'yekwi V move the feet; dance the war dance

tase'yekwi hupia war dance songs

tasimuintseh N [-a] very small black ant with red head living under rocks

tasitoo(n) N [-na] toenail, claw, hoof

tasiyenki N [-'a] carp

tasoni N rug

tasunka'ah TV feel with feet

tatah N [-a] dollar

tatapai N sun (special name sometimes used in myths); *see* tapai

tattahkinah TV smash with foot

tattapaima ADV everyday

tattekih TV step on, walk on; touch with feet

tattekwah TV [tappa'ih pl] hit with a hard object

tatto'ih TV crowd out

tattoko N big toe

tattua N [-'a] little toe

tattunaittseh TV push hard with the feet

tattutai" TV stretch with the feet

tatsa N, ADV summer, in the summertime

tatsawai IV [song form] be like summer, be early summer

tatsii N [-'a] nit(s)

tatsiki V shine

tatsempi(n) ~ tatsinnompi(n) ~
  tatsiyempi(n) N [-tta] star(s)

tatsokkwaih TV pound, pulverize

tattsaka TV knock out with hard object

tattsannih IV stumble

tatsiki IV shine; *see* patatsi(ki), mapataatsi, namapataatsi

tattsinko'no N ankle

tattsokwaih ~ tatsokkwaih TV pound

tattsuhnippeh ADJ strong-legged

ta'uta TV find

ta'utappeh ADJ found

ta'wah N [-a] flour

taweh PRO 1st dl incl [tahi obj, taha(n)
  poss] we two

ta wehe'neki nekkanna ~ mamakkoi N
  bear dance, rasping dance

tawe(n) N [-na; tatawe pl] hole, opening

tawenenuki TV kick around (like a baby)

-tawaih ~ -tawih INSTR V open; *see*
  tsattawai" ~ tsattawi", wettawai" ~
  wettawi"

tawiih ~ tahwii TV [tappaitih ~ paiti" pl]
  throw aside or down

tawiih(tain) TV [tappaitih(tain) pl]
  throw away

tawintsa N ankle

tawituha TV wear out (shoes)

ta yakain nekkanna N cry dance

tai ~ tammi PRO 1st pl incl us

taikka N hole, dwelling place

taikwa" TV [taikkwa dur; niweneh pl]
  speak, talk; pray

taikwahni N [-a] chief, spokesman,
  leader, boss

taikwankta(n) TV speak to, talk to

taikwa(nna) N words, speech, talk,
  language

taikwappeh ADJ spoken, said

taikwawoppih N [-a] speaker, talker,
  spokesperson

taina IV be a hole

tainna N [-nna] man

tainnappe N [-a] old man

tainte(n) N [-ti] hole

taipo N, ADJ [-a] white person,
  Caucasian; English (language); White

taipo taikwa" TV speak English
  E ha taipo taikwante?
  Do you speak English?
  — Haa'a, ne taipo taikwa
    sumpana'inna.
  — Yes, I know how to speak English.

taitsi N brother-in-law of a man [also of
  a woman by some]

taiyumpeh N [-a] in-law

tea(n) ~ tease(n) ADV, CONJ also, too,
  and also, again

-tea AUX V ask (to do)

te'ahwaih TV say, point out, tell,
  explain; *see* tsitte'ahwaih

te'ahwainka(n) ~ te'ahwainke(n) TV tell,
  say to, explain to (about)

te'ahwainkappeh ~ teahwainkeppeh ADJ
  told, explained

te'ahwaippeh ADJ told

Te'akate(n) TOP 'Serviceberry Place' =
  Three Fork or Dry Lake on Duck
  Valley Reservation

te'ampai N speech sound

te'ampaito'ih IV make speech sounds

te'ampih N [-a] serviceberry

tea(n) ~ tease(n) ADV, CONJ also, too,
  and also; again

te'api(n) N [-tta] serviceberry bush

tease(n) ~ tea(n) ADV, CONJ also, too,
  and also, again

te'awi IV miss shooting

Teai TOP 'Little One' = Deeth, NV
  north of Elko

teaika V paint, put makeup on

teaikappeh ADJ painted, made up

teaite(n) ~ teite(n) (teai) ADJ, N [-tt,
  teteaitee(n) pl] small, little; child,
  infant

teaitettsi ADJ tiny

teaiwoppih N [-a] the smallest

teaiyu(n) ~ teiyu(n) IV be small, be tiny

teekkwinuhi N [-a] key; *see* wekkwinuhi

teesua(tekih) IV [teesuatekki dur]
  think through; think deeply; be disappointed from waiting; *see*
  wesuatekih

teesunaih IV sweep, comb; *see* wesunaih

teettemate(n) N [-i] policeman; see
wettemah

teettempokkah IV button; see wettempokkah

teetto'ippeh ~ teetto'ihtaippeh N [-a]
garbage, trash, rubbish, refuse; see
wetto'ih

teettutua N stretcher (e.g., fence
stretcher); see wettutua

teeyaahpunku N [-i] workhorse, draft
horse

te'eyan/h V fear, be afraid (of)

te'eyanna N fear

te'eyante(n) ADJ afraid, scared

te'eyapekka IV be afraid, be scared

teeyottah IV plow, till; see weyottah

tehapi IV [tekwapi pl] stay the night,
spend the night

teheya N [-'an] deer

teheyah N [-a] horse

teheyampeh N [-'a] elderberry

tehu'i(kan) ~ tuhu'i(kan) V be angry at

tehuppeh ~ tuhuppeh ADJ mean, angry

tei N [-'a; tetteyanneweh dl,
tetteyannee(n) pl] friend

E aisen ne tei.

You are my friend.

tei IV [tetei pl] be little

teihaih N [-a] crow

teiku ADJ, ADV [-a] small, little; quietly

teippe N child

teite(n) ~ teaite(n) (tei) ADJ, N [-ti,
teteitee(n) pl] small, little; child, infant

teitseppuha N sorcerer, possessor of
destructive power

teittse ADJ bad, unpleasant, terrible

teittseh INTRJCT shut up! be quiet

teittse'i(nkuttsi) ADV little bit

teiwaikite(n) ADJ narrow

teiyu(n) ~ teaiyu(n) IV be small, be tiny

tekammii ADJ close, near

tekai" V hunt

tekaimmi'a go hunting

tekaite(n) N [-ti] hunter

tekeppinaippeh ~ tekeppinaihtaippeh ADJ
left over (of food)

teki" TV [tahna" pl, tekih INSTR] put,
place, locate, store; bury; see matekih,

mutekih, pittekih, tattekih,
teesuatekih, tottekih, tsattekih,
tsottekih, wesuatekih

tekikka(n) TV [tahnakka(n) pl] put away,
keep, store

teki(n) AUX V [tekki dur] start, begin; be
seated (dur)

tekipekka(n) IV get skinny

tekipettsi ADJ skinny

tekka'a N eater of (used especially in
names for groups of people); see
Tsoika Tekka'a

tekkah V eat

tekkahpaitseh TV invite to eat

tekkanka(n) ~ tekkanke(n) TV eat for; feed

tekkanompeh TV plate

tekkappeh N [-a] food, bread

tekkahtaippeh ADJ eaten up

tekkawenennemmi IV [tekkatopo'inhka
pl] graze

tekkoappeh ADJ, N enclosed (area)

tekko'i N rock hill, rock peak

tekkooni IV go and turn around

tekoppooh ~ tekuppooh IV brand

tekoppooh ~ tekuppooh N branding iron

tekuhannih IV cook

tekuhanninka(n) ~ tekuhanninke(n) TV
cook for

tekuhannippeh N [-a] cooking, cooked
food

-tekwah INSTR V [-pa'ih pl] hit; see
tattekwah, tottekwah, tsittekwah,
wettekwah

tekuppooh ~ tekoppooh IV brand

tekupooh ~ tekoppooh N branding iron

tekwapi IV pl [tehapi sg] stay the night,
sleep over night

-temah INSTR V close up, lock in; see
matemah, teettemate(n); tsattemah;
tsittemah; wettemah; neettemah

temahai" V go off mad at; go fight with;
pursue; see -mahai

temanakkih TV pay for, pay a bill or
debt

temanakkinka(n) ~ temanakkinke(n) TV
pay to

temapaiah IV do, make, build, create,
prepare, take care of

temapaianka(n) ~ temapaianke(n) TV do for, make for, build for, create for, prepare for, take care of for

temapaiappeh ADJ done, made, built, prepared, created, taken care of

temaseanka(n) ~ temaseanke(n) IV plant (a garden), sow

temaseankante(n) ~ temaseankente(n) N [-ti] farmer

temaseankappeh ~ temaseankeppeh N [-a] plants, garden

tematahain nankuh(ten) ADV, N (on the) right side

tematiyainkappeh N [-a] widow, widower

tematsai ~ tematsia TV help

tematsuhinkante(n) ~ tematsuhninkante(n) N [-i] bully

temawaihyanke'inna N fire starter, what is used to start a fire

temeeh TV buy, pay for; earn

temeehkahni N store

temeehkahnikante(n) store owner

temeenka(n) ~ temeenke(n) TV buy for

temeeppeh ADJ bought, paid for

temeete(n) N [-ti] buyer, shopper

temekai TV curse, harm

temmaih TV taste

temmaih(kan) TV be sick from, be ill from

temmaihkante(n) N, ADJ [-i] sick person, patient; sick, ill

temmaiyu(n) IV get sick, be sick

Tempaa TOP Rock Springs

tempah ADV than

tempahai N venereal disease

tempai N [ø] mouth; lip

tempaihea" TV fish, catch fish

tempaitsa'nika N bridle

tempimpooh V, N write on rocks; rock writing, petroglyph

tempi(n) (ten- ~ te"-) N [-tta] rock

Tempin Kutaha TOP Rock Corral

tempokoh ~ tempo'i N rock mound

tempuih(kan) V watch (as entertainment)

temukku(n) N [-na] rope, cord

temuyakainka(n) IV play a horned instrument

temuyakainkante(n) N [-ti] horn player

tenaa ADV down, downward

tenanka(n) IV listen to, behave

tenapoo N mark

tenihannih IV judge

tenihannite(n) N [-ti] judge

tenimmatenkah IV finish singing or talking

teninnasuntsaa IV make fun of, abuse verbally

tenippuiyih IV sing

tenisua" IV say, talk about (something uncertain), express; ponder about; sound

tenitto'ih IV sing

tenitto'inka(n) ~ tenitto'inke(n) TV sing for

tenittsu'ah IV finish talking

teniwaah TV teach

teniwaate(n) N [-ti] teacher

-tenkah/n INSTR V prepare, finish; *see* mapitenka(n), matenkah, nimmatenkah,, tenimmatenkah

Tenkatsu(n) TOP 'End of the Rocks' – northeast mountain range on the Duck Valley Reservation, which runs parallel with highway 51

tenkainua IV (for rock or cliff to) hang over

tenkaite(n) N [-ti] cliff

tenkwi ADJ thick

tenkwito'ih IV thicken; clot

tenkwisi TV thread (e.g., a needle)

tenkwisippeh N [-a] thread

tenooh IV carry

tenoomi'a IV haul (freight or supplies)

tenoomi'ate(n) N (freight) carrier, hauler, freighter

tenooppeh N [-a] lunch, food carried for meal

tenoote(n) N (freight) carrier, hauler, freighter

tento'ih V climb

te'oi N, ADJ [ø] sickness, illness, disease; sick, ill

te'oikante(n) N, ADJ having a disease; *see* pihyaa te'oikanten

te'oipa'i(n) IV have an illness

te'oipekka(n) IV get sick, be sick

te'oipekkate(n) N [-ti, -teen pl] sick person

tepa" N [-i] pinenut

tepaha(n) TV bet, wager

tepahanka(n) ~ tepahanke(n) TV bet (someone) (someone)

tepakkwattsappeh N [-a] pinenut pudding

tepammai V INCORP harvest pinenuts

tepana ADJ late

tepana ~ teppanna P, N beside, on the side of; inside; in the middle of; side

tepanayun V be on the side of; see teppanna

tepannai V INCORP make pinenuts; harvest pinenuts

Tepattekka'a N Pinenut Eaters

tepawaappi(n) N [-tta] pinyon pine, pinenut tree

tepaikkah IV kill (game)

tepaikkammi'a IV go killing

tepaikkanka(n) ~ tepaikkanke(n) TV kill for

tepaikkappeh N [-a] game someone has killed

tepaikkappehkante(n) N [-ti] murderer

tepaiti" IV throw, scatter; sow, plant

tepi(tsi) ADV, ADJ very, really; real, right

tepia N [-i] land owned, real property, field

tepiakante(n) N [-ti] land owner

tepiatekwi IV dwell; stay around not being welcome

tepiha(ka) ADV (in the) middle

tepihante(n) N middle

tepinna ~ tepinni TV [tepinni'i pl] ask (for, about)

tepinniha(n) TV call, name

tepi(tsi) ADV, ADJ very, really; real, right

tepitsi tokoa N [-i] rattlesnake

tepitsi tsaa(n) ADV extremely well, very good

tepooh IV write, inscribe, draw

tepoohpui TV study

tepoo(n) N [-ti] back country, wilderness, desert, barren area

tepoonnompeh N [-a] writing instrument, pen, pencil

tepoontenka N barren country, desert

tepooppeh N, ADJ [-a] paper, letter; written

tepoota IV be born

tepootappeh ADJ born

tepoowoppih N [-a] writer

teppako'aippeh N [-a] split pieces

teppanna ~ tepana N, P side; on the side of; inside of; in the middle of

teppaikia IV fill

teppaikianka(n) ~ teppaikianke(n) TV fill

tepuhainompeh N [-a] binoculars

tepuih IV wake up

tepuihtapu'i: kai tepuihtapu'i; tsaan tepuihtapu'i V be hardly able to see; be able to see well

tese(n) ADV merely, just

Tesi Koi TOP 'Grassy Point' = The Point

Tesikate(n) TOP Grassy Place

tesippeh N [-a] a kind of grass

tesu'aimeah IV be mentally ill, be disoriented

tesu'aimeate(n) ADJ, N [-ti] mentally ill (person)

tesumpite TV pay attention to, notice

tesuyekwi IV think

tetahain naappeh N [-a] (rat) urine powder—a medicine

tetakunai IV iron

tetappo'ihapinka(n) ~ tetappo'ihapinke(n) TV lay/make a footpath

tetappo'ihapinkappeh ~ tetappo'ihapinkeppeh N [-a] well-worn footpath

tetawenne IV stand scattered about; place posts scattered about

tetea V ask to work

teteai V work

teteaiwoppih N [-a] worker, helper

tetei IV pl be little (kids)

teteiku QUANT a little bit

teteitee(n) ~ teteaitee(n) ADJ pl [-tii, teite(n) sg] small, little

tetekkah TV steal, rob

tetena(n) N [-na ~ -ni] root

tetepinna(han) TV ask for or about

tetesih ~ pettitah N [-a] potato

tetetsee IV count

tette'aika N jam

tette'aikanai V INCORP make jam

tetteha(n) N, ADJ, ADV grief; pitiful(ly), awful

tettehampekka(n) V INCORP suffer from grief, grieve, have grief

tettehan(ten) ADJ, N pitiful, sad, mournful, grieving; grief, sadness, pity

tettehantempeh N [-a] orphan

tettehannaakkante(n) ADJ poor (person)

tetteyanneweh dl, tetteyannee(n) pl N [tei sg] friends

tetuah IV, TV be born; bear a child

tetsakkenah IV sew, (to) thread, (to) string

tetsa'moih ~ tetse'oih ~ tetsoih N [-a] hat

tetsannuhkinka(n) ~ tetsannuhkinke(n) IV drive

tetsayakainka(n) ~ tetsayakainke(n) IV play a piano or accordion

tetsayakainkante(n) ~ tetsayakainkente(n) N [-ti] piano/accordion player

tetsee TV count

tetse'oih ~ tetsoih ~ tetsa'moih N [-a] hat

tetsii N a type of grass; *see* piatetsii

tetsikkoappeh N [-a] fence

tetsimmuka N, ADJ sharp point(ed)

tetsiyaanompeh N fork

tetsoih ~ tetse'oih ~ tetsa'moih N [-a] hat

tettsohnai N canyon

tewekkwintui IV stir, churn, swirl; paddle

tewene(ten) N rock face, cliff

tewenenka(n) ~ tewenenke(n) V park (a vehicle)

teweyakainka(n) ~ teweyakainke(n) IV play a violin or stringed instrument

teyekwi IV do, gather, go after

tiih N [-a] tea

timma(sen) ADV pertaining to (previously mentioned topic)

tipoh N [-a] table

tiyaih IV [koi" pl] die

tiyaihkwa'i IV become unconscious

tiyaimmi'a IV die slowly, be dying

tiyaippeh ADJ, N [-a; koippeh pl] dead, deceased; body

tiyoih ~ tiyohih TV send

tohatekka('a) N flour

to"- INSTR PRFX with the fist or hand violently

toi TV [song form of **tahwi**] throw

to'ih N [-a] pipe

to'ih IV, INSTR V, AUX [toto'ih dl, kea" pl] emerge, come out, come up, rise, go out; appear; become; future tense; *see* aato'ih, hunnito'ih, kuttento'ih, muto'ih, oosaanto'ih, pato'ih, pimmito'ih, tahmato'ih, tatto'ih, tenitto'ih, tento'ih, tsatto'ih, tsitto'ih

to'iki(n) IV [keakin pl] come up, come out

to'inka(n) ~ to'inke(n) V come over, go over (used in numbers)

to'ippeh N [-a] cattail (with edible stalk)

tohopi(n) N [-tta] thigh

tokai" ~ tokwai" ADJ right, correct, proper, true, exact, perfect

tokai sunnikku ADV exactly that way

tokainku ~ tokwainku ADV right, really, truly, truthfully, properly

tokaintempai ~ tokwaintempai ADV the right time

tokainte(n) (tokai"-) ~ tokwainte(n) ADJ right, correct; enough, exactly, correctly

tokaippaika(n) ~ tokwaippaika(n) N right amount

tokaise(n) ~ tokwaise(n) ADJ, ADV right, truthful; really, truly

tokaittunnaa(n) ~ tokwaittunnaa(n) ADJ, ADV straight; straightforward, straight ahead

tokaiyu(n) ~ tokwaiyu(n) IV be enough

Tokkapatih N Duck Valley

tokkih N [-a] turkey

tokkuhuyah V peek

toko N [-'a] maternal grandfather; grandchild of man

tokoa N [-i] snake, rattlesnake

Tokoa Tekka'a N [-a] Snake Eaters

Tokoa Wiittsi NAME Snake Knife

tokoan kuna" ~ tokoan taiyumpeh N [-a] Indian paintbrush

tokwai" ~ tokai" ADJ right, correct, true, exact

-tokwai INSTR V see kettokwai

tokwai sunnikku ADV exactly that way

tokwainku ADV right, really, truly, truthfully

tokwainte(n) (tokwai"-) ~ tokainte(n) ADJ right, correct, straight; enough, exactly

tokwaintempai ~ tokaintempai ADV the right time

tokwaippaika(n) ~ tokaippaika(n) N right amount

tokwaise(n) ~ tokaise(n) ADJ, ADV right, truthful; really, truly

tokwaittapaini ADV noon, midday

tokwaittunnaa(n) ~ tokaittunnaa(n) ADV straightforward, straight ahead

tokwaiyu(n) ~ tokaiyu(n) IV be enough

tommo N, ADV winter, in the wintertime; year

tommoh(ka) IV winter, spend the winter

tommohki IV (for year to) come; be a certain age

Tonammutsa N Battle Mountain, NV

Tonampaa N Tonopah, NV

Tonapappayeyekwi TOP Greasewood Lakes

tonappi(n) N [-tta] greasewood

tona" TV poke, stick, prod, inject

to'nampih N [-a] chokecherry

tonikah TV stick in; partake

tonnuyuah TV push away, move

tontsia N [-'a] flower

tontsiah(ka) IV bloom, flower

tookka IV for animals to stand around

tookkahnih N winter house; see tommo, kahni

toomoah IV get cloudy, become overcast

toomoahka(n) IV be cloudy

toomoahkante(n) ADJ cloudy, overcast

toonkisappeh N [-a] chokecherry bush

tooppa'i(n) V (for there to) be clouds

tooppeh (too") N [-a; tootompi pl distr] cloud

tootopo'ih V pl [toowene sg] graze

toottatawene V shine through clouds in spots; (for light to) filter through clouds

tootsa N [-'a] Indian balsam

toowene V [tootopo'ih pl] graze

toppata N loin cloth, g-string

topihka IV pl/dl [wene" sg, tsatsakki dl] stand, stay, stop

topo'ih(kan) IV pl/dl [wene" sg, tsatsakki dl] stand, be upright, stop

topo'ihtekih IV pl/dl [wenettekih sg, tsatsakkihteki(n) dl] stop walking

toppa'ih TV pl [tottekwah sg] beat up, hit with fist

toppaikkwah ~ toppaihkwah TV pile up

toppaitihtai(n) TV pl [towiihtai(n) sg] throw away, throw out, pour out

topputuhi ~ topputuh(tain) TV blow up

Tosa Isa N White Wolf, Jesus Christ (in Native American Church)

tosakaih(yun) IV be white

tosakammu N [-i] white tailed jackrabbit

Tosa Konoki TOP 'White Hollow' = Tuscarora, NV; Independence Valley, NV

Tosan Natsattawih TOP White Gate

tosapihte(n) (tosa"-) ADJ white

tosappo'antuah IV become covered with white

Tosawihi(n) N [-na] White Knife Shoshoni

tosi'a TV put, stick, place somewhere

tosittoya N [-a] wild iris (lavender flowers, poisonous)

toto'ih IV dl [to'ih sg, kea" pl] emerge, come out, go out

totompeen(tsi) N cloud wave; see tooppeh, yuwan totompeentsi

totowaantsi IV pl song word stand; see topo'ih(kan)

totsa" ~ totsa(n) ADJ [song form of tosa"] white

totsantsi TV song cleanse; see tosa"

tottanihka TV pound on

tottahka(n) TV keep laced up

tottainka TV pierce, perforate

tottani'i TV pile up on top of

tottantaki ~ tottontaki TV knock on; peck

tottekih TV put, place with hand

tottekwah TV [toppa'ih pl] hit with fist

tottepekki TV dig

tottohna" TV lace up in a cradle board

tottohnakkante(n) ADJ laced up in a cradle board; bundle up

tottontaki ~ tottantaki TV knock on; peck

tottsakwakkiyu TV sop up (gravy, soap)

tottsappeh ~ tuttsappeh N, ADJ [-a] dirt; dirty, unclean

tottsapikkah V make a crashing sound

tottsatekkah TV push along (as water)

tottsattsi N dirty spot; crotch

tottsayekwi" TV clean up

tottsema TV wipe off, sponge off

tottsi'ah TV peck

tottsohtia TV [towe'waini pl] empty into

towehtiah TV pour out, spill

towene TV place a post or object in a hole

towenenka(n) ~ towenenke(n) TV place in a hole standing up

towiih TV [toppaitih pl] throw aside or away

towiihtai(n) TV [toppaitihtai(n) pl] throw away, throw out, pour out

toyaah TV carry off/along; *see* pantoyaah

toyaahka(n) TV (for a bird to) carry in mouth or beak

toya'ana N mountain top

toyahapite(n) N [-i] mountain range

toyahunupi(n) N mountain canyon

toyakatete(n) N [-i] mountain sitting alone

toyakaite(n) N [-na] thunder

toyakainnai IV thunder

toyakwana N mountain plant with strong pleasant smell

toyanewe N [-i] dwarf-like mythological being

toyapainkwi N brown mountain trout

toyapaitu(n) ADV towards the mountains

toyapayakwahni N [-'a] bull frog

toyapi(n) (toya-) N [-tta] mountain

Toyataipo N [-a] Basque

Toyatepia N [-i] Mountain Dwellers, Shoshoni living near Jarbridge, NV and surrounding mountains

toyatukkupittseh N [-a] mountain lion

toyawaiki(n) N mountain area

toyo(n) N [-na] neck, throat

-ttu(n) ~ tu(n) P through, for; *see* sattu(n), saittu (n), sittu(n), sottu(n), suttu(n)

tua N [tua'a obj; tutua(neen) ~ tutuattsinee(n) ~ tuannee(n) pl] child, baby

tua" N [tu'ai ~ tua'a obj; tutua(neen) ~ tutuattsinee(n) ~ tuannee(n) pl] son

tuah TV become, turn into, change into, engender, accumulate, gain, develop

tuannai V [tutuanai pl] have a baby, give birth

tuannaikahni N birthhouse

tuantsi N child, young, offspring (poetic)

tuappe N [-a] young son

tuattsi N [tuattsi'a obj] baby, newborn; rebirth, new growth

tuhu'ih(kan) ~ tehu'ih(kan) TV be angry at

tuhuppeh ~ tehuppeh ADJ mean, angry

tuhupekka(n) IV get angry

tuhupihte(n) ~ tuupihte(n) (tuu"-) ADJ black, dark

tuhusuahka(n) V think angrily

tuhuwa'i IV (for one's anger to) diminish or calm down

tui N cousin, kin, mate

tuineppe N [-a; pihianneweh dl, pihiannee(n) pl] small boy

tuintsi N youth, young (of animal); young man

tuipittsi N [-a; tuipittsi'ance(n) ~ tuttuipittsi'anee(n) pl] young man

tuittsi(ttsi) N [-a; tuittsianee(n) pl] young man

tuka N night

tukama(n) ADV all night, with the night

tukani ADV at night, in the nighttime

tukan tepana ADV in the middle of the night

tukattepiha ADV (at) midnight, middle of the night

Tukkahpaa TOP Deep Spring

tukka(n) P, ADJ [tukkai, tukkanku, tukkantu(n), tukkante(n), tukkanti] under, below; less than, shorter than, smaller than; deep; see **matukka(n)**, **pentukka(n)**, **(s)utukka(n)**

tukkante(n) (tukkah-) ADJ deep; true

tukku N [-i] flesh, body, meat

tukku kammanka(n) care for, feel for, love, cherish, adore

Soten natian newi tukku kammankante. He/she really cares for people.

tukkukante(n) ADJ true

tukkumpai (tukkun-) QUANT lots, a lot, very much

tukkumpaiyu(n) IV be a lot

tukkupittseh N [-a] bobcat, wildcat

tukuh ADV just, only; must

tukumpeh ~ tukumpi(n) ~ tukumpana(n) (tukun-) N [-a ~ -pitta] sky, heaven

tukumpiwaa N sky sickness, epilepsy

tukumpiwaapekkah IV be afflicted with sky sickness or epilepsy

tukunkuha N sky husband

tukunkwee N [-i] sky wife

tukuppeh ADJ straight up

tu(n) (-ttun) P through, for; see **sattu(n)**, **saittu(n)**, **sittu(n)**, **sottu(n)**, **suttu(n)**

tunnaa(n) ADJ, ADV straight; right away

tunuhinni N firedrill

tupittsih N quarter, two bits, twenty-five cents

tusi" IV spit

tusippeh N [-a] saliva, spit

tusu" TV grind

tusunnompeh N [-a] pestle, mano

tuttuipittsiannee(n) ~ tupittsiannee(n) N pl [tuipittsi sg] young men

tuttukama ADV every night

tuttumpih N [-a] Mormon tea, ephedra

tutua ~ tutuanee(n) ~ tutuattsinee(n) N pl [tutua'a obj, tua" sg] babies, children

tutuakante(n) ADJ, N [-ti] having children, parent

tutuanai V INCORP pl [tuanai sg] give birth, have babies, have children

tutuanaite(n) ~ tutuammi'ate(n) N woman who has children

Tutuapainkwi Paa TOP 'Little Fish Creek' = Indian Creek

tuttsappeh ~ tottsappeh N, ADJ [-a] dirt; dirty, unclean

tuu rhythmical song word

tuu" ADJ, [tuupihte(n)] black, dark; dark shadow, dark silhoutte

Tuuhaappai TOP Black Parsnip NV

tuukkwi'naa N golden eagle

tu'ummi'akki(n) IV walk stooped over

tuun nekenta(n) N [-na] Canadian goose

tuupihte(n) ~ tuhupihte(n) (tuu"-) ADJ black, dark

tuuttaipo N [-a] black, negro

tuuku N marrow

tuuppantsuku N [-'a] mink

tuuppi(n) N [-tta] obsidian, flint

TS

tsa(') EMPH emphatic particle

tsa"- INSTR PRFX with the hand grasping

tsaa(n) ADJ, ADV good, nice, pretty; well, really, kindly, clearly, so

tsaa . . . mee" TV cure, make well

tsaa . . . sua" TV like, think well of; be happy about

tsaa suanka(n) ~ tsaa suanke(n) V think well about, love

Ne en tepitsi tsaa suankanna. I love you very much.

tsaa witsa ADV hopefully

tsaan naha" IV get well

tsaan napuite(n) ADJ good-looking, pretty, handsome

tsaan napunni IV look good, be pretty, be handsome

tsaan neesunkanna v feel good
Ne tsaan neesunkanna.
I feel good.

tsaan temayahnainte(n) ADJ humorous
(person), comic (by action)

tsaan teniyahnainte(n) ADJ humorous
(person), comic (by words)

tsaan tepuihtapu'i v be able to see well

tsaan tuittsi N handsome man

tsaanku ADV well, fine

tsaannaahkante(n) ADJ well-to-do

tsaante(n) (tsaan) ADJ, N, ADV [-ti obj]
good, nice, pretty; good things, nice
things, goodness; so

tsaantenka(n) N-P [tsaantenkahte(n)]
at, in, or to a good place

tsaappai ADV really, actually, especially,
in particular

tsaasuanka(n) ~ tsaasuanke(n) TV like,
think well of, feel good about; love
Ne en tepitsi tsaasuankanna.
I love you very much.

tsaattei N best friend, good friend

tsaawoppih N [-a] the best one

tsaayu(n) IV be good, be well

tsaayunna N goodness, wellness

tsahapinka(n) ~ tsahapinke(n) TV lay
down, have (someone) lie down

tsahimi TV pl [tsa'uhtuh sg] give

tsahimippeh ADJ pl given

tsahittsaa TV lift grasping with hand

tsahopi'i TV pull hair out

tsahotah TV dig

tsahoyonki TV loosen

tsahuyuyu(ki) TV sprinkle (around)

tsa'i IV be good, be OK
Ne ma'i tsa'i.
I'm OK
Aisom ma'i tsa'i.
This is good. = Thank you.

tsakaasih N [-a] jackass, donkey

tsakka'ah TV [tsapponka'ih ~
tsa(p)paittih pl] break by pulling apart

tsakka'anka(n) ~ tsakka'anke(n) TV break
off for; break the spell of

tsakkatenkah ~ tsakkatenkeh TV set,
place

tsakkea" TV pl [tsatto'ih sg] take out,
pull out, dig out, bring out; reveal

tsakkenah TV [tsakkeni'ih pl] sew, (to)
thread, (to) string

tsakko(n) TV grind; *see* yontsakko(n)

tsakko'inka(n) TV bring back

tsakkopah TV [tsakkopai'ih pl] break
by pulling apart

tsakkoyontsako(n) TV grind softening

tsakkwaiha(n) TV touch

tsakkwai'a TV take off, skin, strip off;
yank out

tsakkwaitu'ah TV take off, loosen, strip
off

tsakkwantupi TV wrap up

tsakkwintsunah TV [tsakkwintsuni'ih pl]
curl with hand, twist

tsakkwinuhi TV wind, turn around; stir,
mix around

tsakkwisinkah ~ tsakkwisinke(n) TV
strangle

tsammayaa TV mix together, mix up

tsammeih TV fail to move, can't
budge

tsammetekki TV turn over with hand

tsammito'ih TV turn inside out

Tsanimmanih ~ Tsanittsih N [-a]
Chinese (person)

Tsanimmanihan Nakaha Tetse'oih TOP
Lesser Chinaman's Hat

Tsanimmanihan Tetse'oih TOP
'Chinaman's Hat' = Hat Butte

Tsanittsih ~ Tsanimmanih N [-a]
Chinese (person)

tsannah TV lead

tsannanpite TV bring

tsannehki TV tighten

tsannoo'i TV pluck

tsannuhkinka(n) ~ tsannuhkinke(n) TV
drive (a vehicle)

tsapaittih ~ tsappaittih ~ tsapponka'ih
TV pl [tsakka'ah sg] break in pieces,
break by pulling apart

tsappahai" TV drop, let drop

tsappahkih TV stick to

tsappaikka(n) TV [tsawase pl] kill with
bow

tsappa̱itih TV pl [tsawiih sg] throw in different directions

tsappa̱itihtai(n) TV pl [tsawiihtai(n) sg] throw away

tsappaittih ~ tsapaittih TV pl [tsakka'ah sg] break in pieces

tsappa̱itse TV beckon with hand

Tsappanniih N [-a] Japanese

tsappatah TV [tsappati'ih pl] spread out by hand

tsappe'ah TV let go

tsappe'a(n) ~ tsappe'ase(n) ADV less, to a lesser degree, less than; a little better (in health)

tsappisuta TV drag pulling in hand

tsappoah TV pick

tsapponka'ih ~ tsappaittih TV pl [tsakka'ah sg] break by pulling apart; break in pieces

tsappuinuinuh TV spin with hand

tsasitu'ih TV scratch, claw

tsasiwah TV tear, rip

tsaso'ih TV soften pulling on; scratch

tsasua(n) IV be likely, be apt to

tsasuakkwaiyah TV choke; see suakkwaiyah

tsasuna̱ih ~ tsasu'na̱ih TV scratch, claw

tsattainka(n) TV open; dig with hand; make a hole

tsattamah TV [tsattami'ih pl] tie (up)

tsattanah TV [tsattani'ih pl] TV place, put, locate

tsattawa̱i" ~ tsattawi" TV open

tsattawa̱ippeh ~ tsattawippeh ADJ open, opened

tsattekih(kan) TV place with hand, put, locate

tsattekinka(n) ~ tsattekinke(n) TV bring to, present to; place (something) for (someone); (help) deliver a baby

tsattemah TV [tsattemi'ih pl] close

tsattempokkah TV [tsattempohka'ih pl] fasten, button

tsattempono'i TV tie in a bundle

tsatto'ih TV [tsakkea" pl] take out, pull out, dig out, bring out; reveal

tsattono'ih TV bundle up, compact, wrap up

tsattoyah(tain) TV turn loose, let loose

tsattunaittseh TV pull with hands

tsattutai" TV stretch by pulling with hands

tsatsakki IV dl [wene" sg, topo'ih pl/dl ~ tsattsakai pl] stand, be upright

tsatsakkihteki(n) IV dl [wenettekih sg, topo'ihtekih pl/dl] stop walking

tsattsakai ~ topo'ih IV pl [wene" sg, tsatsakki dl] stand, be upright

tsattsi'ah TV pinch

tsattsino'a TV [tsattsino'ih pl] peel by hand

tsattsuhnippeh ADJ strong handed

tsa'uhtuh TV [tsahimi pl] give

tsawaini TV hang up

tsawainkeh ~ tsawainkah TV bring down or lessen (pain, swelling or illness)

tsawainuah TV hang on to

tsawase TV [tsappa̱ikkan sg] kill with bow

tsa'weah(ku) V have muscle cramps

tsawenenka(n) ~ tsawenenke(n) TV stop, make stop, make stand, park

tsawiih TV [tsappa̱itih pl] throw down or aside

tsawiihtai(n) TV [tsappa̱itihtai(n) pl] throw away

tsayaah TV get, obtain; carry in hand

tsayakainka(n) ~ tsayakainke(n) TV play a piano or accordion

tsayetseh TV raise up

tsai ADV completely, entirely

tsai" TV hold, grasp, catch

tseke(n) N pika rabbit, pygmy rabbit

tsekkah IV get stuck

tsekkahka(n) IV be stuck

tsekke'i TV stick, push in

tsennenneki(n) IV move about moving up and down

tsi"- INSTR PRFX with a sharp or pointed instrument

tsi'ah INSTR V occlude; see kettsi'ah, tottsi'ah, tsattsi'ah, wettsi'ah

tsi'ampeh N [-a] hip

tsi'ampih N [-a] wild rose hip

Tsi'apaa TOP 'Wild Rose Spring' = Lambs Reservoir

tsi'api(n) N [-tta] wild rosebush

tsi'atontsia N [-'a] rose blossom

tsihipinka(n) ~ tsihipinke(n) TV make drink

tsihotah TV dig with a pointed instrument

tsikenneh ~ tsikkinna N [-na] chicken

tsikih N [-a] squirrel, golden mantled squirrel

tsikka'ah TV [tsipponka'ih pl] cut (flex obj)

tsikkatenke(n) ~ tsikkatenka(n) TV set up (e.g., a tent)

tsikkeah TV pl [tsitto'ih sg] dig out with a sharp pointed object

tsikkinna ~ tsikenneh N [-na] chicken

tsikkitsa'a TV smash with pointed instrument

tsikkoa TV fence in

tsikkopah TV [tsikkopai'ih pl] cut (rigid obj)

tsikuttih ~ tsikkwettih TV hit with something pointed

Tsikuttih NAME (man's)

tsikkwinuhi TV stir; screw with a screwdriver

tsikkwintuih TV stir

tsikkwintuihpui TV thicken

tsimmetekki TV turn over with something sharp or pointed

tsimmianka(n) ~ tsimmianke(n) TV chase away; let get away; let go, pass up, miss out on

tsimmito'ih TV turn inside out with something pointed

tsinnehki ~ tsi'nika TV stick in

-tsinno'a INSTR V [-tsino'ih pl] *see* tsattsino'a, wettsino'a

tsippahunakoi TV starve

Tsippani N Mexican

tsippatah TV [tsippati'ih pl] spread out with something pointed

tsippih N [-a] ground squirrel

tsippimah TV cover

tsipponka'ih TV pl [tsikka'ah sg] cut (flex obj)

tsippooh TV write or draw with finger (e.g., in sand or dirt)

tsippunka'ih TV pl [tsikka'ah sg] cut

tsippunni(kin) TV poke (around) to see

tsisunaih TV scratch

tsisunka'ah TV feel, probe with a pointed object

tsitattaki(n) IV scream; *see* wettsitattaki(n)

tsittainka(n) TV pierce, perforate

tsittatawene TV punch holes in

tsittekwah TV poke, stick

tsittemah TV [tsittemi'ih pl] close

tsitte'ahwaih TV point; *see* te'ahwaih

tsitto'ih TV [tsikkeah pl] dig out with a sharp pointed object

tsittona TV poke, stick

tsittuuh IV pour out

Tsitsaseh N Jesus

tsittsukah TV point to, point out

tsittsukanka(n) ~ tsittsukanke(n) TV point out to

tsittsukanompeh N [-a] index finger

tsiwoh(ki) TV stick in; thread

tsiwenenka(n) ~ tsiwennehka(n) TV stand up, make stand up

tsiyaah TV pick up or carry with a pointed instrument

tsiyakaih TV make cry

tsiyuuma(n) TV pitch in

tsiyuppu'i TV prod in the back; goose

tso"- INSTR PRFX with the head

tso'a ADJ spooky, frightening

tsoaika ~ tsoika N [-i] breadroot

tso'apittseh N, TOP [-a] monster (mythological being); Jarbridge mountain range

tso'appatuntsih ~ tso'appuntunkih N [-a] moth

tsoappeh N [-a] shoulder

tso'appeh N [-a] ghost

tso'appuntunkih ~ tso'appatuntsih N [-a] moth

tso'ayaah TV haunt

tsohannih V lift head up

tso'i TV gather, pick

tsoika ~ tsoaika N [-'i] breadroot

Tsoika Tekka'a N 'Breadroot Eater(s)' = Nez Perce Indian(s)

tso'immai ~ tso'mai TV pick

tsokkohno(n) N hood of cradle basket

-tsokkw**ai**h INSTR V mash; *see*
ketsokkw**ai**h, tatsokkw**ai**h

tso'm**ai** ~ tso'imm**ai** TV pick

tsoo N [-'a; tsoonee(n) pl] great-grandparent, great-grandchild

tsoo(n) N [-na] beads

tsopp**ai** N back of head

tsoppiteki'i N pillow, headrest

tsoppitekihapi" V [tsoppitekihappi dur]
lay head on (pillow)

tsottekih V place head on

tsottekinke(n) ~ tsottekinka(n) TV place
head on

tsottekuttih ~ tsottekwettih TV bump
head on something

tsowainuah IV (for head) to hang down

tso'wintukih V nod head

tsoyaah TV carry on the head, wear on
the head

tsu EMPH emphatic particle

tsu'ah ~ tsumah IV, INSTR V run out of,
be out of; *see* tenittsu'ah, nakettsu'ah,
matsu'ah

tsu'appeh ADJ empty, all gone, no more

tsuhni N [ø] bone

tsuhnippeh N [-a] strong, strength

tsukuppe(ttsi) N [-a] old man

tsumah ~ tsu'ah IV run out of, be out
of; *see* nakettsumah

tsututtsutu N [-'a] black cricket

U

u PRO [u(n) poss] it, him, her; its, his,
her

u- DEM/LOC BASE [su-] that, there (not
visible); *see* ute(n), uteweh, utee(n),
use(n), uitte(n), ukkuh, uma(n), uma'ai,
umanku, unai, unni, up**ai**, up**ai**ka,
upuhni, uttu(n), uwa'ih

u'ana DEM-LOC [su'ana] that place;
there somewhere not visible

uhoi DEM-LOC around it, around that

u'imaa ADV next morning

uitte(n) DEM [uitti obj] that (special)
kind out of sight

ukka ~ ukki DEM obj [ute(n) subj,
ukka(n) poss] that (not visible)

ukka CONJ if, when

ukki ~ ukka DEM obj [ute(n) subj,
ukka(n) poss] that

ukkuh DEM-LOC [ukkuhte(n), ukkuhti]
there out of sight

ukkuhte(n) DEM [ukkuhti obj]
therein; about that

¹uma(n) DEM-DEM-P on it/that

²uma(n) DEM-DEM-P with that (instrument)

uma'ai DEM-DEM-P [uma'aihku] with
it/that (person)

umanku(n) for it/that, from it/that;
about that

umante(n) DEM-DEM-P [umanti obj]
some of it/that, part of it/that, member of that (family)

umantu(n) P [ma(n)] to it/that, towards
it/that, through it/that

u(n) PRO its, his, her

Un Kwahai(n) TOP 'Its Back' = Owyhee,
NV

unai(sen) DEM-LOC from there (towards
here)

unni DEM-ADV that way, like that (not
seen)

upa'a(n) DEM-LOC [supa'a(n)] above it,
above that, over it, over that

up**ai** DEM-LOC around there out of sight

up**ai**ka(n) DEM-DEM-P that amount, that
much (out of sight)

upi DEM-LOC around there out of sight,
thereabouts

upika(nten) DEM-DEM-P that much, that
amount

upitaa(nku) ADV slow(ly)

upuhni ~ upu(n) DEM-LOC over that way
(out of sight)

use(n) DEM that (not seen is the one)

usen taka ADV that's all

ute(n) DEM [ukka obj, ukka(n) poss] that
out of sight

utee(n) DEM [utii obj, utee(n) poss]
those out of sight

uteweh DEM [utehi obj, utehe(n) poss]
those two out of sight

uttuh TV [himi pl] give

uttuppeh ADJ given

uttu(n) DEM-LOC over that way out of sight

uttuse(n) ADV times past

utukka(n) DEM-LOC [sutukka(n)] under it, under that

u'ukapa (taka) ADV (only) sometimes

uwa'ih DEM-ADV like that out of sight

uwaka(n) DEM-LOC [uwakante(n)] to him or her, towards him or her

W

waahni N [-'a] fox

Waakkate(n) TOP Juniper Mountain

waako ~ piawaako N bullfrog

waappi(n) N [-tta; waa"-] juniper, cedar

waappitta sanappi(n) N [-tta] cedar pitch

waata N wild rye

waatontsippeh N [-a] rye grass

Waatontsippeham Po'i" TOP Rye Grass Trail

waha pia seemaahte(n) NO two hundred

wahamaahte(n) (wahamaah-) NO [wahamaayente(n)] twenty

Wahan Nawookkah N Tuesday

wahatte(n) (waha-) NO, N two; hemophrodite

-wa'i AUX able to, can, could

wa'ih P [wa'ihte(n), wa'ihku, wa'ise(n), wa'ihkuse(n)] like; see sawa'ih, saiwa'ih, siwa'ih, sowa'ih, suwa'ih

wa'ippe N [-'a; waimpe(ntsi) song form] woman

waka(n) P [wakante(n), wakantu(n), wakayente(n)] to, towards, with (someone); see suwakan(ten)

wakapite TV come to see or visit

wakappi(n) ~ sakappi(n) N [-tta] type of willow

wampu N [-i] trap

wampuni N [-'a] type of woodpecker

wana N [-i] net, trap, web

wanakahni N tent, tepee

wanappeh N [-a] cloth, weaving

wanatsawaini ~ natsawaini N [-'a] oriole

Wankanewe N [-i] Chinese

wankasu'attsih N [-a] spider

wantapasa N false hellebore, skunk cabbage

wantatah N one dollar

wantekwai V be in pain

wantsi N [-'a] buck antelope

wapuih V aim (at), take aim (at)

wasa(n) N [-na] blue heron

Wasannan Kahni TOP Heron's Nest

wase" TV pl [paikkah sg] kill

waseppi(n) ~ waseppeh N [-tta ~ -a; song form watsempin] mountain sheep

waseppin tsukuppe N [watsempin tsukumpe song form] hunter

wasettaippeh ADJ pl all killed

watekih V lack, miss

watsempi(n) N [song form of waseppi(n)] mountain sheep

watsempin tsukumpe N [song form of waseppin tsukuppe] hunter

watsi" IV hide, be hidden, be lost, get lost; see suwatsi", nasuwatsih, niwatsi", naniwatsi"

watsimpite IV go hide

watsinkᴂ(n) ~ watsinke(n) TV lose

watsinkappeh ~ watsinkeppeh ADJ lost

watsippuih TV spy on, watch secretly

watsittua" N illegitimate child

wattsewi pia seemaahte(n) NO four hundred

wattsewihte(n) (wattsewi-) NO four

wattsewimaahte(n) (wattsewimaah-) NO [wattsewimaayente(n)] forty

Wattsewin Nawookkah N Thursday

Wattsi Kahni N (NAME) man's Sagebrush Bark House

wattsimokottsi N gunny sack

wattsippeh N [-a] sagebrush bark, burlap

wawaha N [-'a; wawahaneweh dl, wawahanee(n) pl] twin(s)

wa'wata(n) N [-na] mosquito

wa'yapoo ~ wai'yapoo N [-'a] nighthawk

wayapputunkih N [-a] butterfly

wai" IV [waih- comb] come down, diminish, go away; see nawaih;

tsawainkah, paikwiwainkah,
kammawaih, namatsawai(kin)

waihya" ~ waiha" IV [waiwaihya" pl]
burn

Waihya Po'a Katenua TOP Burnt Cover
Hill, NV

waihyanka(n) ~ waihyanke(n) ~
waihanka(n) TV [waiwaihyanke(n) pl]
burn

waihyante(n) ~ waihante(n) N, ADJ [-ti]
fire; burning

waihyappeh ~ waihappeh N, ADJ [-a]
fire; burned

waiki(ten) N area, side of

waikia TV meet, encounter

Waiki Hunupi(n) TOP 'Side of Canyon' =
Yellow Huni, north of Duck Valley
Reservation in Idaho

waikippu(n) ADV sideways

waikite(n) (waiki) N [-ti] area, side of;
see piawaikite(n), teiwaikite(n)

waikki(n) TV look for, search for

waikkumpittseh N [-a] buzzard, turkey
vulture

waiku" IV pl [ya'ih ~ yua" sg, yaya'i dl]
enter, go in, go down

waimpentsi N song word for woman

wainna(h) rhythmical song word; see
haiya wainna, yaaya wainna

wainua" IV swing

Waipo NAME (man's) Huevo

waiti TV singe; purify with smoke

wai'yapoo ~ wa'yapoo N [-'a]
nighthawk

waiwaihya IV pl [waihya" sg] burn

we"- INSTR PRFX with a long instrument; with a generic instrument

we'a" N penis

weai" IV, N storm

we'annih TV knock down with long
instrument

we'aimea(nkan) TV knock dizzy with a
blunt object, disorient

weainna N, ADJ storm, stormy

we'antoko ~ we'awekkwintsuna N [-'a]
large solitary ant

weehpaippeh N [-a] frost

wehanninkah(tain) TV make disappear

wehawo'ih TV hollow out

wehekanke" TV cool off/down

wehekiah(ka) TV give shade to, shade

wehe'neki"(kkin) V make a rasping
sound; rub together making a rasping
sound

wehe'neki nekkah IV dance the rasping
(= bear) dance; see ta wehe'neki
nekkanna

wehuittsi V vomit violently

wehuitsittsiki(n) V vomit vigorously
repeatedly

wekka'ah TV [wepponka'ih pl] cut,
chop (flex obj); see paiwekka'ah

wekki'ah TV nick, make a little cut in

wekkahninai ~ wekkahnittsinaih TV
make a house

wekkamma(n) TV hurt

wekkatenkah ~ wekkatenke(n) TV pile
up, set, place

wekkatookka(n) TV [wenkato(mpi) song
form] spread out

wekkenah TV cover

wekkih ~ wikkah ~ wikkih V crash, wreck

wekkisinah TV wreck

wekkitsa'a TV smash

wekkoa TV enclose

wekkoappeh ADJ enclosed

wekkopah TV [wekkopai'ih pl] cut,
chop, break (rigid obj)

wekkumpahku TV swat

wekkuhnai" TV throw away

wekkwaitu'ah TV take off with tools,
loosen with tools

wekkwantupi TV wrap in a bundle, roll up

wekkwatsia TV brush

wekkwintuih TV stir up, churn, swirl;
paddle

wekkwintsunah TV [wekkwintsuni'ih pl]
curl, coil, wind

wekkwinuhi TV turn a wrench, turn key
in lock

wekwenai TV scrape off

wemmahka TV drive off, drive with
(e.g., a stick)

wemmapuhi TV fan

wemmapuisi" TV purify with something
(e.g., a feather, smoke, or ashes)

wemme'ekki TV move repeatedly

wemmei TV fail, be unable to do

wemmiha" IV get tired, be tired; run short of, lack

wemmihakkante(n) ADJ tired

wemmutsia TV sharpen

we'napi(n) N desert

wene" IV [**wenne** dur, **tsatsakki** dl, **topo'ih** pl/dl ~ **tsattsakai** pl] stand (up), be upright; stop

wene" N stand of trees

wenekka(n) IV stand still

wenekki(n) IV stand around

wenettai(n) IV stop

wenettekih IV [**tsatsakkihtekih** dl, **topo'ihtekih** pl/dl] stop walking

we'nia ~ wennia TV dip up liquid

wennehki ~ we'nika TV lock up, confine

wennia ~ we'nia TV dip up liquid

wennua TV move

wentsituih V shake rhythmically

weppahkah TV [**weppako'i(n) ~ weppako'ai(n)** pl] slice, split

weppa'ih TV pl [**wettekwah** sg] spank, slap, hit, whip

weppako'i(n) ~ weppako'ai(n) TV pl [**weppahkah** sg] slice, split

weppatah TV [**weppati'ih** pl] spread out

weppatekkih TV wet, sprinkle, anoint

weppaihtai(n) ~ weppaitihtai(n) TV pl [**wiittai(n)** sg] throw away

weppaikoah TV cut out; operate on

weppaitih TV pl [**wiittain** sg] throw down or aside

weppaitihtai(n) TV pl [**wiittai(n)** sg] throw away

weppetette(kin) TV flutter

weppihah TV [**weppiyu'ih** pl] break, shatter

weppimah TV cover

weppinooh(kan) TV carry on the back

weppisuta TV drag

weppiyu'ih TV pl [**weppihah** sg] break, shatter

wepponka'ih TV pl [**wekka'ah** sg] cut, chop (flex obj)

weppuinuinuh TV spin around

wesipi TV shave

wesitu'ih TV scratch

weso'ih TV soften beating on

wesuatekih TV [**wesuatekki** dur] miss (someone)

wesumpana'ih TV wait for

wesunaih TV comb, sweep, brush

wesunka'ah TV feel with something

wesunkanna TV make feel

wesuntapu'i TV perceive

weta N [**-'a**] bear

wettai(ni) TV winnow

wettamah TV [**wettami'ih** pl] tie tight, secure, fasten

wettantaki TV knock out with something, tap

wettataah V have legs spread apart

wettawai"(tain) ~ wettawi"(tain) TV open (up)

wette'aika TV spread on

wettekwah TV [**weppa'ih** pl] hit, slap, whip

wettemah TV [**wettemi'ih** pl] lock up

wettempokkah TV [**wettempohka'ih** pl] button

wettenta'ni TV winnow

wettiah TV pour, spill

wettiyainkah TV knock out, knock unconscious

wetto'ih V vomit

wetto'ippeh N [**-a**] vomit

wettono'ih TV amass, gather together, pile up

wettutai" TV stretch; *see* **neettutai**

wettutua TV stretch; *see* **teettutua**, **neettutua**

wettunaittseh TV pull away, pull forward

wettsaka TV knock out with club

wettsi'ah TV hatch

wettsino'a TV [**wettsino'ih** pl] peel with knife

wettsitattaki(n) TV beat on making (someone) scream

wettsiyu'i TV slice up/open, split into splinters

wettso'appeh N [**-a**] whirlwind

wewainih TV hang up

wewehekittsi N [**-a:** story word] shadow

weyaah TV carry; spread out; *see* seeweyaa, paseeweyaa

weyakainka(n) ~ weyakainke(n) TV play a violin or stringed instrument

weyannai TV winnow

weyempih N [-a] buffalo berry

weyottah TV plow, till

weyunki TV drive away/off

wia N mountain pass; place, stand (of trees); *see* wiya

wihi(n) N [-tta; wii(n)- comb] knife

wihinai INCORP V make a knife

wihnu CONJ then, and then, but; myth marker

wihtuha ~ wituha IV wear out; pass away, die

wihupi(n) ~ wihyupi(n) N [-tta] needle, bee stinger, syringe

wiih INSTR V *see* mawiih, nimmawiih, niwiih(tain), tawiih(tain), towiih(tain), tsawiih(tain)

wiihimpeh N [-a] metal, iron, steel

wiittai(n) ~ wiihtai(n) TV [paittai(n) ~ weppaitihtai(n) pl] throw away, cast away

wika N blanket

wikkah ~ wikkih V break away, break loose, give way (like a bridge); *see* pawikkah

winnooki(n) ~ wi'nooki(n) IV walk with head bobbing up and down

wisaa INTRJCT a purifying or cleansing word

wisu N string

wittua N [-i] drum; pot, bucket

wituha ~ wihtuha IV wear out; pass away, die

wituha'ihkante(n) ADJ, N [-na] passed away; deceased

wituhappeh ADJ passed away long ago

witsa N calf of leg

witsa ADV should, might

wiya N [song form of wia] mountain pass; place

wo'api(n) N [-tta] worm, maggot

woho N [-'a] enemy, opponent

wo'ih N [-a] chipmunk

wokaipi(n) ~ wokwaipi(n) N [-tta] cactus, peyote

Wonko Senkwi TOP 'Pine Trees on One Side' = a mountain near Mountain City, NV

wonkopi(n) N [-tta] tall pine, spruce, douglas fir, evergreen

Wonkopitta Wene" TOP Evergreen Stand, NV

wookkah V, N work for wages

wookkahtea TV hire, employ, give a job, ask to work

wookkapi(n) N [-tta] work, job

wookkawoppih N [-a] worker for wages

wooppih ~ wookki ADJ striped, lined

wooppihte(n) N stripe, line

woosewi pia seemaahte(n) NO eight hundred

woosewihte(n) (woosewi-) NO eight

woosewimaahte(n) (woosewimaah-) NO [woosewimaayente(n)] eighty

wooyompa V [song form] splash

wopi(n) N [-tta] board, log; wagon, car

wopin tottontaki N woodpecker

woppimpono N [-'a] type of woodpecker

wosa N [-i] burden basket

woyoah(ka) IV pl walk in single file one behind the other

Y

yaa" TV sg, INSTR V [hima" pl, -yaah comb] carry, take; keep; *see* keyaah, piyaah, toyaah, toyaahka(n), tsayaah, tsiyaah, tsoyaah, weyaah

yaakka(n) TV [himakka(n) pl] hold, keep, carry

yaakki(n) TV sg [himakki(n) pl] bring here

yaanka(n) ~ yaanke(n) TV [himanka(n) ~ himanke(n) pl] take away from, take for

yaappite TV bring back

yaawikkwa(n) TV grab, grasp

yaaya wainna rhythmical song words used to bless songs

yaainno(h) meaningless rhythmical song
word

yahammai INCORP V go after ground-
hogs or woodchucks

yaha(n) N [-na] groundhog, woodchuck, rock chuck

Yahannam Peta TOP Groundhog's Arm

yahnai" IV [nayahnai pl] laugh

yahnaisuah IV smile

yahnaisuante(n) N smile

ya'ih ~ ya'i" ~ yu'a" IV [yaya'ih dl,
waiku" pl] enter, go in, go down

ya'iti GREETING [ya'i pemme pl; ya'i
peweh dl] goodbye

yakai" IV [yakkai dur, nawoih pl] cry

yakainka(n) ~ yakainke(n) TV cry for

yakainnekka V cry-dance

yakainnekkate(n) N person doing the
cry dance

yakwahni · payakwahni N frog

Yakwahnim Paa N TOP 'Frog's Water' =
Riddle, ID

yamani TV cross over

yampa N [-i] wild carrot; *see* payampa

yanna meaningless rhythmical song
word

yantu(n) N [-na] winnowing tray or basket

yawise(n) ADV in a hurry, right away;
hurry up!

yaya'i IV dl [ya'i sg, waiku" pl] enter, go
in

yaittoko ~ yeittoko N [-'a] sage thrush

yehapittseh N [-a] pocket gopher

yehne(n) ~ yehnettsi N [-na ~ -a]
porcupine

yeikka (yei"-) ADV evening, in the
evening

yeippaitu(n) ADV towards evening

yeittekkah V eat dinner, eat supper

yeittoko ~ yaittoko N [-'a] sage thrush

yekwi" IV pl [yekkwi dur, yeyekwih distrib pl; kate" sg] sit (down), stay

yekwi" TV do, gather, go after

yekwi" TV [yekkwi dur, niweneh pl] say

yekwippeh N, ADJ speech; said

yeme"(kin) IV move, wander, roam,
travel

yemeka(n) IV move, travel, wander,
roam; live

yenka IV pl [nemi sg, yeyenkah dl]
travel, wander, roam; live

yepani N, ADV fall, autumn; in the fall
time

yepantu N fall, autumn (song word)

yetse" IV [yettse dur; yoyoti, yoti" pl]
fly (off/away); get up, arise, rise up

yetsekki(n) [yotikki(n) pl] IV fly along

yewampontsi TV track, take aim (song
word); *see* nampuih, nayaa, wapuih

yewe" V swallow

yeyekwi IV pl [yekwi" pl, kate" sg] sit

yeyenkah IV dl [nemi sg, yenka pl]
travel, wander, roam; live

yokappeh N [-a] phlegm, mucus

yoko" V copulate, fornicate, have sex,
make love

yokottsɪ N [-a] rascal, comic, joker

Yokottsi NAME (man's)

yommannai IV wave in the wind (as
grass or wheat)

yontsakko(n) TV grind softening

yontsoka(nten) ADJ soft, pliable, flexible

yoo- ADJ [song form of yuu(n)] gentle,
peaceful

yooti" IV pl [yotti dur; yetse" sg] fly
(off/away); get up, arise, rise up

-yottah TV plow, till

yoyoha ADV in a hurry, quickly

yoyoti IV dl [yetse" sg, yoti" pl] fly
(off/away); get up, arise, rise up

yua" IV [yuyuah dl, waiku" pl] enter, go
in

yuampiteh IV enter arriving, go in
arriving

yu'aih IV [yuwai(n) ~ yuwa(n) song forms]
be warm

yu'ainaihte(n) ADV from the south

yu'ainankuhte(n) ADV south

yu'ainka(n) ~ yu'ainke(n) TV warm up;
see kuyu'ainka(n)

yu'aippaitu(n) ADV southward, towards
the south

yuhu N [-i] grease, oil

yuhukante(n) ADJ fat, fatty

yuhupekkah IV get fat

yuhuppeh ADJ [**yuyuhuppehnee(n)** pl] fat

yuhuppettsi N [**-a**] fat one

yu'inahannemmi IV move slowly because of being weak, paralysis or physical disability

yu'ito'ih IV get weak, weaken; become paralyzed, atrophy

yu'ito'ihtaippeh ADJ weak, weakened; paralyzed, atrophied

yummah IV fall (from tree)

yunah TV carry, take

yunahki(n) TV bring

yunahku(n) TV take away

yunka(n) ~ yunki(n) V move away (from)

yunnah TV scoop (a liquid), dip (a liquid), ladle

yuppu INSTR V jiggle, wiggle; *see* **payuppuka, piyuppuki(n), tsiyuppu'i**

yuu(n) ADJ, ADV [**yoo-** song form] gentle, peaceful, still, soft

yuumpittseh N [**-a**] gentle animal

yuun kate sit still

yuu wene stand still

yuwain ~ yu'aih [**yuwan** song form] IV be warm

yuwannan totompeentsi N heat wave

yuunnaahka IV live in peace

yuyuah IV dl [**yua"** sg, **waiku"** pl] enter, go in

English to Shoshoni

A

a few (times) he'eh(ten)

a little better (in health) tsappe'a(n) ~ tsappe'ase(n)

a little bit teteiku, heheiku; mapiku(sen)

a long time ago peai

a lot soo(n), soonte(n), soose(n); tukkumpai

able to -wa'i

about ma(n) [mannai, manku, mantu(n), mante(n), mayente(n)]; ka" [kai, kakku, kattu(n), katte(n), katti, kayente(n)]

about it or that umanku(n)

about that ukkuhte(n), sakkuhte(n); summa(n) ~ suma(n) [sumanku, sumayente(n)]; supa'a(n) [supa'ante(n)]

about this sima(n) ~ simma(n) [simanku]

about this time si'apai

about which pempa'a(n)

above pa'a(n) [pa'ai, pa'anku, pa'antu(n), pa'ante(n)]

above it or that upa'a(n) ~ supa'a(n)

abuse nasuntsaa

abuse verbally nanisuntsaa ~ ninnasuntsaa, teninnasuntsaa

abused nasuntsaappeh

accept natea

accept as relative nanatea

according to mankuse(n)

accordion player tetsayakainkante(n) ~ tetsayakainkente(n)

accumulate tuah

accumulate (water) paatua(mpite)

ache kamma(n) ~ kammah; kammahpuinna

act naha"

active(ly) pehai(ten)

actually tsaappai

adore tukku kammanka(n)

adult nahnappeh

affirmative haa('a), maaikkuh

afraid te'eyante(n), kwikkwiya'wente(n)

after pa'a(n) [pa'ai, pa'anku, pa'antu(n), pa'ante(n)]

after a few days he'e hapikkante(n)

after a while napaisai ~ napisai

again tea(n) ~ tease(n); pinna

ahead of munnai

aim altiki(n)

aim at wapuih

alert iyampeh

alfalfa soni(ppeh)

all oyo(n) ~ oyose(n), oyointe(n); ooyoku(sen) ~ oyoku(sen) ~ ooyote(sen);

all alone sewese(n) ~ semese(n)

all gone kaihaiwa(n), tsu'appeh

all gone (of food) kettsu'appeh ~ kettsumappeh; nakettsu'appeh ~ nakettsumappeh

all night tukama(n)

all over attu(n); peaise(n)

all right maaikkuh, ha tukuh

alone taka(n)

along with other people nenneema'ai

already peaise(n)

also tea(n) ~ tease(n)

although noo(n)

always ooyoku(sen) ~ oyoku(sen) ~ ooyote(sen), oyo(n) ~ oyose(n)

amass wettono'ih

amazing nanasuwekai(n), nana-suwekainte(n)

among kapa(n), mante(n)

amount paika(nten) ~ pika(nten)

and ma'ai ~ mai ~ ma'i [ma'aihku, ma'aise(n)]

and also tea(n) ~ tease(n)

and that (one) suma'ai [suma'aihku]

and then wihnu

and this (one) sima'ai

anger to diminish or calm down
    tuhuwa'i

angle worm pahunkwitsa(n)

angry tehuppeh ~ tuhuppeh

animal sokopittan nanewe

animal mother piapeh

ankle tawintsa, tattsinko'no

annoy masunai" ~ ma'sunai"

annoy verbally nisu'nai

anoint weppatekkih

anoint oneself neeppatekki(n),
    namapatekki, neemapatekki(n)

another (one) seepatte(n)

answer (back to) naniwaiki'a

ant a'ni(n) [song form annita(n)];
    hu'nita(n) ~ hunnita(n)

antelope kwahate(n)

antler aa(n)

anus kwitattainna

any hii(n) ~ hinni, hinna; noo

any amount himpaikan(ten)

any kind hakaitte(n), noohakaitte(n)

any old way susu'a

anybody hakate(n), hakkai" ~ hakki";
    noohakate(n), noohakkai

anybody else noohihiintsinee(n)

anybody's hakka(n)

anyhow hakanni, hakai, noohakai

anyone hakate(n), hakkai" ~ hakki";
    noohakate(n), noohakkai

anyone else noohihiintsinee(n)

anyone's hakka(n)

anything hii(n) ~ hinni, hinna; noohii(n),
    noohinna

anytime himpai, hakapai, noohimpai

anyway hakannikku, noohakanni(kku)

anywhere hakappu(n), haka'ana, himpai,
    noohimpaika; noohakka, noohakattu(n)

apart na'antappu(n)

appeal to (someone) for
    nanittsawainka(n) ~ nanittsawainke(n)

appear napuih ~ napuni [nanapui pl];
    to'ih [toto'ih dl, kea" ~ nakea" pl]

appear (instilling feeling)
    nanapuisunka'a(n)

appearance napuippeh, napuinna

appearing napuite(n)

apple appo(n)

archer hoakkante(n) ~ huakkante(n)

area waiki(ten)

argue nanamannippahai(kkan), nippahai"

argue back and forth nanippitenka(n)

arise yetse" [yoyoti dl, yoti" pl]

arm peta

armless petawatte(n)

armpit ahnatukka

around hoi [hoiten, hoiti]

around here ipi ~ ipai, sipai ~ sipi

around it or that uhoi

around it or this mahoi

around there opai ~ opi, sopai ~ sopi

around there out of sight supi ~ supai,
    upi ~ upai

around there yonder api ~ apai, sapai ~
    sapi

arrive pite [pippite dl]

arrive at noopite

arrogant nasu'yekwite(n)

arrow paka(n)

arrowhead paka(n), napaka(n)

arroyo hunupi(n)

artery pai

as ni(sen) [-nni]

ashes kuttuhsippeh, kusippeh

ask suntehai

ask for natea, niwaih

ask for or about tepinna ~ tepinni
    [tepinni'i pl], tetepinna(han)

ask someone for suntehainka(n)

ask to do -tea

ask to gather together nikkawi

ask to help nanittematsai

ask to stand niwenenka(n) ~
    niwenenke(n)

ask to work tetea, wookkahtea

aspen sennapi(n)

at ka" [kai, kakku, kattu(n), katte(n), katti,
    kayente(n)]

at midnight tukattepiha

at night tukani

at noon tapaini

at once sewese(n) ~ semese(n)

at some point (in time) su'ana nahate(n)

at that time back then apuse(n)
at the end katsunka
at this time mai'ukka, eki"
at which penka [penkayente(n)]
atrophied yu'ito'ihtaippeh
atrophy yu'ito'ih
attempt mapuih
aunt (father's sister) paha
aunt (mother's sister) piattsi
automobile atamuh
autumn yepani
awaken suapitai(n)
aware iyampeh
away antase(n)
away from antappu(n) ~ antappuse(n)
away from each other nana'anta(hku)
awesome nanasuwekai(n),
    nanasuwekainte(n)
awful nanatetteha(n), tetteha(n)
awhile noo(n)

B

baby ohaa(ttsi), pipih, tuattsi; tua"
    [tutua(neen) ~ tutuattsinee(n) ~
    tuannee(n) pl]
babysit nokatenka(n)~nokatenke(n)
¹back kwahaimpeh
²back pittuse(n)
back and forth nanappittuse(n)
back country tepoo(n)
back of head tsoppai
back out pimmito'ih ~ pimpito'ih
back then apai, apaise(n)
backbone kwahaintsuhni
backwards pimpippu(n)
bad atsa, teittse; kaitsaan(ten)
    [kaitsaayente(n)]
bad(ly) kaitsaanku
badger huna(n)
bag mokottsih
bake nokko(n) ~ nokkoh
baked nanokkoppeh
ball takapoo
Bannock Pannaihte(n)
bar pakahni
bark po'a(n)
barn punkukahni

barn owl heehni
Barn Swallow Canyon Pasokompii'a
    Hunupi(n)
barren land tepoo(n), tepoontenka
basket pasekkittah
basket (burden) wosa
Basque Pasekkoh, Toyataipo
bat henapittseh
bathe koitsoih ~ koitsohi
bathe oneself nakoitsoih ~ nakuitsoih
bather pahapite(n)
Battle Mountain, NV Tonammutsa
be naa" [naah AUX], naakka(n), naha";
    nanaah, nanahaitah(kan)
be a body of still water pakateh ~
    pakate(n)
be a certain age tommohki
be a hole tainna
be a lake or pool pakateh ~ pakate(n)
be a lot tukkumpaiyu(n)
be able to see well tsaan tepuihtapu'i
be afflicted with -pekka(n)
be afflicted with epilepsy
    tukumpiwaapekkah
be afraid te'eyapekka
be afraid of te'eyan/h
be alert iya'ih
be amazing nanasuwekai(n)
be angry at tuhu'ih(kan) ~ tehu'ih(kan)
be anointed namapatekki,
    neeppatekki(n), neemapatekki(n)
be apt to tsasua(n)
be asleep eppeihka(n) [ekkoihkan pl]
be awesome nanasuwekai(n)
be beaten nanakwaha(n)
be bet natepaha(n)
be blue puhikaih
be born tepoota; tetuah
be bought natemeeh
be branded nakoppooh(kan)
be built namapaiah
be buried natekih(ka)
be burned nawaihyanka(n) ~
    nawaihyanke(n) ~ nawaihanke(n)
be called naniha(n), niakka(n) ~ nihakka(n)
be closed natsattemah
be clouds tooppa'i(n)
be cloudy toomoahka(n)

be cold eitse'i"
be constipated kwitattemi
be created namapaiah
be crooked kwipuntah(kan)
be cured napuhanai
be dangerous nanate'eya(n)
be different antappuyu(n)
be disabled katettai(n), katettaiippeh; kai
  tattekinaattaippeh
be disappointed from waiting teesuatekih
be dishonest itsanahayu
be disoriented aimeah, tesu'aimeah
be done nahannih, nameeh, namapaiah
be done cooking (of food) kukkwase
be dressed namahannihka(n), namasuahka, kwasu'uhka(n)
be drunk pa'aimeah(kan), aimeahka(n),
  hipikka(n)
be dying kaihaiwan naammi'a; tiyaimi'a
be early summer tatsawai
be empty hawo'ih
be enough tokaiyu(n) ~ tokwaiyu(n)
be explained nate'ahwaikka(n)
be finished namatenkah
be fixed nahannih
be frightened kwiya'a
be frostbitten or frost burned sewaiha
  ~ sewaihya
be gathered nameeh
be given away nahimihtai(n)
be given away (food) namakah(tain)
be good tsaayu(n), tsa'i
be going to (future tense) to'ih
be green puikai(yun), puhikaih
be handsome tsaan napunni; tsaan tuittsi
be hanging neewainihka(n)
be happy about tsaa . . . sua"
be hardly able to see kai tepuihtapu'i
be healed napuhanai
be heard nananka"
be heavy petteeyu(n)
be held in high regard naninnakkih ~
  naninnahki"
be hidden watsi"
be hollow hawo'ih, kono'ih
be hot etei(n)
be very hot kusuai
be how much himpaika'i

be hungry pahupekka(n) ~ pahu-
  napekka(n) ~ pahopekka(n)
be very hungry pahotiyaih ~ pahutiyaih
  [pahoko'ih ~ pahunakoih pl]
be ill (from) temmaih(kan)
be in heat (of an animal) napi'ai(yun)
be in pain kamma(n) ~ kammah;
  wantekwai
be in (emotional) pain maneettsikkwa
be infected pisi"
be injured e'atua, namahoitah
be insistent nittunaitseh
be lacking nahawatekih
be large piayu
be left over pinnaih(ka)
be left up to hittsaah
be light napuih ~ napuni [nanapui pl],
  napuikka(n)
be like summer tatsawai
be like that sunniyu(n)
be likely tsasua(n)
be little tei [tetei pl]
be located natekih(ka), natsattekih(kan)
be locked up neettemah
be lost watsi"
be made nahannih, nameeh, namapaiah
be made sick eating nakettemmaih
be mentally ill tesu'aimeah
be missing nahawatekih
be naked maniyu(n)
be named naniha(n), niakka(n) ~
  nihakka(n)
be no more kaihaiwayu(n)
be numb sese'ni
be obvious (that) nanapuisunka'a(n)
be okay tsa'i
be on the side of tepanayu(n)
bo only one pennaih
be open natsattawih
be out of tsumah ~ tsu'ah
be packed nanoote'aikka
be paid for natemeeh
be piled up natoppaikkah
be piled up (of rocks) natakkoa
be placed natekih(ka)
be placed (with hand) natsattekih(kan)
be prepared nahannih, namapaiah,
  namatenkah

be pretty tsaan napunni
be quiet teittseh
be put natekih(ka), natsattekih(kan)
be recognizable nanapuisunka'a(n)
be ripe (of fruit) kukkwase
be scared te'eyapekka
be scattered nanahaitah(kan)
be seated teki(n)
be seen napuih ~ napuni [nanapui pl],
   napuikka(n)
be setting (of a chicken) nohappi
be sick temmaiyu(n), te'oipekka(n)
be sick from temmaih(kan)
be sleeping eppeihka(n) [ekkoihkan pl]
be sleepy eppeipekkah(kan)
be small teaiyu(n) ~ teiyu(n)
be smokey kwiiweneh
be so much himpaika'i
be sore kamma(n) ~ kammah
be spanked neeppa'ih
be spring tahmato'ih
be startled kwiya'a
be stashed nanoote'aikka
be sticky sanappa'i(n)
be stored nanoote'aikka
be strange antappuyu(n)
be stuck tsekkahka(n)
be surprised kwiya'a
be swollen paikwikka(n)
be tangled kwisi"
be teary-eyed papuih(ka)
be that amount or that much supaika'i
be that way sunniyu(n)
be the height of paika'i
be thirsty takuppekka(n), takwittsih
be (very) thirsty takuttiyaih [takukkoih
   pl]
be thrown off (a horse) neeppahih
be tiny teaiyu(n) ~ teiyu(n)
be tired of neemai
be tired of eating nakenneemai
be told nate'ahwaikka(n)
be treated (for an illness) napuhanai,
   nanattahsu'a
be unable to do wemmei, meih ~ menih
be unable to urinate siittemi
be used nahannih, nameeh
be valued naninnakkih ~ naninnahki"

be vehement nittunaitseh
be visible napuih ~ napuni [nanapui pl],
   napuikka(n)
be warm yu'aih [yuwain ~ yuwan song
   forms]
be well tsaayu(n)
be wet patso'i
be white tosakaih(yun)
be wilted takwittsih
be wonderful nanasuwekai(n)
beads tsoo(n)
bear weta
bear a child tetuah, ohaanai
bear dance ta wehe'neki nekkanna ~
   mamakkoi
bearberry sokoteheyampehe
beard motso(n)
beat kwakkuhu(n) ~ kwakkwaha(n)
beat on making (someone) scream
   wettsitattaki(n)
beaver a'nii
because pehnah/n
because of maayunte(n)
because of that suma(n)~ summa(n)
   [sumanku, sumayente(n)]
beckon with hand tsappaitse
[1]become naa" [naah AUX], naha",
   nanaah; tuah; naakki(n), naakkwai(n),
   nanahaitah(kan)
[2]become to'ih [toto'ih dl, koa" ~ nakea"
   pl]
become an old lady hepittsipekka
become covered with frost aikkapo'antuah
become covered with white tosappo'antuah
become infected pisi"
become light kuttapaitua(n), napuikki(n) ~
   napuimpite(n)
become morning imaayu(n)
become overcast toomoah
become paralyzed yu'ito'ih
become rotten pisi"
become something hiintuah
become spring tahmato'ih
become unconscious tiyaihkwa'i
bed kappai
bedbug kappaipusia

bedding kappaisoni
bedroll kappaisoni
been naappeh(kanten)
beer piiya, sosipaa
before kaise(n), munnai
beg for niwaih
begin teki(n)
behave tenanka(n)
behind pinnaih, pinnanku
behind (buttocks) kwita", pittehku
behind each other nanappinnai
behind the house kappainnanku
being naakkante(n) [naakkantee(n) pl]
believe nankapitsia(n)
belly sappeh [sasappeh pl]
belongings oyonte(n) ~ oyontettsi
beloved relative nanewettsi
    [nanewettsinnee(n) pl]
below tukka(n) [tukkai, tukkanku,
    tukkantu(n) tukkante(n)]
belt nekki
bend kwipuntah(kan)
bend over pippupuah(kan), nopontah
bent kwipuntahkante(n)
berry pokompih
beseech nanittsawainka(n) ~ nanitt-
    sawainke(n)
beside nanku ~ nankwa, tepana ~
    teppanna
best friend tsaattei
[1]bet tepaha, tepahanka(n) ~ tepahanke(n)
[2]bet natepahappeh
between kapa(n) [kapai(ten), kapanku,
    kapantu(n), kapante(n)]
big pia [pipia pl]; piante(n) [pipiante(n) pl];
    piappehte(n) [pipiappete(n) pl]
Big Foot Pianampai
big one piaittsi
big toe tattoko
bigger than makuppa(n), ka'wi
binoculars tepuhainompeh
bird kwi'naa
bird (small) huittsuu
bird (large) piakwi'naa
birthhouse tuannaikahni
bite kettsia, kekkate"
[1]bite in two kekka'ah [kepponka'ih pl]
[2]bite in two kekkopah [kekkopai'ih pl]

bite many times keso'ih
bite once kettsi'ah
bitter muha
bitterbrush henapi(n)
bitterroot kana(n)
black tuupihte(n) ~ tuhupihte(n) [tuu"-]
black (person) tuuttaipo
black ant a'ni(n) [song form annita(n)]
black ant (very small with red head)
    tasimuintseh
black cricket tsututtsutu
Black Parsnip, NV Tuuhaappai
black tailed jackrabbit kamme ~ kamme
    [kammuntsi song form]
blackbird pakantsukkih; saipakantsukkih
bladder siimmokottsih
blanket ehe, wika
bleed peekkih
bless (with) suntehai, suntehainka(n)
blessed relative nanewettsi [nanewettsin-
    nee(n) pl]
blind kai puite(n), puihwatte(n)
blood peeppi(n) [pee"-]
blood vein(s) paikwakkwapih ~
    peekkwakwapih
blood vessel pai, paihapinna
bloodletting tan napaiwekka'anna
bloodline peehapinna
bloom tontsiah(ka)
blow neai"
blow away po'ayaah
blow out (of nose) mosotto'ih
blow up topputuhi ~ topputuh(tain)
blue puhipihte(n) [pui comb]
blue grouse kaha(n)
blue heron wasa(n)
bluish chalk pui aipi(n tempin)
bluish white aipuipihte(n) [aipui"-]
board wopi(n)
boat sai
bobcat tukkupittseh
body tukku
body (dead) tiyaippeh [koippeh pl]
body (one's own) natukku
body of water pakatete(n)
bog payuppuka
boil saa", kuttento'inka(n) ~
    kuttento'inke(n)

boil sizzling kusaakakakai"
boil up kuttento'i(n)
boiled (food) saappeh
boiling pot saannompeh, saawittu'a
bone tsuhni
born tepootappeh, tetuappeh
boss taikwahni
both namiante(n)
bother masunai" ~ ma'sunai"
bother verbally nisu'nai
bottle osa ~ pa'osa
bought temeeppeh
bovine (song form) pimmaa
bow aiti, hoa" ~ hua"
bow and arrow huu'aiti, hoa'aiti ~ hua'aiti
bowman hoakkante(n) ~ huakkante(n)
box pookkuse ~ pookkusih
boy tuineppe [pihianneweh dl,
    pihiannee(n) pl]
boyfriend haintseh
boyfriend and girlfriend relationship
    nahaintsehneweh
braid tankwisi
brain kupisi
brand koppooh ~ kuppooh, tekoppooh ~
    tekuppooh
branded nakoppooppeh ~ nakuppooppeh
branding iron tekoppooh ~ tekuppooh
bread tekkappeh, nokkoppeh
breadroot tsoaika ~ tsoika
break tappihah [tappiyuih pl]; weppihah
    [weppiyu'ih pl]
break (flex obj) ka'ah [ponka'ih pl]
break (rigid obj) kopah [kopi'ih ~ -
    kopai'ih pl]; wekkopah [wekkopai'ih pl]
break away wikkah ~ wikkih
break away (water, as in a flash flood)
    pawikkah ~ pawikkih
break (flex obj) by pulling apart
    tsakka'ah [tsapponka'ih ~ tsa(p)paittih
    pl]
break (rigid obj) by pulling apart
    tsakkopah [tsakkopai'ih pl]
break down by sitting on piyuttsa
break from cold (flex obj) sekka'ah
    [sepponka'ih pl]
break from cold (rigid obj) sekkopah
    [sekkopai'ih pl]

break from heat (flex obj) kukka'ah
    [kupponka'ih pl]
break from heat (rigid obj) kukkopah
    [kukkopai'ih pl]
break loose wikkah ~ wikkih
break (one's own) nose mukopah
    [mukkopai'ih pl]
break off kwai'ah
break off for tsakka'anka(n) ~
    tsakka'anke(n)
break the spell of tsakka'anka(n) ~
    tsakka'anke(n)
break wind pisuuh, pukkiih
break (rigid obj) with behind pikkopah
    [pikkopai'ih pl]
break (flex obj) with rock takka'ah
    [tapponka'ih pl]
break (rigid obj) with rock takkopah
    [takkopai'ih pl]
break with teeth kekka'ah [kepponka'ih
    pl]
break (rigid obj) with teeth kekkopah
    [kekkopai'ih pl]
breast pitsi
Breast Hill Pitsi Ko'i
breastfeed pitsinka(n) ~ pitsinke(n)
breath suappeh
breathe sua" [suan AUX]
breathe hard suakki
breathe repeatedly suakikki
bridge poseke(n) ~ posika(n)
bridle tempaitsa'nika
bring noo", tsannahpite, yunahki(n)
bring (a person) paitseppite
bring back noopite ~ nooppite, panipite,
    toaldo'inka(n), yaappite
bring down (pain, swelling or illness)
    tsawainkah
bring here yaakki(n) [himakki(n) pl]
bring out tsatto'ih [tsakkea pl]
bring to tsattekinka(n) ~ tsattekinke(n)
bring to consciousness suapitai(n)
broth hupa
brother (older) papi
brother (younger) tami
brother (woman's) samuppe ~ samappe
brother-in-law of a man [also of a
    woman by some] taitsi

brothers (relationship) nana papinewe
[nana papi(ttsi)nee(n) pl]
brown ontempihte(n) [onten-]
brown mountain trout toyapainkwi
brrh (in response to cold) eitsee
brush wekkwatsia, wesunaih
buck antelope wantsi
buck deer aan kuha ~ aan kuhma
buckaroo pakkatuuh ~ pakkiata
bucket wittua
buckskin pikappeh
buddy tui, taka
buffalo piakuittsu(n)
buffalo berry weyempih
build mapaiah, temapaiah, -nai
build a corral kutahanaih
build a house kahninai
build fire to keep (someone) warm
kottoonka(n) kottoonke(n)
build for mapaianka(n) ~ mapaianke(n),
temapaianka(n)
building kahni
built temapaiappeh; naippeh
bull puuteh
bull snake kokko(n) ~ pasikkokko(n)
bullet paka(n), napaka(n)
bullfrog waako ~ piawaako,
toyapayakwahni
bully matsuhinka(n) ~ matsuhninke(n)
bully tematsuhinkante(n) ~
tematsuhninkante(n)
bulrush saippeh
bump head on something tsottekuttih ~
tsottekwettih
bunchgrass piasonippeh
bundle neekkwantupihkanna
bundle up tsattono'ih, tottohna"
buried nakuuppeh
burlap wattsippeh
burn kottooh; waihya" ~ waiha" [waiwai-
hya" pl]; waihyanka(n) ~ waihyanke(n)
~ waihanka(n) [waiwaihyanke(n pl]
burn one's hand mawaihyanke(n)
burned waihyappeh ~ waihappeh, nawaihyankappeh ~ nawaihankeppeh
burning waihyante(n) ~ waihante(n)
Burnt Cover Hill, NV Waihya Po'a
Katenua

burp akwate'i"
bury kuu"; teki" [tahna" pl, tekih instr]
but pinnah; wihnu
butt kwita", pittehku ~ pittuhku
butter pata
buttercup tahma isampeh
butterfly wayapputunkih
buttocks pittehku ~ pittuhku
button tsattempokkah [tsattempohka'ih
pl]; wettempokkah [wettempohka'ih
pl], teettempokkah
buy temeeh
buy drinks for patemeenka(n) ~
patemeenke(n)
buy for temeenka(n) ~ temeenke(n)
buyer temeete(n)
buzzard waikkumpittseh
by mayente(n); kemaka ~ kemahka ~
kematu
by and by su'ana nahate(n)
by cold se"-
by fire or heat ku"-
by means of ma" ~ ma(n) [mante(n),
manku]
by talking ni"-
by thinking sun-

C

cactus aikopi(n), wokaipi(n) ~ wokwaipi(n)
calf of leg witsa
call mai [maiti]; nia" ~ niha ~ nihya,
niakka(n) ~ nihakka(n); tepinniha(n),
ninnapunni ~ ninnapui; nimma'i(kki)
call out to paitse"
call to paitsenkakki
calm someone upset by talking to
nimma'anka(n) ~ nimma'oonka(n);
nimma'i(n) ~ nimma'ikki
camas pasikoo
can -wa'i
can't meih ~ menih; kee . . . -wa'i
can't budge tsammeih
Canadian goose tuun nekenta(n)
candy kantih
candy jawbreakers monoo
cane poto(n)
canvas pahki ~ pakki, pahkiwanappeh

canyon tettsohp<u>ai</u>

canyon (narrow) hunupi(n)

car atamuh, wopi(n)

carbonated water sosipaa

care for mayekwi; kammanka(n) ~
  kammanke(n); tuku kammanka(n);
  mapitenka(n) ~ mapitenke(n);
  nokatenka(n) ~ nokatenke(n)

carp tasiyenki

carrier tenoote(n) ~ tenoomi'ate(n)

carry yaa" [hima" pl, -yaah comb],
  yaakka(n) [himakka(n) pl]; weyaah;
  yunah; nookka(n), noommi'a, tenooh

carry a cradle board neenooh(kan)

carry along toyaah

carry along (water) pantoyaah

carry back (home) kopakko'ih

carry hither nookki(n)

carry in arms kopa" ~ kwapa"

carry in beak toyaahka(n)

carry in hand tsayaah

carry in mouth monooh(kan), keyaah(kan)

carry in truck noo"

carry off toyaah

carry off (water) pantoyaah

carry on back noo", pinnoo(n/h),
  weppinooh(kan)

carry on the behind or on the tail or in
  back piyaah

carry on the head tsoyaah

carry oneself around neemeennooh,
  neeyekwimmi'a(kwain)

cast away mawiih(tain); wiittai(n) ~
  wiihtai(n) [p<u>ai</u>tittai(n) pl]

cast away for mawiih(tai)nka(n)

cast away mentally or spiritually
  niwiih(tain)

cast out of the mind suwiih(taih)

cat keti(h)

catch hea", tsai", kwisinka(n) ~
  kwisinke(n)

catch fish painkwihea, temp<u>ai</u>hea"

caterpillar pi'ake(n)

catfish motsom p<u>ai</u>nkwi

cattail (with edible stalk) to'ippeh

Caucasian talpo

cease makia(han); peattai(n) ~ peaittai(n) ~
  puittai(n)

cedar waappi(n) [waa"-], sanawaappi(n)

cedar pitch waappitta sanappi(n)

ceremonial house puhakahni, pahu(n)

certain (other) seepatte(n)

chair katennompeh

chalk aipi(n)

change into tuah

change into a person naninnewetuah

characterized by -kante(n)

chase mianka(n) ~ mianke(n)

chase away tsimmianka(n) ~
  tsimmianke(n)

chase down kimmanke(n) ~ kimmanka(n)

cheek so'o

cherish tukku kammanka(n)

chest nenkappeh ~ nennappeh

chew ketsokkw<u>ai</u>h

chew making noise keppeittseiki(n)

Cheyenne Indian Pakannapoo

chicken tsikkinna ~ tsikonneh

Chico (NAME) Chikko

chide nittehu'i(n) ~ nittuhu'i(n)

chief t<u>ai</u>kwahni

child tua [tutua(neen) ~ tutuattsinee(n) ~
  tuannee(n) pl]; teaite(n) ~ teite(n) [teai
  teteaitee(n) pl]; teippe

child (poetic) tuantsi

chin keppatantsih, keppikko'o(n)

Chinese (person) Tsanimmanih ~
  Tsanittsih, Wankanewe

chipmunk wo'ih

choke pitsakka'a; tsasuakkwaiyah

choke on haikku

chokecherry to'nampih

chokecherry bush toonkisappeh

chomp making noise keppeittseiki(n)

chop (flex obj) wekka'ah [wepponka'Ih
  pl]

chop (rigid obj) wekkopah [wekkopai'ih
  pl]

chop (flex obj) with rock takka'ah
  [tapponka'ih pl]

chop (rigid obj) with rock takkopah
  [takkopai'ih pl]

Christian nanisuntehaite(n)

chubby pono'ihkante(n)

church nanisuntehai kahnikatte(n)

churn wekkwintuih, tewekkwintuih

cigarette pahu(n)
circular puinui
city soonkahni
claw tsasitu'ih, tsasun<u>ai</u>h ~ tsasu'n<u>ai</u>h,
    tasitoo(n)
clay patekwinappeh
clay (white chalky) aipi(n)
clean up tottsayekwi"
cleanse mapuisi", totsantsi
cleanse oneself namapuisi"
cleansing word wisaa
clear papumpihte(n) [papun]
clearly tsaa(n)
cliff tenkaite(n), tewene(ten)
climb tento'ih
climb down nawaih
clock tap<u>ai</u>
close -temah, matemah; tsattemah
    [tsattemi'ih pl], tsittemah [tsittemi'ih pl]
close (near) tekammii
close by mii(sen)
close to kemaka ~ kemahka ~ kematu
clot tenkwito'ih
cloth wanappeh
clothes namasuappeh, namahannihkappeh
clothing oyonte(n) ~ oyontettsi
cloud tooppeh [too"- comb, tootompi pl
    distrib]
cloud wave totompeen(tsi)
cloudy toomoahkante(n)
coals kuttsippeh [kotsimpoo song form]
coat kuuta(n)
coffee koppih ~ koppii
coil wekkwintsunah [wekkwintsuni'ih pl]
coil up neekkwintsunah [neekkwintsuni'ih
    pl]
cold eitse'i(h), eitse'inte(n)
cold (illness) ohippeh
Cold Springs Eitse'ippaa ~ Eitse'ihpaa
colt punkum tua
columbine pawaaka
comb wesun<u>ai</u>h, teesun<u>ai</u>h
combine together mayaah
come kimma" [kikimma dl]
come (of a new year) tommohki
come after kimmanke(n) ~ kimmanka(n)
come and go kooni [kokooniyenka dl,
    kooniyenka pl]

come back pite [pippite dl], ko'ih [koko'ih
    dl]
come down wai" [waih- comb]
come off kwai'ah
come out to'ih [toto'ih dl, kea" ~ nakea"
    pl]; to'iki(n) [keakin pl]
come out the nose muto'ih
come over (used in numbers) to'inka(n)
    ~ to'inke(n)
come to suapitai(n)
come to be naakkwai(n), nahapite
come to know sumpana'ihki(n)
come to know (how to) sumpana'aipite
come to see wakapite
come to understand sumpana'ihki(n)
come together ka'wimpite
come up to'ih [toto'ih dl, kea" ~ nakea"
    pl]; to'iki(n) [keakin pl]
come up (of sun) tap<u>ai</u>tuah
comedian nisummampeh, yokottsi,
    niyokottsi
comic yokottsi, niyokottsi
comic (by action) tsaan
    temayahnainte(n)
comic (by words) tsaan teniyahnainte(n)
commit suicide nap<u>ai</u>kkah [nanawase" pl]
commodities meeppeh
compact tsattono'ih
complete matenkah
completed matenkappeh
completely seme ~ sewe ~ semme,
    sewese(n) ~ semese(n); tsai; peaise(n)
composer of songs hupiakante(n)
conceal suwatsi"
conceited nasu'yekwite(n)
confine wennehki ~ we'nika
consume kettsumah ~ kettsu'ah,
    nakettsu'ah ~ nakettsumah
consumed nakettsu'appeh ~
    nakettsumappeh
continuously seme ~ sewe ~ semme
cook kuhannih, tekuhannih, kwase"
cook for tekuhanninka(n) ~ tekuhanninke(n)
cooked kwasepeh, kuppe'appeh,
    kukkwaseppeh
cooked food tekuhannippeh
cooking tekuhannippeh
cooking pot saannompeh

cool down hekankah ~ hekanke(n)

cool down/off pakuyu'ai(n), wehekanke"

copulate yoko"

copulate (of animals) nanakai ~ nanaki

copy manakki(n)

cord temukku(n)

corpse tiyaippeh [koippeh pl]

corral kutiha ~ kutaha, koappeh

correct tokai" ~ tokwai"

correctly tokainte(n) ~ tokwainte(n)

cost natemeeh

cottontail rabbit tapu(n) ~ taputtsi

cottonwood sohopi(n)

cough ohi"

could -wa'i

could be noha kia, sunni kia

count tetsee, tetetsee

count as relative nanatea, nanateate

couple (married) nanakweenneweh ~
    nanakwehennewe

cousin nanatea, taka, tui; samuppe

cousin (close older female) patsi

cousin (close older male) papi

cousin (close younger female) nammi

cousin (close younger male) tami

cover kenah, wekkenah, weppimah,
    tsippimah, matemah

cover with hand makenah

cover with rock takkenah

covet nasuyakai

cow kuittsu(n)

coward piapeh

cowboy pakkatuuh ~ pakkiata

coyote itsa, itsappe

Coyote Fur (NAME) Itsapehe

Coyote White Man (NAME) Itsataipo

crackle in a fire kuppeittseittseiki(n)

cradle basket (or board) kohno(n)

crane koanta

crash wekkih ~ wikkah ~ wikkih

crawl nuyuah

create -nai, mapaiah, temapaiah

create (people) manemenai

create for mapaianka(n) ~ mapaianke(n);
    temapaianka(n) ~ temapaianke(n); -
    nainka(n) ~ -nainke(n)

created mapaiappeh, namapaiappeh,
    temapaiappeh; naippeh

Creator of People Newi
    Manemenaippehkante

creature sokopittan nanewe [sokopittan
    nanewenee pl]

Cree Aanoo

creek okwaite(n)

criticize nimmakwittsi

crooked kwipuntahkante(n)

cross (over/through a body of water)
    mani(yun)

cross over yamani

crotch tottsattsi

crow teihaih

crowd out tatto'ih

crush with foot takkitsa'ah

cry yakai" [nawoih pl]

Cry Dance ta yakain nekkanna

cry-dance yakainnekka

cry for yakainka(n) ~ yakainke(n)

cup awe ~ awo

cure puhanai, napuhakante(n), tsaa . . .
    mee"

curing (service or ceremony)
    napuhanainna

curl wekkwintsunah [wekkwintsuni'ih pl]

curl up neekkwintsunah
    [neekkwintsuni'ih pl]

curl with hand tsakkwintsunah
    [tsakkwintsuni'ih pl]

currant pokompih, pampi kamma'a,
    ainkappata

curse nitteah, temekai

cursed nitteappeh

cut (flex obj) tsikka'ah [tsipponka'ih ~
    tsippunka'ih pl]; wekka'ah
    [wepponka'ih pl]

cut (rigid obj) tsikkopah [tsikkopai'ih pl];
    wekkopah [wekkopai'ih pl]

cut a blood vessel paiwekka'ah

cut grass sonitsikka'ah

cut hair pampitsikka'ah

cut out weppaikoah

D

dance nekkah

dance around nekkakwai ~ nekkanemi

dance place nekkatenka

dance the bear dance wehe'neki nekkah
dance the war dance tase'yekwi
dance time nekkatenkappai'i
dancer nekkawoppih
dangerous nanate'eyante(n)
dark tuupihte(n) ~ tuhupihte(n) [tuu"-]
daughter paite"
daughter-in-law huttsimpia
day tapai
day before yesterday kekkentuse(n)
day of week nawookkah
daytime tapai, tapaini, tapaima
dead tiyaippeh [koippeh pl]
dead body   tiyaippeh [koippeh pl]
deceased naappeh(kanten), tiyaippeh
    [koippeh pl]; wituha'ihkante(n)
decide nihannih [nimmeeh pl]
deep tukka(n)
Deep Spring Tukkahpaa
deer teheya
Deeth, NV (north of Elko) Teai
defecate kwita" [kwikkwihtu(n) distrib]
defecate loosely and continuously
    pihuitsittsiki
defecate loosely and quickly pihuittsi
defend ninnaha ~ ninnaah
delicacy na'kamma'a
deliver panittaih ~ panittai(n)
deliver a baby tsattekinka(n) ~
    tsattekinke(n); pui" ~ punni"
deliver for paninkah(tain) ~ panittainka(n)
    ~ panittainke(n)
deny niwatsi", naniwatsi"
depending on mankuse(n)
descend nawaih
desert tepoo(n), tepoontenka, we'napi(n)
desire nasuyakai, sunkwitanka(n)
destroy -'aipui ~ -'aipunni, ma'aipui
destroy with words ni'aipui ~ ni'aipunni
detain takkooni
detain for takkooninke(n)
develop tuah
develop a sore or wound e'atua
devil kwasi appe, saampunku
diabetes pihyatukku ~ pihatukku
diaper pisoni
didn't kai

die tiyaih [koi" pl]; suakkimmaah, wihtuha
    ~ wituha; nekkamaih
die from cold settiyaih [sekkoih pl]
die from heat kuttiyaih [kukkoih pl]
die giving up on life nasuntiyaih
die of thirst takuttiyaih [takukkoih pl]
die slowly tiyaimmi'a
different antappunte(n) [anta", antappu(n)]
different (one) kemmai [kekkemmai pl]
different things nanasumma(nten)
different(ly) antananku, antappu(n) ~
    antappuse(n)
differently from each other nana'an-
    tappu(n)
difficult natia(n)
dig ahwai ~ ahwi ~ awi; hotah, tsahotah;
    tottepekki
dig out tsatto'ih [tsakkea pl]
dig out with a pointed object tsitto'ih
    [tsikkeah pl]
dig with a pointed instrument tsihotah
dig with hand tsattainka(n)
digging stick poto(n)
digit -sitoo(n), masitoo(n), tasitoo(n)
diminish wai" [waih- comb]
diminish (pain) kammawaih
Dinner Station Penka Tan
    Tapaitekka'inna
dip up liquid wennia ~ we'nia, yunnah
dirt sokoppeh; tottsappeh ~ tuttsappeh
dirty tottsappeh ~ tuttsappeh
dirty spot tottsattsi
discuss nihannih [nimmeeh pl],
    nisunka'ah, ninnapunni ~ ninnapui
discuss with each other nanatemu'i ~
    nanateme'i
discussed nihannippeh
disease te'oi
dish awe ~ awo
dislike (kai) sumpitsappih ~ (kai)
    sumpaitsappih
dismiss suwiihtaih
disorient we'aimea(nkan)
disparage nanisuntsaa ~ ninnasuntsaa
disregard suwiihtaih
distant maanankwah ~ manakkwah
distressfully natianku

ditch hunupi(n)
dive kuu"
divide up nanahoih
divorce napuittai(n) ~ na'puittai(n) ~
  napuihtai(n); neempuihtai(n)
divorced napuittaippeh ~ napuihtaippeh
do hannih, mapaiah, temapaiah, mee" ~
  mehe(n); yekwi", teyekwi, mayekwi,
  naa", naha", nanaah
do for nahanke(n), mehenka(n) ~
  mehenke(n), meenka(n) ~ meenke(n);
  hanninka(n) ~ hanninke(n),
  mapaianka(n) ~ mapaianke(n);
  temapaianka(n) ~ temapaianke(n)
do poorly kai tapu'i
do with the mouth kennaawai
dock plant (Rumex crispus)
  ainkappawia
doctor nattahsu'unkante(n), puhakante(n)
  [puppuhakantee(n) pl]; nattahsu'a,
  puhanai
doctor (one's own) napuhakante(n)
doctor oneself nanattahsu'a
doctoring napuhanainna
doesn't kai
dog satee
Dog Eaters (Plains tribe) Satee Tekka'a
dog owner sateekante(n)
doggy sateettsi
doings nahappeh
dollar tatah, pikkontatah
done mapaiappeh, namapaiappeh,
  temapaiappeh, hannippeh; nahappeh,
  meeppeh, nameeppeh
done (of food) kukkwaseppeh,
  kwaseppeh
donkey tsakaasih
don't kai
door natsattawih, natsattema
door (at the) kammuyenka(ten)
doubtfully noha kia
douglas fir wonkopi(n)
dove haiwi ~ haaiwi
down peesi
down(wards) tenaa
doze off eppeikki(n)
draft horse teeyaahpunku

drag weppisuta
drag pulling in hand tsappisuta
dragonfly pakantutuh
draw pooh, tepooh
draw with finger tsippooh
drawing napooppeh
dream napuisunaih
¹dress kwasu'u(n)
²dress kwasu'unke(n) ~ kwasu'unka(n),
  namahannih, namasuah
dress (someone) namahanninke(n)
dried pasappeh
dried things pasankappeh ~ pasankeppeh
dried up pasattaippeh
¹drink hipi"
²drink paa [pa- comb, pappa distrib]
drinker hipite(n)
drip patsokki
drip repetitively pattsokki(kin)
drive (a vehicle) tsannuhkinka(n) ~
  tsannuhkinke(n); tetsannuhkinka(n) ~
  tetsannuhkinke(n)
drive away/off weyunki
drive off wemmahka
drive on foot tammahka
drive together takkooni
drive together for takkooninke(n)
drive with (e.g., a stick) wemmahka
drop tsappahai"
drop down pahai" ~ pahi" [papahi dl,
  sawe'i pl]
drop down (for the hand to) mapahai"
drop off panittai(n)
drop off for paninkah(tain) ~ panit-
  tainka(n) ~ panittainke(n)
drum wittua
drunk hipite(n), hipittaippeh,
  nahipittaippeh, pa'aimeahkante(n)
drunk completely nahipittaippeh ~
  hipittaippeh
drunk up kettsu'appeh ~ kettsumappeh
drunkard hipittsuku
¹dry pasappeh
²dry pasanka(n) ~ pasanke(n)
Dry Lake on Duck Valley Reservation
  Te'akate(n)
Dry Spring, NV Paam Pasa

dry up pasa"
dry up from heat kuppasa
dry with wind po'appasanka(n) ~ po'ap-
  pasanke(n)
duck pehye(n) ~ peye(n)
duck (small reddish) sokopehye(n)
Duck Valley Tokkapatih
dug out hotappeh
dumb kaisuante(n)
dung kwitappeh
duratively noo(n)
during pempai
dust hukkumpeh, kusippeh
dusty kusippeh [kotsim song form]
dwarf-like mythological being toyanewe
dwell kahnikante(n), kahnipa'i(n),
  tepiatekwi
dwelling kahni
dwelling place taikka

E

each other nana"
each separately nana'anta(hku)
eagle piakwi'naa
ear nankih ~ nainkih
earache nankih kammanna
earless nainkiwatte(n) ~ nankiwatte(n)
early in the morning imaase(n)
earn temeeh
earth sokoppeh ~ sokopi(n)
easily anta"
east tapaito'inankuhte(n)
eastward tapaito'ippaitu(n)
easy anta"
eat tekkah
eat dinner or supper yeittekkah
eat for tekkanka(n) ~ tekkanke(n)
eat pudding-like food kwini"
eat up kettsu'ah ~ kettsumah
eatable natekkate(n)
eaten up tekkahtaippeh, kettsu'appeh ~
  kettsumappeh; nakettsu'appeh
  nakettsumappeh
eater of (used for groups of people)
  tekka'a
echo nankah, nananka"
edge katsu(n), kemah

edible food natekkate(n)
egg noyo
eight wooosewihte(n) [wooosewi-]
eight hundred wooosewi pia seemaahte(n)
eighteen seemayente wooswihtemman
  to'inkanna
eighty wooosewimaahte(n)
  [wooosewimaah-, wooosewimaayente(n)]
either . . . or (else) noon tea . . . noon tea
ejaculate huittsi, noittsi'i
elastic sanakkoo
elbow kiippeh
elderberry kunukippeh, teheyampeh
elderly relative napeaittempeh
  [napeaittempehnee(n) pl]
eleven seemayente semmeman to'inkanna
elk pateheya
Elko, NV Atakkuh, Natakkoa
else antappu(n) ~ antappuse(n)
elsewhere antappu(n) ~ antappuse(n)
emerge to'ih [toto'ih dl, kea" ~ nakea" pl]
emphatic particles pe, tsa('), tsu
emphatically ma'i
employ wookkahtea
empty matsu'ah, hawo, tsu'appeh
empty into tottsohtia [towe'waini pl]
enclose wekkoa
enclosed wekkoappeh, nawekkoappeh
enclosed (area) tekkoappeh
encounter waikia; takkamah
end katsu(n)
end of a green place puhiam paikwasi
enemy woho
engender tuah
English (language) taipo
enough tokainte(n) ~ tokwainte(n)
ensnare kwisinka(n) ~ kwisinke(n)
ensnared kwisi"
entangle kwisinka(n) ~ kwisinke(n)
enter ya'ih ~ ya'i" ~ yua" [yaya'ih ~
  yuyuah dl, waiku" pl]
enter arriving yuampiteh
enterprising natia(n)
entirely tsai
ephedra tuttumpih
epilepsy tukumpiwaa
especially tsaappai
even noon tea

even so sampai, noo sunninte sampai
even though noo(n)
evening yeikka [yei"-]
evening (towards) yeippaitu(n)
evergreen wonkopi(n)
Evergreen Stand, NV Wonkopitta Wene"
every oyo(n) ~ oyose(n); ooyoku(sen) ~
  oyoku(sen) ~ ooyote(sen)
every day nana'imaa, tattapaima
every morning nana'imaa
every night tuttukama
every time oyo(n) ~ oyose(n)
evil atsa
exact tokai" ~ tokwai"
exactly tokainte(n) ~ tokwainte(n)
excrement kwitappeh
exhausted enuhi
exist naakka(n)
explain ninnapunni ~ ninnapui,
  naniwaiki'a, te'ahwaih
explain to (about) te'ahwainka(n) ~
  te'ahwainke(n)
explained te'ahwainkappeh ~
  teahwainkeppeh
express nisua", tenisua"
express exuberance nanippunuhaki
express lack of confidence in/low opinion of (kai) nittapu'i
extreme natia(n), natianku
extremely naketsa natia(n), natianku
extremely well tepitsi tsaa(n)
eye puih
eyebrow puisih, putusippeh
eyelash puisippeh
eyeless puihwatte(n)

F

face kopai
fade aato'ih
faded aato'ihtaippeh
fail wemmei
fail to meih ~ menih
fail to move tsammei
falcon kinii
fall (season) yepani
fall asleep eppeih [ekkoih pl], eppeikki(n)
fall down annih [kwampi ~ yuma pl]

fall down or over hapikku
fall from yummah
fall off pahai" ~ pahi" [papahi dl,
  sawe'i pl]
fall off (for the hand to) mapahai"
fall on behind pittakkai
fall out (hair) hopi'i
fall time (in the) yepani
false hellebore wantapasa
fan wemmapuhi
far away maanankwah ~ manakkwah
farmer temaseankante(n) ~
  temaseankente(n)
fart pukkiih; pisuuh; pisuuppeh
fast kettaa(nten)
fasten wettamah [wettami'ih pl];
  tsattempokkah [tsattempohka'ih pl]
fat yuhuppeh [yuyuhuppehnee(n) pl],
  yuhukante(n)
fat one piaitlsi, yuhuppettsi
father appe
father and mother appe ma'ai pii
father and son relationship nana
  appeneweh
father's brother haih
father's sister paha
father-in-law atattsi
fatty yuhukante(n)
fatso piaittsi, yuhuppettsi
favorite food na'kamma'a
Fawn Creek Koanta Paa Hunupi(n)
fear te'eyan/h; te'eyanna
fear from hearing something
  nankakwiya'a
fearfully natianku
feast pia tekkahi tam pia tekkanna
feather siapi(n) ~ siappi(n)
feces kwitappeh
feed maka", namakah(tain, tekkanka(n) ~
  tekkanke(n)
feel sua" [suan AUX]; -sunka'a(n) ~ -
  sunka'ah; neesunka'ah ~ neesunkan(na)
feel bad kaitsaan neesunkanna
feel for kammanka(n) ~ kammanke(n);
  tuku kammanka(n)
feel good tsaan neesunkanna
feel good about tsaasuanka(n)
  tsaasuanke(n)

feel hearing nankasua(n)

feel in mawai

feel not well kaitsaan neesunkanna

feel one's way down namatsawai(kin)

feel out with words nisunka'ah

feel seeing puisunkanna

feel very hot kusuai

feel with feet tasunka'ah

feel with hand masunka'ah ~ masunka'a"

feel with pointed object tsisunka'ah

feel with something wesunka'ah

female piapeh

fence tetsikkoappeh

fence in tsikkoa; kutaha ~ kutiha

fence stretcher teettutua

fetch -mai ~ -mahai; noonnii

few he'eh(ten)

field tepia

fifteen seemayentem manekihtemman
to'inkanna

fifteen cents na'piyaa

fifty manekimaahte(n) [manekimah-,
manekimaayente(n)] ~
manaikimaahte(n) [manaikimah-,
manaikimaayente(n)]

fight napitenkah ~ napitenkeh

fill teppaikia; teppaikianka(n) ~
teppaikianke(n)

filter (light) through clouds
toottatawene

finally sunni taka

find ta'uta

fine tsaanku

fine dust ottappeh

fine fur peesi

finger maseki

fingernail masitoo(n)

finish -tenkah/n, matenkah

finish singing or talking tenimmatenkah

finish talking nimmatenkah, nittsu'ah,
tenittsu'ah

finished matenkappeh, namatenkappeh

fir wonkopi(n)

fire kuna", kottooppeh; waihyappeh ~
waihappeh, waihyante(n) ~ waihante(n)

fire drill kosopi(n), tunuhinni

fire starter kuttsihanni, temawaihyanke'inna

firewood kuna"

first enkinaa(n)

fish painkwi; painkwihea, tempaihea"

fish (with green stripes) puiwoo ~
puhiwoo [puipaawoo song form]

five manekihte(n) [maneki-] ~
manaikihte(n) [manaiki-]

five hundred maneki (~ manaiki) pia
seemaahte(n)

fix hannih

fixed nahappeh

flat takkinahkan(ten)

flatten with foot takkintsai" ~
takkintsaih, tahiipa

flesh tukku

flexible yontsoka(nten)

flint tuuppi(n)

float pahapi; hapi" [kwapi" pl,
kwakkwappi pl distrib]

flood(ing) okwaite(n)

flour ta'wah, hopittseh, tohatekka('a)

flow okwai"

flow (blood) peehapi"

flower hepinkeppeh, tontsia; tontsiah(ka)

flowing okwaite(n)

flutter weppetette(kin)

flutter (poetic) petette(kin)

fly a'nimuih

fly (off/away) yetse" [yoyoti dl, yoti" pl]

fly along yetsekki(n) [yotikki(n) pl]

Fly Head A'nimuiham Pampi

foam saattointsi; pasaattointsi

foamy soosi, saattointsi

fog pakenappeh [pakenna ~ pakenaa
song form]

folktale natekwinappeh [nanatekwinappeh
pl], newe natekwinappeh

food tekkappeh; tan tekkanna

food carried for meal tenooppeh

fool itsapaikkah

foot nampai

for manku [ma(n)]; nai [naiten]; tu(n)
(-ttun); pehnah/n

for a drum to be beating tantantak(k)i(n)

for example kwa'i witsa

for pain or soreness to go away
kammawaihkwai(n)

for some reason hakannikku

for some time noo(n)
for that suttu(n)
for that (reason) suma(n ~ summa(n)
  [sumanku]; umanku(n)
for that reason sunni
for this (reason) sima(n) ~ simma(n)
  [simanku]
for whatever reason hakanniyun(ten) ~
  hakanniu(ten)
forceful natianku
ford mani(yun)
forehead ka'i
foreign antapittseh
foreigner antapittseh, kemmai
  [kekkemmai pl]
foretold nate'ahwaikkante(n)
forget nasuwatsih
fork tetsiyaanompeh
former naappeh(kanten)
fornicate yoko"
forty wattsewimaahte(n) [wattsewimaah-,
  wattsewimaayente(n)]
found ta'utappeh
four wattsewihte(n) [wattsewi-]
four hundred wattsewi pia seemaahte(n)
fourteen seemayente wattsewihtemman
  to'inkanna
Fourth of July Tam Puittsuhtaippai'i
fox waahni
foxtail plant pi'utua
freeze to death settiyaih [sekkoih pl]
freight carrier tenoote(n) ~
  tenoomi'ate(n)
freighter tenoote(n) ~ tenoomi'ate(n)
fresh eke
Friday Maneikin Nawookkah
friend naintseh; tei [tetteyanneweh dl,
  tetteyannee(n) pl]
friend relationship nahaintsehneweh dl
  [(na)nahaintsehnee(n) pl]
friends with one another nanatei
friendship nanatei
frighten makwiya'a
frightened kwikkwiya'wente(n)
frightening tso'a
frightful enee
frog yakwahni ~ payakwahni
from manku ~ mannai [ma(n)]; nai

from above pa'annaih
from back then until now apai
  mannaise(n) ~ apai mannise(n)
from hereabouts sinai, sainai
from somewhere hakannai
from that sumanku [suma, susumanku
  pl], umanku(n)
from that direction sonai, sunai
from the east tapaito'inaihte(n)
from the north kwinahainaih(ten)
from the south yu'ainaihte(n)
from the west tapaiyuanaihte(n)
from there (towards here) unai(sen)
from thereabouts sonai; sanai
from thereabouts out of sight sunai
from this direction sinai, sainai
from way back (in time) aattuse(n)
from which pemmanku, pemmayente(n)
from whom pemmanku, pemmayente(n)
front of the house kammuyenka(ten)
frost aikkappeh [aikka-], weehpaippeh
fry kuttsawene
funny nisummaappeh
fur pehe
furry peesi
fuss about nittehu'i(n) ~ nittuhu'i(n);
  nananittehu'i(n)
future tense to'ih

G

g-string toppata
gain tuah
gall bladder pu'ih
game someone has killed tepaikkappeh
garbage teotto'ippoh ~ teettu'Ihtaippen
garden temaseankappeh ~
  temaseankeppeh
gas (intestinal) pisuuppeh
gate natsattawih, natsattema
gather yekwi", teyekwi; tso'i; mee" ~
  mehe(n); hannih; -mai ~ -mahai
gather firewood kukki
gather for mehenka(n) ~ mehenke(n)
gather together ka'wi, ka'wimpite, ooki,
  wettono'ih
gathered meeppeh, nameeppeh
gelding kuha ~ kuhma

gentle yuun [~ yoo- song form]
gentle animal yuumpittseh
get hannih, nanahaitah(kan), tsayaah;
   naa" [naah AUX], naakki(n),
   naakkwai(n), naha"
get a cold ohipekka(n)
get a sore or wound e'atua
get angry tuhupekka(n)
get blurry pakenaih(kan)
get burned nawaihyanka(n) ~
   nawaihyanke(n) ~ nawaihanke(n)
get cloudy toomoah
get crooked kwipuntah(kan)
get dressed namasuah, namahannih
get (someone) dressed kwasu'unke(n) ~
   kwasu'unka(n)
get drunk aimeah, pa'aimeah(kan)
get fat yuhupekkah
get foggy pakenaih(kan)
get light kuttapaitua(n)
get lost watsi"
get married (of a man) kweettu ~
   kwehettu
get married (of a woman) kuhatu
get rusty oosaanto'ih
get sick te'oipekka(n), temmaiyu(n)
get sick eating nakettemmaih
get skinny tekipekka(n)
get sleepy eppeipekkah(kan)
get stuck tsekkah
get tired wemmiha"
get up yetse" [yoyoti dl, yoti" pl]
get weak yu'ito'ih
get well tsaan naha"
get worse kai tapu'i
ghost tso'appeh
girl (little) nai'pi(n)
girl (teenage) naipi(n) [nai'yannee(n) pl]
girlfriend haintseh
give uttuh [himi pl]; tsa'uhtuh [tsahimi
   pl]; hanninka(n) ~ hanninke(n)
give (especially food) maka"
give a job wookkahtea
give birth tuannai [tutuanai pl]
give drink to pamaka
give (away) food namakah(tain)
give shade to wehekiah(ka)
give value to ninnakkih ~ ninnahki"

give way (like a bridge) wikkah ~ wikkih
given uttuppeh [(tsa)himippeh pl];
   na'uttuppeh
given (especially food) makappeh;
   namakappeh
given away na'uttuhtaippeh [nahimih-
   taippeh pl]
glove(s) masetto'o(n)
gluteus maximus pittuhku
go mi'ah ~ miah [mimi'ah dl]
go after yekwi", teyekwi; -mai ~ -mahai
go after ground hogs or woodchucks
   yahammai
go along miannooh, mi'aki(n), poyoha
go and return ko'inii
go and turn around tekkooni
go away mi'akwa(n), mi'ahtai(n); wai"
   [waih- comb]
go away (pain) kammawaih
go back ko'ih [koko'ih dl; pipuntu song
   word]
go down ya'ih ~ ya'i" ~ yua" [yaya'ih ~
   yuyuah dl, waiku" pl]
go fight with temahai"
go get -mai ~ -mahai; noonnii
go get (a person) paitse"
go get rations or commodities mee ~
   mehe(n)
go hide watsimpite
go home ko'ih [koko'ih dl]
go hunting tekaimmi'a
go hunting and gathering nemi
   [yeyenkah dl, yenka ~ yeme" pl]
go in ya'ih ~ ya'i" ~ yua" [yaya'ih ~
   yuyuah dl, waiku" pl]
go in arriving yuampiteh
go killing tepaikkammi'a
go off mad at temahai"
go on a vision quest puha yaami'a
go out to'ih [toto'ih dl, kea" ~ nakea" pl]
go over (used in numbers) to'inka(n) ~
   to'inke(n)
go to seek supernatural power puha
   yaami'a
gold money ohamunih ~ ohamoonih
golden ohappihte(n) [oha"-]
golden eagle sanakwi'naa, tuukkwi'naa
gone mi'appeh

gone away mi'ahtaippeh

good tsaa(n)

good-looking tsaan napuite(n)

good friend tsaattei

good place (at, to, or in) tsaantenka(n) [tsaantenkahte(n)]

good to eat natekkate(n)

goodbye ya'iti [ya'i pemme pl; ya'i peweh dl]; pinnanku tease puinnuhi; Em puinnuhi ~ Ne noohimpai puinnuhi

goodbye (dl) mehi puinnuhi

goodbye (pl) me(mm)i puinnuhi

goodness tsaayunna

¹goose nekenta(n)

²goose tsiyuppu'i

gopher (pocket) yehapittseh

Gosiute Shoshoni Kusiyuttah

grab yaawikkwa(n)

graceful(ly) pehai(ten)

grand pia [pianten, niniante(n) · pipia pl]

grandchild of a man kenu, toko

grandchild of a woman huttsi, kaku

grandfather (maternal) toko

grandfather (paternal) kenu

grandmother (maternal) kaku

grandmother (paternal) huttsi

grasp tsai", yaawikkwa(n)

grass puhippeh ~ puippeh; soni(ppeh); tesippeh, tetsii; sihu(n) ~ sihuh

grass (bunch) piasonippeh

grass (rye) waatontsippeh

grass seed (large) patuntsi

grasshopper attankih

Grassy Place Tesikate(n)

grave nakuuppeh

gravy kuttsaappeh ~ kottsaappeh ~ kwattsaappeh

gray aisempihte(n) [aisen-]

graze kenno'ai; tekkawenennemmi, [tekkatopo'ihka pl]; toowene [tootopo'ih pl]

grease yuhu

greasewood tonappi(n)

Greasewood Lakes Tonapappayeyekwi

great natia(n); pia [pianten, pipiante(n) ~ pipia pl]

great horned owl muumpittseh ~ muhumpittseh

great-grandchild tsoo [tsoonee(n) pl]

great-grandparent tsoo [tsoonee(n) pl]

green puhipihte(n), puitte(n) ~ puhitte(n) [puhi- ~ pui- comb]

green aspen (leafing in the spring) puisenna

green grass puhippeh ~ puippeh [puih- comb]

green place puhitenka(n) ~ puitenka(n)

greenery puhipihte(n), puitte(n) ~ puhitte(n) [puhi- ~ pui- comb]

grief tetteha(n), tettehan(ten)

grieve tettehampekka(n)

grieving tettehan(ten)

grievous nanatetteha(n)

grievously nanatettehase(n)

grind tusu", tsakkon, yontsakko(n), tsakkoyontsako(n)

grinding stone potto(n)

ground sokopi(n), sokoppeh

ground squirrel keempai

ground up natusuppeh

groundhog yaha(n)

Groundhog's Arm Yahannam Peta

grove of trees huuppi(n) [huu"-]

grow sea"

grow (of humans and animals) nahna"

grow older nahnapite

grow up nahnammi'a

grown up nahnappeh

gruel kottsaappeh ~ kuttsaappeh ~ kwattsaappeh

¹guard hoawoppih ~ huawoppih

²guard puitamah ~ puihtamah

gum sanakkoo

gun aiti

gunny sack wattsimokottsi

guts kohai ~ kohi

H

hair pampi

half na'ahpu(n)

half dollar poopitsih

halfway na'ahpu(n)

hand mo'o

handgame tan naaiyawinna

handsome tsaan napuite(n); tsaan tuittsi

hang down (head) tsowainuah
hang on to tsawainuah
hang (meat) out to dry ina" ~ inna"
hang (meat) out to dry for inanka(n) ~
    innanke(n)
hang over (of rock or cliff) tenkainua
hang up tsawaini, wewainih
happen naa" [naah AUX], naha"
hard kettaa(nten), natia(n)
hardly able to see kai tepuihtapuinte(n)
harm temekai
harvest -mai ~ -mahai
harvest pinenuts tepammai
has been naappeh(kanten)
hat tetsa'moih ~ tetse'oih ~ tetsoih
Hat Butte Tsanimmanihan Tetse'oih
hatch wettsi'ah
hateful person cho'appeh
haul noo"; tenoomi'a
hauler tenoote(n) ~ tenoomi'ate(n)
haunt tso'ayaah
have -pa'i(n); -kante(n)
have a baby ohaanai; tuannai [tutuanai
    pl]; pipihnai
have a big meal pia tekkah
have a cold ohipekka(n)
have a fire burning kottoohka(n)
have a headache pampi kamma(n)
have a house kahnikante(n), kahnipa'i(n)
have a period hunnapekkayu(n), hunni-
    to'ih ~ hunnitu'ih
have a sore e'attsihpa'i(n), e'atua
have a sore throat kuittsehpekka(n),
    kuittseh kamma(n)
have a toothache taman kamma(n)
have a wife kweeppa'i(n) ~ kweheppa'i(n)
have a wound e'apekka(n),
    e'attsihpa'i(n), e'atua
have an earache nankih kamma(n)
have an eye infection or disease
    puihpekka(n)
have an illness te'oipa'i(n)
have an injury e'attsihpa'i(n)
have blurry eyes pakenapuih(kan)
have canker sores in mouth painam-
    pekka(n)
have cramp(s) itsawene(kku)
have diarrhea piwea, kohipekka(n)

have grief tettehampekka(n)
have legs spread apart wettataah
have (someone) lie down hapinka(n) ~
    hapinke(n); tsahapinka(n) ~ tsa-
    hapinke(n)
have (someone) make -nainka(n) ~ -
    nainke(n)
have muscle cramps tsa'weah(ku)
have property oyontempa'i(n)
have rouge or red face paint on
    napisah(ka)
have sex yoko"
have (someone) stand niwenenka(n) ~
    niwenenke(n)
have taken away from nayaanka(n) ~
    nayaanke(n)
haver of -kante(n)
having -kante(n)
having a disease te'oikante(n)
having a wife kweekkante(n) ~
    kwehekkante(n)
having an appearance
    napuippehkante(n)
having children tutuakante(n)
having sugar diabetes pihyaa
    te'oikante(n)
hawk kinii
hay soni(ppeh); soniwekka'ah
he mate(n)
head pampi
head lice pampi pusi'a
headache pampi kammanna
headrest tsoppiteki'i
heal puhanai
healer puhakante(n) [puppuhakantee(n)
    pl]
healing napuhanainna
healing ceremony napuha [puha]
healing ceremony to be held napuhanai
healing power puha
hear nankah
hear (with feeling) nankasua(n)
heard nankappeh
heart pihye(n)
heat eteinte(n)
heat up katenkahka(n), kuttseni
heat wave kusuainna, yuwannan
    totompeentsi

heaven tukumpeh ~ tukumpi(n) ~
tukumpana(n) [tukun-]
heavy pettente(n)
heel tappikko'o(n)
help tematsai ~ tematsia
help deliver a baby tsattekinka(n) ~
tsattekinke(n)
helper teteaiwoppih
hem ha
hemophrodite wahatte(n) [waha-]
her u(n), ma, makka [makka(n) poss]
her own pe(n)
here aikkih, saikkih
here and there attu(n)
here somewhere ipai ~ ipi, sipi ~ sipai;
ana
here somewhere nearby ai'ana ~ sai'ana
hereabouts aipi, saipi ~ saipai
heron wasa(n)
Heron's Nest Wasannan Kahni
herself pen taka(sen), pese(n); penne(n) ~
penna(n) ~ pennese(n) pennase(n)
¹hide pehe
²hide watsi"
high pa'a(n) [pa'ai, pa'anku, pa'antu(n),
pa'ante(n)]; pa'attsi
highly natia(n)
Highway 51 (south of Little Valley,
ID) Piappehtem Po'in Nawainnna
hill ko'i, katete(n), nookatete(n), no'opi(n)
[noa-]
him ma, u, makka
himself penne(n) ~ penna(n) ~
pennese(n) pennase(n), pese(n); pen
taka(sen)
hindquarters pittehku ~ pittuhku
hip piwo'sa, tsi'ampeh
hire wookkahtea
his u(n), his makka(n)
his own pe(n)
hit -tekwah [-pa'ih pl]; wettekwah
[weppa'ih pl]
hit with fist tottekwah [toppa'ih pl]
hit with hard object tattekwah [tappa'ih
pl]
hit with something pointed tsikuttih ~
tsikkwettih
hog hoinkeh ~ hoinkih

hold yaakka(n) [himakka(n) pl]; tsai";
hannih
hold a healing ceremony napuhanai
hold down with hand makenah
hold in arms kwapakka(n) ~ kopakka(n)
hold in high regard ninnakkih ~
ninnahki"
hold in the mouth monooh(kan)
hole hotappeh, tainte(n), taikka, tawe(n)
[tatawe pl]
holler paitse"
holler after paitsenkakki
hollow hawo, konoki, kono'ihkante(n)
hollow out wehawo'ih
hollowed out hawo'ihkante(n)
holster huukkuna" ~ huukuna
Hombre (NAME) Amputih
home kahni
Home of the Big Wind Pia Neaippittan
Kahni
honey pihaa ~ pihnaa ~ pihyaa
honeybee pihyaamua
hood of cradle basket tsokkohno(n)
hoof tasitoo(n)
hop pottsi, poppi(n)
hopefully tsaa witsa
horn aa(n)
horn player temuyakainkante(n)
horned toad mattsankih
hornet paina(n)
horny na'isape
horse punku, teheyah
horse owner punkukante(n)
horsefly pi'pihta
horseman punkukante(n)
Horseshoe Bend, NV Newen Topo'ih
horsey punkuttsi
hospital nattahsu'unkahni
hot eteinte(n)
hot embers kuttsippeh [kotsimpoo song
form]
house kahni
house of prayer nanisuntehai
kahnikatte(n)
how hakai, hakanni
how many himpaikan(ten), heette(n)
how much heette(n), himpaikan(ten)
How are you? Hakanni e?

how so hakannikku
however hakanni, noohakai,
    noohakanni(kku)
Huevo (man's name) Waipo
hug kopa" ~ kwapa"
hummingbird piisi
humorous nisummaappeh
humorous (person) nisummampeh;
    tsaan temayahnainte(n), tsaan
    teniyahnainte(n)
hunchback kwipuntahkante(n)
hunchbacked nopontahkante(n)
hunched nopontahkante(n)
Hundred Mile Post, NV Ohattewene"
hunger pahu ~ paho
hungry pahupekkante(n)
hunt tekai", hannih; -mai ~ -mahai
hunter tekaite(n), waseppin tsukuppe
hurry namasohi
hurry up! mayanuhi, yawise(n), pammuuse
¹hurt kamma(n) ~ kammah; kammanna
²hurt manayaha, mahoihta,
    wekkamma(n)
husband kuhappe ~ kuhmappe,
    natainna(n)
husband (affectionately)
    natainnappettsi
husband and wife nanakweenneweh ~
    nanakwehennewe
husbandless kuhawatte(n)
Huukwitsa Spring, NV Huukwitsa
    Patetsoppih

I

I ne
ice paakkappeh
if ukka
ignore suwiihtaih
ill te'oi, temmaihkante(n)
illegitimate child watsittua"
illness te'oi
imitate manakki(n)
in a hurry yawise(n), yoyoha, kaippai(ttsi)
in a little while kaippai(ttsi), napaisai ~
    napisai
in addition noose(n)
in all directions na'appunte(n)

in back of pinnaih
in company with mai ~ ma'ai
in different directions nana'ahpu(n),
    nana'antappu(n)
in equal amounts nanahoi, nahpaikanku
in front of munnai
in half nahpaikanku, na'ahpu(n)
in heat (of an animal) napi'aiyu(n)
in particular tsaappai
in pieces nana'ahpu(n)
in the daytime tapaini; tapaima
in the fall time yepani
in the middle of tepana
in the middle of the night tukan tepana
in the nighttime tukani
in the same amount nanappaikante(n)
in the springtime tahmani
in the summertime tatsa
in the wintertime tommo
in time aattuse(n)
in which penkuppa(n) [penkuppai(ten),
    penkuppayente(n)]
in-law taiyumpeh
incline nawaih
indefinitely noo
Independence Mountain Range Settoya
Independence Valley, NV Tosa Konoki
index finger tsittsukanompeh
Indian neme ~ newe [newenee(n) pl]
Indian balsam tootsa
Indian Creek Tutuapainkwi Paa
Indian dance tan newe nekkanna
Indian Hay Meadows, NV Pia
    Payuppuka
Indian Meadows, NV Pia
    Sennahunupi(n) ~ Pia Hunupi(n)
Indian paintbrush tokoan kuna" ~
    tokoan taiyumpeh
Indian Rock Hill Newe Tekkoi
Indian tobacco newe pahu(n)
inedible kai natekkate(n)
infant ohaa(ttsi); teaite(n) ~ teite(n)
    [teteaitee(n) pl]
inject tona"
injure manayaha, mahoihta
injury e'attsih
inmate neettemahkante(n)
inscribe pooh, tepooh

inscription napooppeh
inside kuppa(n), tepana
inside that sukuppa(n) [sukuppayenten]
insist nittunaitseh
instruct niyekwi
intelligent natia suante(n)
intermingled nanakkapa(n)
intestinal gas pisuuppeh
intestines koh<u>a</u>i ~ kohi
invalid hapittaippeh, katettaiippeh; kai
    tattekinaattaippeh
invite p<u>a</u>itse"
invite to eat tekkahp<u>a</u>itseh
¹iron wiihimpeh
²iron takunaih, tetakunai
it u, ma
it is said m<u>a</u>i [m<u>a</u>iti]
Italian Pappatappisi
itch pihyakih
its u(n)
its own pe(n)
itself penne(n) ~ penna(n) ~ pennese(n)
    pennase(n), pese(n); pen taka(sen)

J

jackass tsakaasih
jackrabbit kamme ~ kamme [kammuntsi
    song form]
jackrabbit (white tailed) piakammu,
    tosakammu
jam tette'aika
Japanese Tsappanniih
Jarbridge mountain range tso'apittseh
jaw ahtahpeh
jerk (meat) ina" inna"
jerk (meat) for inanka(n) ~ innanke(n)
jerky inappeh ~ innappeh
Jesus Tsitsaseh
Jesus Christ (in Native American
    Church) Tosa Isa
jiggle yuppu
job wookkapi(n)
jog nukkinooh, poyoha
joke nisummaa, niyahnai(n)
joke together nananisummaha(n)
joker yokottsi, niyokottsi, nisummampeh,
    nananisummaate(n)

¹judge tenihannite(n)
²judge nihannih [nimmeeh pl], tenihannih
jug osa ~ pa'osa
juice napaa, hupa
juicy paa [pa- comb, pappa distrib]
jump pottsi, poppi(n)
juniper waappi(n) [waa"-]
Juniper Mountain Waakkate(n)
just eke, noo(n), nuha ~ noha, antase(n),
    nanah, tukuh, tese(n), taka(n)
just anything nanah hinna
just the same noo sunninte samp<u>a</u>i

K

keep tekikka(n) [tahnakka(n) pl];
    matemah; meekka(n); yaa" [hima" pl, -
    yaah comb]
keep hand on makateh(kan)
keep in the mouth monooh(kan)
keep laced up tottahka(n)
key teekkwinuhi
kick (for a horse to) tamminkuttih ~
    tamminkwettlh
kick (for a human to) sekkuttih ~
    sekkwettih
kick around (like a baby) tawenenuki
kidney takipoo
kill p<u>a</u>ikkah [wase" pl], tep<u>a</u>ikkah
kill for p<u>a</u>ikkanke(n) ~ p<u>a</u>ikkanka(n);
    tep<u>a</u>ikkanka(n) ~ tepaikkanke(n)
kill oneself nap<u>a</u>ikkah [nanawase" pl]
kill with bow tsapp<u>a</u>ikkan [tsawase pl]
kill with feet takkumpa
kill with mouth or teeth kettokwai
killdeer pantei
killed p<u>a</u>ikkappeh, nap<u>a</u>lkkappeh
    [wasettaippeh, nawasettaippeh pl]
kin tui
kindly tsaa(n)
kiss mutehai(n)
kitten ketian tua"
kitty ketian tua"
knee tannappeh ~ tankappeh
kneel down tannahottoo
knife wihi(n) [wii(n)- comb]
knock dizzy with a blunt object
    we'<u>a</u>imea(nkan)

knock down with long object we'annih
knock on tottantaki ~ tottontaki
knock out or unconscious wettiyainkah
knock out with club wettsaka
knock out with hand matsaka
knock out with hard object tattsaka
knock out with something wettantaki
knoll ko'i
know sumpana'ihki(n)
know (how to) sumpaatu(n),
   sumpana'ih(kan)
know how to -pana'in/h ~ -pana'ai(n)
know how to do mapana'ai(n) ~
   mapana'aih(kan)
know how to do by hand mapanatuh
know how to say nimmapana'ai(n)

L

lace up tottohna"
lace up shoes tammuhkah
laced up in a cradle board
   tottohnakkanten
lack watekih, wemmiha"
lacking nawate'inte(n)
ladle yunnah
lamb sippehan tua
Lambs Reservoir Tsi'apaa
[1]land sokopi(n)
[2]land hapikku, kate" [yekwi" pl]
land owned tepia
land owner tepiakante(n)
language taikwa(nna)
large piappehte(n) [pia, pipia pl, pipiap-
   pete(n) pl]; piante(n) [pia comb, pipia,
   pipiante(n) pl]
large crow haih
large solitary ant we'antoko ~
   we'awekkwintsuna
lasso kuuhkinka
last pinnanku
last born nakaha
last year munnanku
late kaiyu(n)
late (deceased) naappeh(kanten)
late at night tukan tepana
later on napaisai ~ napisai
latter pinna

laugh yahnai" [na'yahnai pl]
laugh uproariously nanittiyaih [nanikkoi pl]
lava rock oompi(n) [oon-]
lay a footpath tetappo'ihapinka(n) ~
   tetappo'ihapinke(n)
lay down hapinka(n) ~ hapinke(n);
   tsahapinka(n) ~ tsahapinke(n)
lay head on (pillow) tsoppitekihapi"
lazy kwi'yampeh ~ kwi'ampeh
   [kwikkwi'ampehnee(n) pl];
   kwi'yankante(n) ~ kwi'ankante(n);
   hapinaite(n)
lead tsannah
leader taikwahni
leaf seki; sekituah
leave mi'ah ~ miah [mimi'ah dl],
   mi'ahtai(n), mi'akwa(n); pea", peattai(n)
   ~ peaittai(n) ~ puittai(n); panittai(n)
leave for paninkah(tain) ~ panittainka(n) ~
   panittainke(n)
leave mate or spouse neempeattai(n)
   neempuihtai(n)
left mi'appeh, mi'ahtaippeh
left over pinnaippeh, pinnaih(ka)
left over (of food) tekeppinaippeh ~
   tekeppinaihtaippeh
left side ohainnankuhte(n)
left side (on the) ohainnankuh ~
   ohinnankuh
leftward ohainnankuh ~ ohinnankuh
leg oo(n)
legless oowatte(n)
less tsappe'a(n) ~ tsappe'ase(n)
less than ina; tsappe'a(n) ~ tsappe'ase(n);
   tukka(n) [tukkai, tukkanku, tukkantu(n)
   tukkante(n)]
lessen (pain, swelling or illness)
   tsawainkeh ~ tsawainkah
lesser nakaha
Lesser Chinaman's Hat Tsanimmanihan
   Nakaha Tetse'oih
let be seen manapuih ~ manapunnih
let blood paiwekka'ah
let drop tsappahai"
let get away tsimmianka(n) ~ tsimmianke(n)
let go tsappe'ah; tsimmianka(n) ~
   tsimmianke(n)
let go with mouth keppeah

let loose tsattoyah(tain)
letter tepooppeh
level seeppaite(n)
liar isampeh
lice posia(ttsi) ~ pusia(ttsi)
lick kwini"
lie isa(n), isannai, isannainna
lie (down) hapi" [kwapi" pl, kwakkwappi
   pl distrib]
lie (for a bloodline to) peehapi"
lie around hapinnemmi
lie in state (of a deceased)
   natsattekih(kan)
lie to isannainka(n) ~ isannainke(n)
lift behind up pihittsaah
lift feet up tahittsaah
lift grasping with hand tsahittsaa
lift head up tsohannih
light a fire kottooh, kuttsihtunah
light a match kuppihto
light footed(ly) pehai(ten)
lightly pehai(ten)
¹like -sunka'a(n) ~ -sunka'ah; tsaa . . .
   sua"; tsaasuanka(n) ~ tsaasuanke(n)
²like ni(sen) [-nni]; wa'ih [wa'ihte(n),
   wa'ihku, wa'ise(n), wa'ihkuse(n)]
like each other natsaasuanka(n) ~
   natsaasuanke(n)
like each other na'wa'i [na'wa'iten]
like one semmewa'i(se)
like that owa'ih, sowa'ih; onni, sonni;
   mawa'ih
like that out of sight unni; sunni [sun-
   nikku, sunniunte(n); susunni pl]; uwa'ih;
   suwa'ih [suwa'iten, suwa'ihku(ten)]
like that yonder anni, sanni, awa'ih,
   sawa'ih
like this aiwa'ih, saiwa'ih; mawa'ih
like this nearby ainni, sainni
like this right here iwa'ih, siwa'ih; inni,
   sinni
like what hakanni
likely not kai sampai
line wooppihte(n)
lined wooppih ~ wookki
lip tempai
liquid paa [pa- comb, pappa distrib]
liquor paa [pa- comb, pappa distrib]

listen nankah
listen carefully nankasuanka(n) ~
   nankasuanke(n)
listen thinking about nankasuanka(n) ~
   nankasuanke(n)
listen to tenanka(n)
little teaite(n) ~ teite(n) [teai teteaitee(n)
   pl]; teiku
little bit mapaitettsi; teittse'i(nkuttsi)
little bit at a time mammapaiku
Little Canyon, NV Nakaha Tettsohpai
little finger mattua
little girl nai'pi(n)
little toe tattua
live nemi(kkan) [yeyenkah dl, yenka ~
   nayekwin ~ yeme" pl]; naakka(n),
   nanaahka(n), nanahaitah(kan);
   kahnikante(n), kahnipa'i(n)
live in peace yuunnaahka
lively pehai(ten)
liver newe(n) ~ neme(n)
lizard pokoitsi
loaf nokkoppeh
locate teki" [tahna" pl, tekih instr];
   tsattekih(kan); tsattanah [tsattani'ih pl]
located natsattekihkante(n)
lock in -temah
lock up wettemah [wettemi'ih pl];
   wennehki ~ we'nika
locked neettemappeh
locust kea
log huuppi(n) [huu"-]; wopi(n)
loin cloth toppata
Lone Mountain Anta Katete(n)
long kepetaa(nten)
long ago peai, himpaise(n), apaise(n);
   a'akkuse(n), i'ana hattu(n)
long time eei(ttsi)
look napuih ~ napuni [nanapui pl]
look (instilling feeling)
   nanapuisunka'a(n)
look after manapuih ~ manapunnih
look at punni" ~ pui"; puikka(n);
   puisunkanna
look for antsi, puhai(n), waikki(n)
look good tsaan napunni
looking napuite(n)
looking bad kaitsaan napuite(n)

lookout hoawoppih ~ huawoppih
looks napuinna
loosen tsahoyonki, tsakkwaitu'ah
loosen with tools wekkwaitu'ah
lope poyoha
lose nanakwaha(n); watsinka(n) ~
 watsinke(n)
losings (in a game) nanakwahappeh
lost watsinkappeh ~ watsinkeppeh;
 nawatsinkappeh ~ nawatsinkeppeh
lost (be) watsi"
lots soo(n); soonte(n) [soon- comb,
 sooyente(n)]; soose(n); natia(n),
 tukkumpai
louse posia(ttsi) ~ pusia(ttsi)
love -sunka'a(n) ~ -sunka'ah; tsaa
 suanka(n) ~ suanke(n); tuku
 kammanka(n) ~ kammanke(n)
lunch tapaitekkanna, tenooppeh
lung sonko ~ sonno
lupine kwitakkwana
lying in state (of a deceased)
 natsattekihkante(n)
lying on one's stomach (face down)
 muttehappi

M

made naippeh; mapaiappeh,
 temapaiappeh, namapaiappeh;
 nahappeh, hannippeh
made up
made up (with face paint or makeup)
 teaikappeh; napisappeh
maggot wo'api(n)
magpie kwitawoyo(n)
make hannih, mapaiah, temapaiah,
 naha", mee" ~ mehe(n), -nai
make camp noopite
make ceremonial house pahunkahninai
make crashing sound tottsapikkah
make cry tsiyakaih
make cut in wekki'ah
make disappear wehanninkah(tain)
make drink hipinka(n) ~ hipinke(n),
 tsihipinka(n) ~ tsihipinke(n)
make feel wesunkanna, maneesunka'ah
 ~ maneesunkanna

make fire kottooh
make fire for kottoonka(n) kottoonke(n)
make footpath tetappo'ihapinka(n) ~
 tetappo'ihapinke(n)
make for meenka(n), nahanke(n); -
 nainka(n) ~ -nainke(n); mapaianka(n) ~
 mapaianke(n), temapaianka(n),
 hanninka(n)
make fun of ni'aipui ~ ni'aipunni;
 nanisuntsaa ~ ninnasuntsaa,
 teninnasuntsaa
make function nukkinka(n) ~
 nukkinke(n)
make gravy kuttsaah ~ kottsaah ~
 kwattsaah
make gruel kwattsaah ~ kuttsaah ˜
 kottsaah
make house wekkahninai ~
 wekkahnittsinaih
make jam tette'aikanai
make knife wihinai
make laugh with actions mayahnai(n)
make laugh with words niyahnai(n)
make love yoko"
make music hupianai
make nest noote(n), nottsoninai
make noise nananka", nankah,
 -peittseiki(n)
make noise like nanankasuanka(n) ~
 nanankasuanke(n)
make numb sese'nika(n) ~ sese'ninkeh
make oneself shine namapataatsiki
make pinenuts tepannai
make popping sound pottainnanankah
make pudding kwattsaah ~ kuttsaah ˜
 kottsaah
make rasping sound wehe'neki"(kkin)
make run nukkinka(n) ~ nukkinke(n)
make shine mapataatsi
make sick eating kettemmaih
make speech sounds te'ampaito'ih
make stand (up) tsawenenka(n) ~
 tsawenenke(n); tsiwenenka(n) ~
 tsiwennehka(n)
make stop mawenenka(n), tsawenenka(n)
make well tsaa . . . mee"
Maker of People Nemi
 Manemenaippehkante(n)

male kuha ~ kuhma
mallard duck pehye(n) ~ peye(n)
man tainna
man (one's own, said by a woman)
  natainna(n)
man's nephew/niece haih
mano (pestle) tusunnompeh
many soo(n); soonte(n) [soon- comb,
  sooyente(n)]; himpaikan(ten)
mare piapeh, punkum piapeh
mark tenapoo
marriage nakweekkante(n) ~
  nakwehekkante(n)
married (of a man) kweekkante(n) ~
  kwehekkante(n)
married (of a woman) kuhakante(n)
married couple nanakweenneweh ~
  nanakwehennewe
marrow tuuku
marry (of a man) kweettu ~ kwehettu
marry (of a woman) kuhatu
marry each other na'kweettu ~
  nanakweettu
mash -tsokkwaih
mash with hand makitsa'a
matches mantsih, sonikuna"
mate tui, taka
mate (of animals) nanakai ~ nanaki;
  napi'ai(yun)
maternal grandfather toko
maternal grandmother kaku
mature grass soni(ppeh)
maybe kia ~ ki'a; noo; okia ~ osen kia;
  seepa ~ seepa kia
maybe so noo sampai, sunni kia
me nei, ne
meadow puhitapai(n)
meadowlark hiittoo(n)
[1]mean atsa, tehuppeh ~ tuhuppeh
[2]mean niikwi", ninnapunni ~ ninnapui
meander okkwaikki(nnemmi)
meat tukku, meat pihetsih
medicate oneself nanattahsu'a
medicinal plant (large leaves, white
  flowers) piapoko
medicine nattahsu'u(n)
medicine person puhakante(n)
  [puppuhakantee(n) pl]

medicine power puha
Medicine Woman Puha Wa'ippe
meet waikia
meet each other or together nanawaikia
meet face to face takkamah
melt patehwi ~ patuhi
member of (family) mante(n)
member of this (family) imante(n),
  simante(n)
member of that (family) umante(n),
  sumante(n)
menses hunni
menstrual blood hunni
menstrual flow hunna peeppi(n)
menstrual house hunna kahni
menstruate hunnapekkayu(n), hunnito'ih
  ~ hunnitu'ih
menstruation hunni
mentally ill (person) tesu'aimeate(n)
mention nanikklmma, niikwi"
merchant natemakate(n)
merely tese(n)
Merrit Mountain, NV (northeast of
  Mountain City) Oosaanten Kate(n)
mesquite beans ohpi
metal wiihimpeh
Mexican Tsippani
midday tokwaittapaini
middle tepihante(n), tepiha(ka)
middle (in the) na'akka
middle finger mattepiha
midnight (at) tukattepiha
might noo; witsa
might be noha kia
migrate (of birds) pommi'a
mildew aippo'intsiappeh
milk pitsa
milk cow pitsa kuittsu(n)
milkweed pitsite puhippeh
Miller Creek, NV Kettaa Okwai",
  Kettaa See
mimic manakki(n)
mind suappeh
mink tuuppantsuku
mint pa'kwana
miss (someone) watekih, wesuatekih
miss aim or miss shooting ahwai ~ ahwi
  ~ awi [a'ahwai pl], te'awi

miss out on tsimmianka(n) ~
  tsimmianke(n)
missing nawate'inte(n)
mix around tsakkwinuhi
mix together mayaah, tsammayaa,
  natsammayaappeh
mix up mayaah, tsammayaa,
  natsammayaappeh
moldy aippo'intsiappeh
mole pammuhi, pampo'naih
molt kwayu'i
mom pii ~ pia
mommy pii
Monday Semme Nawookkah
money muunih, nappiasi(n) ~ nappiaseh,
  puhwih
monkey munkih, kwasi taipo
monkey flower (medicinal plant)
  antapittseh kwana
monster tso'apittseh
month mea
moon mea
moon house hunna kahni
more than haiyani, makuppa(n), mayani
  ~ mahyani, ka'wi; pa'a(n) [pa'ai,
  pa'anku, pa'antu(n), pa'ante(n)]
Mormon cricket maiso(n)
Mormon tea tuttumpih
morning imaa
mosquito mooppo, wa'wata(n)
moth tso'appatuntsih ~ tso'appuntunkih
mother pia ~ pii
mother and daughter (relationship)
  nana paitenneweh dl
mother's brother ata
mother's sister piattsi
mother-in-law pahattsi
mountain toyapi(n) [toya-]
mountain area toyawaiki(n)
mountain canyon toyahunupi(n)
Mountain Dwellers (= Shoshoni in
  Jarbridge area) Toyatepia
mountain lion toyatukkupittseh
mountain near Mountain City, NV
  Wonko Senkwi
mountain pass wia [wiya song form]
mountain range toyahapite(n)

mountain range on the Duck Valley
  Reservation Tenkatsu(n)
mountain sheep waseppi(n) ~ waseppeh
mountain sitting alone toyakatete(n)
mountain top toya'ana
mournful tettehan(ten)
mouse po'naih
mouth tempai, natempai
move nua ~ nuwa, noommi'a; tonnuyuah;
  wennua; yeme"
move (away) noomi'a(taih)
move about nooh
move about moving up and down
  tsennenneki(n)
move away (from) yunka(n) ~ yunki(n)
move feet tase'yekwi
move repeatedly wemme'ekki
move slowly from being weak or disabled yu'inahannemmi
moved away noomi'ataippeh
mover noomi'ate(n)
mow soniwekka'ah
much soo(n); soonte(n) [soon- comb,
  sooyente(n)]; himpaikan(ten); natia(n)
much (this/that) paika(nten) ~ pika(nten)
Muchacho (NAME) Muittsaittseh
mucous, mucus yokappeh, mupisippeh
mud pasakwinappeh
muddy pasakkwinapa'i
mudhen saiya(n) ~ saya(n)
mule muuta
murderer tepaikkappehkante(n)
must noo, tukuh
mute kaitai'kwa'a, sua
my ne ~ neai"
my own nease(n)
myself nese(n)
myth natekwinappeh [nanatekwinappeh pl]
myth marker kia ~ ki'a, wihnu

N

naked maniyunte(n)
name naniha(n), nanihanna; niha ~ nihya
  ~ nia"; niha; niakka(n) ~ nihakka(n);
  tepinniha(n); mai [maiti]
name (woman's) Kiiki

names (men's) Amputih, Antannewe, ,
  Chikko, Itsapehe, Itsataipo,
  Muittsaittseh, Pamuseh, Pianampai,
  Tapai Pui, Tokoa Wiittsi, Tsikuttih,
  Tso'apittseh, Waipo, Wattsi Kahni,
  Yokottsi
narrate natekwina, natemu'i ~ nateme'i
narrate to natemu'inka(n) ~
  natemu'inke(n) ~ nateme'inke(n);
  natekwinanka(n) ~ natekwinanke(n)
narrow teiwaikite(n)
nasty atsa
naughty person natekwinappeh
navel punu
near mii(sen)
near here aikkih, saikkih
near here somewhere aipi ~ aipai; saipai
  ~ saipi
neck toyo(n)
necklace kolokki
need sua" [suan AUX]
needle wihupi(n) ~ wihyupi(n)
negative particle kai
negro tuuttaipo
nephew of a man ata
nephew of a woman paha, piattsi
nest nottsoni
nest (laying) nokahni
nest(le) noote(n)
¹net wana
²net kwisinka(n) ~ kwisinke(n)
nettles painke(n)
never kaite(n) ~ kaiti; kai himpai
new eke
new growth tuattsi
newborn tuattsi
newly eke, newly e'eki
next day imaa
next morning u'imaa
next time pinnanku
next to kemaka ~ kemahka ~ kematu;
  paiyekwi
next to each other nanappaiyekwi
Nez Perce Indian(s) Tsoika Tekka'a
nice tsaa(n)
nick wekki'ah
nick oneself neekki'ah

niece of a man ata
niece of a woman piattsi, paha
night tuka
nighthawk wai'yapoo ~ wa'yapoo
nine seewemmihante(n) [seewemmihan-]
nine hundred seewemmiha pia
  seemaahte(n)
nineteen seemayente seewemmihamman
  to'inkanna
ninety seewemmihammaahte(n)
  [seewemmihammaah-]
nipple pitsi ko'i
nit(s) tatsii
no kai
no good kaitsaan(ten) [kaitsaayente(n)]
no more kaihaiwa(n); tsu'appeh
nod head tso'wintukih
noon tapaini, tokwaittapaini
north kwinahainankuhte(n)
Northern Paiute Paiyuti ~ Payuti,
  Papiyotsa
northward kwinahaippaitu(n)
nose mupi(n) ~ muupi(n)
not kai; kaite(n) ~ kaiti
not be strong kai tapu'i
not certain noon (kwa'i) kia
not do well kai tapu'i; kai tapu'inna naakka
not enough kai tokaiyu
not even kai sampai
not ever kai himpai
not good kaikkaitsaa(n)
not like kai sumpaitsappih ~ kai
  sumpitsappih
not love (kai) sumpaitsappih ~ (kai)
  sumpitsappih
not sure noon (kwa'i) kia
not there kai himpai
not well kaitsaan(ten) [kaitsaayente(n)]
not yet kaise(n)
nothing kaihaiwa(n)
notice tesumpite
now eki"; mai'ukka
now then maaikkuh
nowadays ekittapaima ~ ekittapaini
nurse pitsinka(n) ~ pitsinke(n)
nurse (for a mother to) nempitsinka(n)
  ~ nempitsinke(n)

O

obnoxious nasu'yekwite(n)
obsidian tuuppi(n)
obtain tsayaah
occlude tsi'ah
ocean piapaa
offspring (poetic) tuantsi
oil yuhu
okay maaikkuh
old peai ~ peaite(n)
old (person) peaittempeh
  [pepeaittempehnee(n) ~ pepeaitte(n) pl]
old lady hepitsoo(ttsi)
old maid kuhawatte(n)
old man tsukuppe(ttsi), tainnappe
old woman hepitsoo(ttsi)
on ma(n) [mannai, manku, mantu(n),
  mante(n), mayente(n)]
on (top of) pa'a(n) [pa'ai, pa'anku,
  pa'antu(n), pa'ante(n)]
on it mapa'a(n), uma(n)
on one side senkwinanku
on one's back pa'atai ~ pa'ataihku
on one's side senkwippu(n)
on other side of maananku ~ mananku
on that uma(n), suma(n); supa'a(n)
  [supa'ante(n)]
on the right side tematahain nankuh(ten)
on the side of nanku ~ nankwa; tepana ~
  teppanna
on this sima(n) [simanku]; mapa'a(n)
on top of each other nanappa'a(n)
  [nahpa'a(n) dl]
on which pemma(n); pempa'a(n)
once seme ~ sewe ~ semme
once and for all seme ~ sewe ~ semme
once in a while sesewekka ~ semekka
one seme ~ sewe ~ semme
one (someone) ta(n)
one-sided senkwi
one at a time sesemanikku ~ sesema
one dollar wantatah
one from here sainankuhte(n)
one hundred pia seemaahte(n)
one's ta(n)
oneself pesu'a, taka(n), takattsi
onion muha
only nanah, noo(n), tukuh, taka(n)

only one semmettsi, pennaipih, takattsi
only sometimes u'ukapa (taka)
[1]open -tawai" ~ -tawi"; tsattainka(n),
  tsattawaih ~ tsattawih, wettawai" ~
  wettawi"
[2]open tsattawaippeh ~ tsattawippeh,
  wettawaippeh ~ wettawippeh
open legs apart tasaa
open mouth kesaa, kesaapah
open up (of pinecones) ake";
  wettawih(tain)
opened tsattawaippeh ~ tsattawippeh,
  wettawaippeh ~ wettawippeh
opened mouth kesaapappeh
opening natsattawih, tawe(n)
openly pianku
operate on weppaikoah
opponent woho; nanatemmuneweh
or (else) noon tea
Oregon grape sokoteheyampehe
oriole na'tsawaini ~ wanatsawaini
orphan tettehantempeh
other seepatte(n)
other things nanasumma(nten)
otter pantsuku
ouch! ataa, oto'oto
our (excl) nemme(n)
our (incl) tamme(n)
our two (excl) nehe(n)
our two (incl) taha(n)
ourselves (excl) nemmese(n)
ourselves (incl) tammese(n)
ourselves (dl excl) nehese(n)
ourselves (dl incl) tahase(n)
out of tsumah ~ tsu'ah
out of place antananku
outdoors maittenkah(ten)
outer covering pehe, po'a(n)
outhouse kwitakkahni
outside maittenkah(ten), peattenkah
over pa'a(n) [pa'ai, pa'anku, pa'antu(n),
  pa'ante(n)]
over it or that upa'a(n) ~ supa'a(n)]
over that way opuhni ~ opu(n), sopuhni
  ~ sopu(n); ottu(n) ~ sottu(n)
over that way out of sight upuhni ~
  upu(n), supuhni ~ supu(n); uttu(n),
  suttu(n)

over that way yonder apuhni ~ apu(n);
  sapuhni ~ sapu(n); attu(n ~ sattu(n)
over this way ipuhni ~ ipu(n), sipuhni ~
  sipu(n)
over this way nearby aipuhni ~ aipu(n);
  saipuhni ~ saipun; aittu(n) ~ saittu(n)
overcast toomoahkante(n)
overcome matsuhninka(n) ~
  matsuhninke(n) ~ matsuhinka(n)
overpower with the mind
  summatsuhninka(n) ~ summatsuhninke(n)
overpower with words
  nimmatsuhinka(n) ~ nimmatsuhinke(n)
owl (burrowing) pokkoo
owl (great horned) muumpittseh ~
  muhumpittseh
owner of -kante(n)
Owyhee, NV Un Kwahai(n)

P

pacer horse pisenteki
pack noote'aikah, nookka(n)
paddle wekkwintuih, tewekkwintuih
paid for temeeppeh
pain kammahpuinna; kammanna
paint pisa"; teaika
painted teaikappeh
Paiute Paiyuti, Paiyuttsi
pal taka
pale aapihte(n) [aa-]; papumpihte(n)
  [papun]
Pale Point (valley of North Fork, NV)
  Aamutsa
palm mappana
pants kusa
paper tepooppeh
parade natayaa
paralyzed yu'ito'lhtalppeh
parent tutuakante(n)
parents appe ma'ai pii
park (a vehicle) tewenenka(n) ~
  tewenenke(n)
parsnip haappai
parsnip (poison) hattai
part of mante(n)
part of it or that umante(n), sumante(n)
part of this imante(n), simante(n)

partake tonikah
partner taka
pass wia
pass away wihtuha ~ wituha,
  wituha'ihkante(n), kaihaiwan naammi'a
pass on nekkamaih
pass up tsimmianka(n) ~ tsimmianke(n)
pass wind pukkiih, pisuuh
passed away long ago wituhappeh
paternal grandfather kenu
paternal grandmother huttsi
path po'i"
patient temmaihkante(n)
pay a bill or debt temanakkih
pay attention nankasuanka(n) ~
  nankasuanke(n)
pay attention to tesumpite
pay for temeeh, temanakkih
pay to temanakkinka(n) ~
  temanakkinke(n)
payment natepahappeh
peaceful yuu(n)
peak ko'i
peck tottsi'ah, tottantaki ~ tottontaki
pee sii"; siippeh; si'si'we(n)
peek kuhuyah(kan), tokkuhuyah
peel by hand tsattsino'a [tsattsino'ih pl]
peel with knife wettsino'a [wettsino'ih
  pl]
pen tepoonnompeh
pencil tepoonnompeh
penis we'a", paka(n)
people neme ~ newe [newenee(n) pl]
perceive wesuntapu'i
perfect tokai" ~ tokwai"
perforate tsittainka(n), tottainka(n)
perfume na'kwana'a
perhaps noo; kia ~ ki'a; seepa, seepa kia
perhaps not naketsa hattu(n)
persist nittunaitseh
person neme ~ newe [newenee(n) pl]
person afflicted with an eye disease
  puihpekkate(n)
person doing the cry dance
  yakainnekkate(n)
person from Fort Hall, ID
  Pohoko'ikkate(n)
person who prays nanisuntehaite(n)

persuade nimma'i(n) ~ nimma'ikki
pertaining to timma(sen)
pestle tusunnompeh
pet punkuttsi, sateettsi
pet bird kwi'naattsi
petroglyph tempimpooh
peyote wokaipi(n) ~ wokwaipi(n),
    Piyotti(ttsi)
phlegm yokappeh
photo napooppeh
piano tan tetsayakainkanna ~ tan
    tetsayakainkenna
piano/accordion player tet-
    sayakainkante(n) ~ tetsayakainkente(n)
pick tso'i, tsappoah, poma, tso'imm<u>ai</u> ~
    tso'm<u>ai</u>
pick on nasuntsaa
pick up or carry with a pointed instru-
    ment tsiyaah
picture napooppeh
pierce tsittainka(n), tottainka(n)
pig pikih
pika rabbit tseke(n)
pile up koa; topp<u>ai</u>kkwah ~ topp<u>ai</u>hkwah;
    wettono'ih; wekkatenkah ~
    wekkatenke(n)
pile up on top of tottani'i
pile up with frost aikkawekkatuah
pile up with rock takkoa
pillow tsoppiteki'i
pinch tsattsi'ah
pine (cedar or juniper) waappi(n)
    [waa"-], sanawaappi(n)
pine (tall) wonkopi(n)
pine cone kappeh
pine cone hook <u>ai</u>hko(n)
pine jay kaiyattsih ~ kayattsih
pinenut tepa"
Pinenut Eaters Tepattekka'a
pinenut pudding tepakkwattsappeh
pinenut tree tepawaappi(n)
pinyon (piñon) nut tepa"
pinyon (piñon) pine tepawaappi(n)
pipe to'ih
piss sii"; siippeh; si'si'we(n)
pissant a'ni(n)
pistol kepi aiti
pitch sanappi(n)

pitch in tsiyuuma(n)
pitiful tettehan(ten), nanatetteha(n)
pitiful(ly) tetteha(n)
pitifully nanatettehase(n)
pity tettehan(ten)
[1]place himpeh; wia
[2]place teki" [tahna" pl, tekih instr];
    wekkatenkah ~ wekkatenke(n);
    tsakkatenkah ~ tsakkatenkeh;
    tsattanah [tsattani'ih pl]
place for tsattekinka(n) ~ tsattekinke(n)
place head on tsottekih, tsottekinke(n)
place in a hole standing up
    towenenka(n) ~ towenenke(n)
place in a hole tamping in with foot
    tsottekinka(n)
place mouth on mutekih
place post (or other object) in a hole
    towene, tetowenne
place somewhere tosi'a
place with hand matekih,
    tsattekih(kan)
placed natsattekihkante(n)
plant seakkante(n), maseanka(n) ~
    maseanke(n); tep<u>ai</u>ti"
plant (a garden) temaseanka(n) ~
    temaseanke(n)
plant in mountains with strong pleas-
    ant smell toyakwana
plants temaseankappeh ~
    temaseankeppeh
plate tekkanompeh
play nuhi(n) ~ nui(n)
play a horned instrument
    muyakainka(n), temuyakainka(n)
play a piano tsayakainka(n) ~
    tsayakainke(n), tetsayakainka(n)
play a violin or stringed instrument
    weyakainka(n), teweyakainka(n)
play an accordion tsayakainka(n),
    tetsayakainka(n)
play handgame (or stickgame) naaiyawi
Pleasant Valley Canyon Pia Tettsohp<u>ai</u>
please e witsa . . . ne suntehai
pliable yontsoka(nten)
plow -yottah, teeyottah, weyottah
pluck tsannoo'i
pocket pimmokottsih

¹point mutsipi(n); mutsa, ko'i
²point tsitte'ahwaih
point out te'ahwaih; tsittsukah
point out to tsittsukanka(n) ~
   tsittsukanke(n)
point to tsittsukah
poison parsnip hattai
poisonous kai natekkate(n)
poke tona", tsittona; tsittekwah
poke (around) to see tsippunni(kin)
policeman teettemate(n)
ponder about tenisua"
pool pakatete(n)
poop kwitappeh
pooped out enuhi
poor (person) tettehannaakkante(n)
poorly susu'a
poplar sohopi(n)
porcupine yehne(n) ~ yehnettsi
possessions himpeh, oyonte(n) ~ oyontettsi
possessor of -kante(n)
possessor of destructive power
   teitseppuha
possibly seepa
pot wittua
potato pettitah ~ tetesih
potato bug aattoko
pound tatsokkwaih ~ tattsokwaih
pound on tottanihka
pour wettiah
pour out tsittuuh, towehtiah, towiihtain
   [toppaitihtain pl]
powdery stuff homokaite(n)
power puha
power being puha naakkante(n) [puha
   naakkantee(n) pl]
powerful natia(n)
prairie dog keempai
pray nanisuntehai(n); taikwa" [niweneh pl]
pray for nanisuntehainka(n) ~
   nanisuntehainke(n)
prayer nanisuntehai
prayer song nanisuntehai hupia
praying nanisuntehai
preceding pinna
pregnant no'akante(n)
prepare mapaiah, temapaiah; mapitsi'a;
   mayekwi; hannih; -tenkah/n

prepare for temapaianka(n) ~
   temapaianke(n)
prepare oneself namapaiah; namayekwi
prepared nahappeh, namatenkappeh;
   mapaiappeh, namapaiappeh,
   temapaiappeh
present to tsattekinka(n) ~ tsattekinke(n)
pretend nasuyekwi" ~ nasu'yekwi"
pretend to be dead nama'atiyaihku
pretty tsaa(n); tsaan napuite(n)
pretty soon ekise(n)
previous pinna
prisoner neettemahkante(n)
probably kia noo(n); okia ~ osen kia
probe with a pointed object tsisunka'ah
prod tona"
prod in the back tsiyuppu'i
proper tokai" ~ tokwai"
properly tokainku ~ tokwainku
property himpeh, oyonte(n) ~ oyontettsi
protector hoawoppih ~ huawoppih
provide hanninka(n) ~ hanninke(n)
pubic hair suhi
pudding kuttsaappeh ~ kottsaappeh ~
   kwattsaappeh
pull away or forward wettunaittseh,
   neettunaittseh
pull hair out tsahopi'i
pull out tsatto'ih [tsakkea pl]
pull with hands tsattunaittseh
pulverize tatsokkwaih
punch holes in tsittatawene
puppy satee'an tuattsi
purify mapuisi"
purify oneself namapuisi"
purify oneself with smoke nawaiti
purify with (e.g., a feather, smoke, or
   ashes) wemmapuisi"
purify with smoke waiti
purifying word wisaa
purple aikkwimpihte(n) [aikkwin-]
pursue temahai"
pus pisippeh
push along (as water) tottsatekkah
push away mawiih(tain), tonnuyuah
push down or out from within the butt
   pittunaittseh
push hard with the feet tattunaittseh

push in tsekke'i

put teki" [tahna" pl, tekih instr]; tottekih,
    tsattekih(kan); matekih, tosi'a, hannih;
    tsattanah [tsattani'ih pl]; mee" ~
    mehe(n) put away matemah;
    tekikka(n) [tahnakka(n) pl]

put clothes on namahannih

put face paint on pisa"

put in a hole standing up towenenka(n)
    ~ towenenke(n)

put in a hole tamping in with foot
    tannehki;

put makeup on teaika

put post in a hole towene

put priority on doing mapitsi'a

put rouge or red face paint on
    napisah(ka)

put saddle on natenootekih

put water out (for an animal) in a con-
    tainer patsawenneh(kan)

pygmy rabbit tseke(n)

Q

quaking aspen sennapi(n)

quarter (25 cents) tupittsih

question particles ha, hattu(n)

quickly yoyoha, teiku

quill aikopi(n)

quiver huukkuna" ~ huukuna

R

rabbit (cottontail) tapu(n) ~ taputtsi

rabbit (jack) kammu ~ kamme

rabbit (pika or pygmy) tseke(n)

rabbit (snowshoe) piakammu

rabbit brush sipappi(n)

raccoon paakkwitahawo ~ pankwitahawo

race (in a footrace) na'natea

rain ema" ~ pa'emah ~ pa'emeah;
    emate(n) ~ pa'emate(n)

rainbow emappatompittseh, tapai
    patompittseh

raise ma'nahna; tsayetseh

raise up ma'nahayetse

raise up the behind (bending over)
    pippupuah(kan)

rancid ta'oo(n)

rascal cho'appeh, natekwinappeh,
    yokottsi

rasping dance (= bear dance) mamakkoi
    ~ ta wehe'neki nekkanna

rat kaa(n)

rat urine powder (medicine) (kaan)
    tetahain naappeh

rations meeppeh

rattlesnake (tepitsi) tokoa

raven haih

Raven Nest Haihan Nokahni

ravine hunupi(n)

raw saampittseh

real tepi(tsi)

real property tepia

really kettaa(n), kettaanku; naketsa,
    natia(n); naketsa natia(n); haiya;
    tsaappai; tepi(tsi); tsaa(n); tokainku ~
    tokwainku, tokaise(n) ~ tokwaise(n)

really bad kaikkaitsaa(n)

rear ma'nahna

rear up (like a horse) ma'nahayetse

rebirth tuattsi

recently e'eki

recognize puisumpana'ih

rectum kwitattsi

red ainkapihte(n) [ainka"-]

red ant hu'nita(n) ~ hunnita(n)

red face paint pisappi(n)

red ocher pisappi(n)

red-winged blackbird saipakantsukkih

refuse teetto'ippeh ~ teetto'ihtaippeh

regain consciousness suapitai(n)

reject nimmuya'i

relation(s) nanewe ~ naneme
    [nananewenee(n) pl]; newetuhi
    [newetuhinee(n) pl]

relative(s) nanewe ~ naneme
    [nananewenee(n) pl]; nanatea; newe-
    tuhi [newetuhinee(n) pl]; nanewettsi

religion nanisuntehai, nanisuntehaippeh

remain katekka(n) [yekwikka(n) pl];
    naakka(n); pennaihka(n)

remember nasuntamah(kan)

remind niikwi"

renew spiritual power tahma puhatuah

renewed tahma

rest hapinnemmi

rest in the daytime tap<u>ai</u> hapi"

retarded k<u>ai</u>suante(n)

retarded person <u>ai</u>meattsi ~ <u>ai</u>'meattsi

return ko'ih [koko'ih dl]; pite [pippite dl];
noopite ~ nooppite, panipite,
tsakko'inka(n), yaappite

reveal tsatto'ih [tsakkea pl]

revive suapitai(n)

rhythmical song words h<u>ai</u>n<u>ai</u>(h) ~
h<u>ai</u>nna(h), h<u>aa</u>inna(h), h<u>ai</u>na(h);
h<u>ai</u>yo(n), h<u>ai</u>yaho, haaiyuh, h<u>aa</u>iyaanna;
ho, <u>ai</u>yoo, nai, tuu; yanna, yaainno(h),
wainna(h)

rhythmical song words to bless songs
haiya wainna, yaaya wainna

rib amattampeh

Riddle, ID Yakwahnim Paa

ride a horse punku kate"

ride a horse away punku katemi'a

ride a horse hither punku katekki(n)

ride along on a horse punku katenooh

ride around katenooh

ride away katemi'a

right tokai" ~ tokwai", tokainku ~
tokwainku, tokainte(n) ~ tokwainte(n);
haa('a); tepi(tsi)

right amount tokaipp<u>ai</u>ka(n) ~
tokwaipp<u>ai</u>ka(n)

right away sup<u>ai</u>se(n); tunnaa(n);
yawise(n)

right here ikkih, sikkih

right here somewhere i'ana, si'ana

right now ekittsi

right side (on the) tem<u>a</u>tah<u>ai</u>n
nankuh(ten)

rigorous natianku

rigorously natianku

ring ma'nika'a

ring finger mattepiha nankuhte(n)

rip siwah ~ si'wah; tsasiwah

rip with mouth or teeth kesi'wah

ripe kwaseppeh

ripen kwase", kwasenka(n) ~ kwasenke(n)

rise to'ih [toto'ih dl, kea" ~ nakea" pl]

rise up yetse" [yoyoti dl, yoti" pl]

ritual done before round dance tan
natayaanna

road po'i"

roam nemi [yeyenkah dl, yenka ~
nayekwin pl]; yeme"

roam around neminemmi

¹roast kwase"

²roast nokko(n) ~ nokkoh; kwasenka(n) ~
kwasenke(n)

roast in cones kanokkoh(ka)

roasted nokkoppeh, nanokkoppeh

rob tetekkah

robin suikkokko(n)

rock tempi(n) [ten- ~ te"-]

rock chuck yaha(n)

Rock Corral Tempin Kutaha

rock face tewene(ten)

rock hill tekko'i

rock mound tempokoh ~ tempo'i

rock peak tekko'i

Rock Springs Tempaa

rock writing tempimpooh

rogue cho'appeh

roll over on face mukwantuah

roll up makwantupi, wekkwantupi

roll up for makwantupinke(n) ~
makwantupinka(n)

root tetena(n)

rope temukku(n)

rope (an animal) kuuhkinka

rose (blossom) tsi'atontsia

rose hip tsi'ampih

rosebush tsi'api(n)

rot pisi"

rotten pisippeh

round poppontsanite(n), ponopihte(n),
puinui, punnunkaite(n)

round up takkooni

round up (animals) takkamah

round up for takkooninke(n)

rub -kunaih

rub butt against pikunaih, pisun<u>ai</u>h

rub together making a rasping sound
wehe'neki"(kkin)

rub with hand makunaih

rubber sanakkoo

rubbish teetto'ippeh ~ teetto'ihtaippeh

rug tasoni

rump pittehku ~ pittuhku

run nukki [nunukki dl, nutaa(n) pl]

run along nukkinooh
run along slowly nukkikki(nna)
run away namanukkih
run away from namakuhnai"
run fast nukkimi'a
run off kuhnai", namawene
run out of tsumah ~ tsu'ah
run out of breath suakkwaiyah
run short of wemmiha"
rust oosaante(n); oosaanto'ih
rusted oosaanto'ippeh
rusty oosaanto'ippeh
rye grass waatontsippeh
Rye Grass Trail Waatontsippeham Po'i"

S

sack mokottsih
sad tettehan(ten)
saddle natenoo, natenootekih
saddle horn natenoo'am pampi
saddle horse natenoo punku
sadness tettehan(ten)
sage hen huittsaa(n) [huintsaantsi song
    form]
sage thrush yeittoko ~ yaittoko
sagebrush pohopi(n)
sagebrush (large) pakwinompi(n)
sagebrush bark wattsippeh
Sagebrush Bark House (man's name)
    Wattsi Kahni
Sagebrush Butte (near Fort Hall)
    Pohoko'i
said mai [maiti]; taikwappeh; yekwippeh
saliva hettsippeh, tusippeh
salmon akai
Salmon Eaters (Shoshoni on Snake
    River) Akai Tekka'a
salt ohapi(n)
Salt Lake City soonkahni
sand pasiwampi(n) ~ pasiwompi(n)
sand dune pasiwakkatete(n)
Sand Pass (near Horseshoe Bend, NV)
    Pasiwa Wia
sandhill crane koanta
sandpiper kuwii
sass naniwaiki'a
Saturday Naahpain Nawookkah

save makwisunai
say te'ahwaih; nisua", tenisua"; yekwi"
    [niweneh pl]; ninnapunni ~ ninnapui
say to niikwi", nimma'i(kki);
    te'ahwainka(n) ~ te'ahwainke(n)
say(s) mai [maiti]
scare with hands makwiya'a
scare with words nikkwiya'a
scared kwikkwiya'wente(n), te'eyante(n)
scary enee
scary! eenee
scatter tepaiti"
scold nittehu'i(n) ~ nittuhu'i(n)
scold each other nanannittehu'i(n)
scoop (a liquid) yunnah
scorn nimmakwittsi
scorpion kwipuntsih
scoundrel cho'appeh
scout hoawoppih ~ huawoppih
scrape off wekwenai
scratch -situ'ih, tsasitu'ih, wesitu'ih;
    tsaso'ih; tsasunaih ~ tsasu'naih;
    tsisunaih
scratch oneself natsasunaih
scream nikkwitah; tsitattaki(n)
screw with a screwdriver tsikkwinuhi
scurry petette(kin)
sea piapaa
search antsi
search for puhai(n); waikki(n)
secure -tamah [-tami'ih pl]; wettamah
    [wettami'ih pl]
see pui" ~ punni"
see with feeling puisunkanna
see you all later memmi puinnuhi
see you later Em puinnuhi ~ Ne
    noohimpai puinnuhi
see you two later mehi puinnuhi
seed paihai
seed beater tanihku
seed pod kappeh
seem napuih ~ napuni [nanapui pl]; sua"
    [suan AUX]
seen napuippeh
Sees the Sun (man's name) Tapai Pui
sego lily sikoo
self pesu'a, taka(n), takattsi
sell natemaka

sell to natemakanke(n) ~ natemakanka(n)

seller natemakate(n)

semen noittsi'ippeh, noittso'i(ppeh), takka(n)

send tiyoih ~ tiyohih

send away nimmawiih(tain)

sentinel hoawoppih ~ huawoppih

separate (a couple) napuittai(n) ~
na'puittai(n) ~ napuihtai(n)

separate from neempeattai(n) ~
neempuihtai(n); takka'ah [tapponka'ih
~ tappunka'ih pl]

separated napuihtaippeh ~ napuittaippeh

separately antakku ~ antananku,
na'antappu(n)

separately from each other
nana'antappu(n)

serviceberry te'ampih

serviceberry bush te'api(n)

set tsakkatenkah ~ tsakkatenkeh;
wekkatenkah ~ wekkatenke(n)

set a trap hea"

set aside katenkahka(n)

set hand on makateh(kan)

set on fire kottooh

set up (e.g., a tent) tsikkatenke(n) ~
tsikkatenka(n)

seven taattsewihte(n) [taattsewi-]

seven hundred taattsewi pia
seemaahte(n)

seventeen seemayenten taattsewihtemman to'inkanna

seventy taattsewimaahte(n)
[taattsewimaah-, taattsewimaayenten]

several (times) he'eh(ten)

sew tsakkenah [tsakkeni'ih pl], tetaaldenah

sexual intercourse (have) yoko"

sexually aroused na'isape

shade heki; weheklah(ka)

shade house hekikahni

shadow heki, wewehekittsi

shake rhythmically wentsituih

shall (future tense) -to'ih

shaman puhakante(n) [puppuhakantee(n)
pl]

share nanahoih

sharp edge kemah

sharp-edged kemappeh

sharp point(ed) tetsimmuka

sharp-pointed mutsippeh, mutsikante(n)

sharpen wemmutsia

shatter tappihah [tappiyuih pl]; weppihah
[weppiyu'ih pl]

shave wesipi

shave (oneself) neesipi

she mate(n)

shed kwaitu'a, kwayu'i

shed fur or hair hopi'i

sheep sippeh

shine tatsiki, patatsi(ki)

shine (of sun) tapaituah

shine through clouds in spots
toottatawene

shiver kwippikka(n)

shiver from cold sekkwippiki(n)

shiver furiously from cold
sekkwipippiki(n)

shoe nampeh

shoestring tammuhka

shoot kuttih ~ kwettih

shoot at aiti kuttih

shopper temeete(n)

short kepihte(n) [kepih]; kepi wenete(n);
pono'ihkante(n)

short and stocky pottsa'ni (weneten)

short-legged dog ma'nii

shorter than ina; tukka(n) [tukkai,
tukkanku, tukkantu(n) tukkante(n)]

Shoshoni neme ~ newe [newenee(n) pl];
Sosoni

Shoshoni in Jarbridge mountains area
Toyatepia

Shoshoni story newe natekwinappeh

should witea

shoulder tsoappeh

shoulder blade sikkumpeh

shut up teittseh

sibling samuppe ~ samappe;
nanasamunneweh

sick te'oi; temmaihkante(n)

sick person te'oipekkate(n),
temmaihkante(n)

sickness te'oi

side nanku ~ nankwa; tepana ~
teppanna; senkwi

side of waiki(ten); kemaka ~ kemahka ~
kematu

sideways sikki, senkwippu(n), waikippu(n)

silver money aisemmunih

silverish aisempihte(n) [aisen-]

similar to ni(sen) [-nni]

similar to each other na'wa'i
[na'wa'iten]

simpleminded person aimeattsi ~
ai'meattsi

since way back in time apai mannaise(n
~ apai mannise(n)

sinew tammu

sing hupianai, nitto'i(n), tenitto'ih,
tenippuiyih

sing for nitto'inka(n), tenitto'inka(n) ~
tenitto'inke(n)

singe waiti

singer hupiakante(n)

single mother kuhawatte(n)

Sioux Pampittsimminna

sissy piapeh

sister (man's) samuppe ~ samappe

sister (older) patsi

sister (younger) nammi

sister-in-law of man pahampia

sister-in-law of woman atantohi

sisters (relationship) nana nammineweh

sit katekka(n) [yekwikka(n) pl]

sit around katettai(n)

sit down kate" [yekwi" pl]

sit on top of pikkenah

sit still kateppui; yuun kate"

sitting in a row nanappaiyekwi

six naahpaihte(n) [naahpai-]

six hundred naahpai pia seemaahte(n)

sixteen seemayenten naahpaihtemman
to'inkanna

sixty naahpaimaahte(n) [naahpaimaah-,
naahpaimaayente(n)]

size paika(nten) ~ pika(nten)

sizzle kusaakakakai", kuppeittseittseiki(n)

¹skin po'a(n)

²skin tsakkwai'a

skinny pasampeh, tekipettsi

skinny one pasampettsi

skunk pohni'attsih

skunk cabbage wantapasa

sky tukumpeh ~ tukumpi(n) ~
tukumpana(n) [tukun-]

sky husband tukunkuha

sky sickness (epilepsy) tukumpiwaa

sky wife tukunkwee

slanted sikki

Slanted Mountain Sikkikate(n)

slap matakki ~ mattakki; wettekwah
[weppa'ih pl]

slap around matakihka

sleep eppeih [ekkoih pl]

slice weppahkah [weppako'i(n) ~
weppako'ai(n) pl]

slice up/open wettsiyu'i

slingshot sanakkoo aiti

slip on slippery surface takkwitihku

slow(ly) upitaa(nku)

small teaite(n) ~ teite(n) [teteaitee(n) pl];
teiku

small amount heite(n), mapaitettsi

small boy tuineppe [pihianneweh dl, pihi-
annee(n) pl]

small lone hill in valley po'a katenoa

small reddish duck sokopehye(n)

small sunflower with gray-green leaves
kusiakke(n)

small yellow bird ohahuittsuu

smaller than ina; tukka(n) [tukkai,
tukkanku, tukkantu(n) tukkante(n)]

smallest teaiwoppih

smart natia suante(n)

smart aleck nasu'yekwite(n)

smash wekkitsa'a

smash by sitting on pikkitsa'a

smash with foot tahiipa; takkitsa'ah;
takkintsai" ~ takkintsaih; tattahkinah

smash with hand makitsa'a

smash with pointed instrument
tsikkitsa'a

smell ekwi"; kwana"

smell (for breath to) kekkwanah

smell rancid ta'oon kwana"

smell rotten pisikkwanah

smile yahnaisuah, yahnaisuante(n),
mu'yahnaisuah

smoke kwiippeh

smoke oneself nawaiti

smoke tobacco pahu'i

smokey colored aikkwimpihte(n)
[aikkwin-]

smolder kukkwiikkih, kwiiweneh
smooth seeppaite(n)
smudge waiti
smudge oneself nawaiti
snake tokoa
Snake Eaters Tokoa Tekka'a
Snake Knife (NAME) Tokoa Wiittsi
snakeweed kwitawoyampeh
snap at kennaaw<u>ai</u>
sneak up on mahoi(n)
sneeze akwisi"
sniff (around) ekkwikki(n)
snort out mosotto'ih
snot mupisippeh
snow takkapi(n) [takka]; takkatuah,
    takkaweai"
snowbird takkahuittsuu
so kwa'i; tsaa(n)
so be it ha tukuh
¹soak patekkih; patsawenneh(kan)
²soak patsawennenka(n) ~
    patsawennenka(n)
sock tappih<u>a</u>(a) ~ tappihyaa
soft yuun [~ yoo- song form];
    yontsoka(nten)
soften beating on weso'ih
soften pulling on tsaso'ih
soil sokoppeh
sold natemakappeh
sole of foot tappana
some he'eh(ten; himpeh; noo; sesema;
    hii(n) ~ hinni [hinna obj, hinna(n) poss]'
some kind hakaitte(n), noohakaitte(n)
some of mante(n)
some of it or that umante(n), sumante(n)
some of this imante(n), simante(n)
some(times) sesewekka ~ semekka
somebody hakate(n) [hakk<u>ai</u>" ~ hakki"
    obj]; noohakate(n) [noohakk<u>ai</u> obj]; ta
    [ta(n) poss]
somebody's hakka(n); ta(n)
somehow hakai, noohakai; hakanni;
    noohakanni(kku)
somehow weird hakaitte(n),
    noohakaitte(n); noohakanni(kku)
someone hakate(n) [hakk<u>ai</u>" ~ hakki" obj];
    noohakate(n) [noohakk<u>ai</u> obj]; ta [ta(n)
    poss]

someone's hakka(n); ta(n)
something himpeh; noohii(n) [noohinna
    obj]; hii(n) ~ hinni [hinna obj, hinna(n)
    poss]; ta [ta(n) poss]
something there sukkuhte(n)
sometime himp<u>ai</u>, noohimp<u>ai</u>
sometimes nanakkapa(n); u'ukapa (taka)
someway noohakanni(kku)
somewhere himp<u>ai</u>, noohimp<u>ai</u>ka;
    noohakka; noohakattu(n); haka'ana,
    hakappu(n); a'ate(n), a'ayente(n)
son tua" [tutua(neen) ~ tutuattsinee(n) ~
    tuannee(n) pl]
son-in-law munappe
song hupia ~ nahupia
song of nahupia
Song Woman Hupia Waimpe
sop up (gravy, soap) tottsakwakkiyu
sorcerer toitseppuha
sore e'attsih
sore throat kuittseh kammanna
soreness kammahpuinna
sorrowful nanatetteha(n)
sorrowfully nanatettehase(n)
soul mukua(pin)
sound nankah, nisua", nananka"; tenisua"
sound like nanankasuanka(n) ~
    nanankasuanke(n)
soup saappeh
south yu'ainankuhte(n)
Southern Paiute Paiyuttsi ~ Payuttsi
southward yu'aipp<u>ai</u>tu(n)
sow maseanka(n) ~ maseanke(n);
    temaseanka(n) ~ temaseanke(n);
    ten<u>ai</u>ti"
sparkle patasikaih
sparrow huittsuu
speak t<u>ai</u>kwa" [niweneh pl], ninnaah
speak English taipo t<u>ai</u>kwa"
speak Shoshoni newe t<u>ai</u>kwa", sosoni
    t<u>ai</u>kwa"
speak tenderly or kindly to nittehai
speak to t<u>ai</u>kwanka(n)
speak with nimma'i(kki)
speaker t<u>ai</u>kwawoppih
speech t<u>ai</u>kwa(nna), yekwippeh
speech sound te'amp<u>ai</u>
spend the night tehapi [tekwapi pl]

spend the winter tommoh(ka)

sperm noittsi'ippeh, noittso'i(ppeh),
    takka(n)

sphere poono ~ pono, takapoo

spherical punnunkaite(n), ponopihte(n)

spider wankasu'attsih

spill wehtiah ~ wettiah, mawehtiah,
    neettiah, towehtiah

spin puinuinuh

spin around punuhaki,
    kuppunnunnukki(n), neeppuinuinuh;
    wepuinuinuh, tsappuinuinuh,
    tappuinuinuh

spine kwahaintsuhni

spinal cord kwahain kupisi

spirit mukua(pin), namukua

spirit (being) ene'e

spiritual medicine puha

¹spit hettsippeh; tusippeh

²spit tusi"

spit out muto'ih

splash pakwittsu'ih; wooyompa (song form)

spleen haikwi

split weppahkah [weppako'i(n) ~
    weppako'ai(n) pl]

split into splinters wettsiyu'i

split open paikko'ah ~ paikoah [paiko'ih
    pl]

split pieces teppako'aippeh

spoken taikwappeh

spokesman taikwahni, taikwawoppih

spokesperson taikwawoppih, taikwahni

sponge off patottsema, tottsema

sponge oneself off napatottsema,
    natottsema

spook makwiya'a

spooky tso'a

spoon kwininnompeh; sippunneh

spread legs apart tasaa

spread on wette'aika

spread out -patah [-pati'ih pl], neeppatah
    [neeppati'ih pl]; weppatah [weppati'ih
    pl]; weyaah; wekkatookka(n)
    [wenkato(mpi) song form]; natekotah

spread out by hand tsappatah
    [tsappati'ih pl]

Spread Out Lava Rock Hill Oon
    Natsippata

spread out with something pointed
    tsippatah [tsippati'ih pl]

¹spring patetsoppih ~ patetsoppeh

²spring tahma, tahmani

Spring Creek Puhi Paa Hunupi(n)

spring forth paatua(mpite)

spring water patetsoppih ~ patetsoppeh

sprinkle weppatekkih

sprinkle around tsahuyuyu(ki)

sprout leaves sekituah

spruce wonkopi(n)

spurt huittsi

sputter in a fire kuppeittseittseiki(n)

spy on watsippuih

spy on (song word) pui'awatsi

squirrel (ground) tsippih

squirrel (golden mantled) tsikih

squirt noittsi'i

staff poto(n)

stag aan kuha ~ aan kuhma

stalk hoami'a ~ hoamahaih ~ huamahaih

stalker hoawoppih ~ huawoppih

stallion noyopunku

stand (up) wene" [tsatsakki dl,
    topo'ih(kan) ~ tsattsakai ~ topihka pl]

stand around wenekki(n); tookka

stand by itself on end (e.g., feather,
    stick) namattsiwene

stand of trees huuppi(n) [huu"-]; wene"

stand scattered about tetawenne

stand still wenekka(n); yuu wene

stand up tawene; tawenenuki; tawe-
    nenka(n) ~ tawenenke(n); tsiwenenka(n)
    ~ tsiwennehka(n)

star(s) tatsempi(n) ~ tatsinnompi(n) ~
    tatsiyempi(n)

start teki(n)

start a fire mawaihyanke(n)

start to burn mawaihyanke(n)

start to run kuhnai"

startle makwiya'a

startle with words nikkwiya'a

¹starve pahotiyaih ~ pahutiyaih
    [pahoko'ih ~ pahunakoih pl]

²starve tsippahunakoi

stash noote'aikah

stay naakka(n); katekka(n) [yekwikka(n)
    pl], kateppui

stay around katettai(n)

stay around not being welcome
tepiatekwi

stay at home nokateh

stay the night tehapi [tekwapi pl]

steal tetekkah

steam aikotooweneh,
aikotooweneh(pui)te(n)

steel wiihimpeh

stepfather natsuku

step on tattekih

¹stick huuppi(n) [huu"-]

²stick tona"; tsittekwah, tsittona; tosi'a;
tsekke'i

stick arrow huuppaka(n)

stick in tonikah; tsinnehki ~ tsi'nika;
tsiwehki

stick on matsappaki

stick to tsappakih

stick up behind (e.g., like a stinkbug)
piwonua

stick up for ninnaah ~ ninnaha

stickily noitsai [nointsai song form]

sticky sanakkante(n) ~ sanankante(n)

sticky (as feet in mud) noitsai

still ekise(n); yuu(n)

still (of water) pakatete(n)

stinger (e.g., of bee) wihupi(n) ~ wihyupi(n)

stinkbug pipusi

stir -kwintuih, -kwinuhi; wekkwintuih,
tewekkwintuih; tsakkwinuhi,
tsikkwinuhi, tsikkwintuih

stocking tappiha(a) ~ tappihyaa

stocky pottsa'ni (weneten)

stocky-shaped pono'ihkante(n)

stomach sappeh [sasappeh pl]

stone tempi(n) [ten- ~ te"-]

stoop over piwonua

stoop over with legs spread apart
pittataah

¹stop wene" ~ wenettai(n) [tsatsakki dl,
topo'ih(kan) ~ tsattsakai ~ topihka pl];
peattai(n) ~ peaittai(n) ~ puittai(n)

²stop makia(han); mawenenka(n) ~
mawenenke(n); tsawenenka(n) ~
tsawenenke(n)

stop breathing suakkwaiyah,
suakkimmaah

stop drinking keppeah

stop the swelling paikwiwainkah

stop walking wenettekih [tsatsakkihtekih
dl, topo'ihtekih pl/dl

¹store temeehkahni

²store teki" [tahna" pl, tekih instr];
tekikka(n) [tahnakka(n) pl]

store owner temeehkahnikante(n)

storm weai", weainna

stormy weainna

story natekwinappeh [nanatekwinappeh pl]

stove kottoonnompeh

straight tokaittunnaa(n) tokwaittunnaa(n);
tunnaa(n)

straight ahead tokaittunnaa(n) tokwait-
tunnaa(n)

straight up tukuppeh

straightforward tokaittunnaa(n)
tokwaittunnaa(n)

strange antapittseh; antappunte(n)
[anta", antappu(n)]

stranger antannewe, antapittseh

strangle tsakkwisinkah ~ tsakkwisinke(n)

straw hat saitetsoih

stream okwaite(n)

strength tsuhnippeh

strengthen mapitsi'a

strengthen with words nimmapitsi'a

stretch wettutai"; wettutua

stretch by pulling with hands tsattutai"

stretch oneself neettutua ~ neettutai"

stretch out arms mattutua

stretch with the feet tattutai"

stretcher (e.g., fence stretcher)
teettutua

¹string wisu

²string tsakkenah [tsakkeni'ih pl],
tetsakkenah

stringed instrument ta weyakainkanna ~
ta weyakainkenna

strip off tsakkwai'a, tsakkwaitu'ah

stripe wooppihte(n)

striped wooppih ~ wookki

strong natia(n), natianku; tsuhnippeh

strong-arm matsuhinka(n) ~
matsuhinke(n) ~ matsuhninka(n)

strong-armed mattsuhnippeh

strong-handed tsattsuhnippeh

strong-legged tattsuhnippeh
strongly natianku
study tepoohpui
stuff himpeh, oyonte(n) ~ oyontettsi
stumble tattsannih
suck pitsih [pintsi song form]
suck out mupitsi
sucker fish mukate
suckle pitsih [pintsi song form], pittsi"
suffer kamma(n) ~ kammah;
    maneettsikkwa
suffer from -pekka(n)
suffer from grief tettehampekka(n)
suffering kammanna
sugar pihaa ~ pihnaa ~ pihyaa
sugar diabetes pihyatukku ~ pihatukku
summer tatsa
Summit Creek Koanta Paa
sun tapai
sun (ritually) appe
sun (special name sometimes used in
    myths) tatapai
Sunday Nasanti" ~ Nasuntih ~ Taattsewin
    Nawookkah
sunflower akke(n)
supernatural power puha, napuha
    [puha]
supplicate nanittsawaih(kan)
supplicate (someone) for
    nanittsawainka(n) ~ nanittsawainke(n)
sure haa('a)
surely naketsa
surely not kai (kia) naketsa
surround koappeh
survive kwitsunaih
[1]swallow yewe"
[2]swallow pasokompii
swat wekkumpahku
sweat takusippeh, takusito'ih
sweaty takusito'ihtaippeh(ttsi)
sweep wesunaih, teesunaih
sweet pihaa ~ pihnaa ~ pihyaa
sweet cicely pasokwai
swell paikwi"
swim pahapi
swimmer pahapite(n)
swing wainua"
swirl wekkwintuih, tewekkwintuih

swirl around pampunua
swirling water pampunuaniite(n)
swollen paikwippeh
swollen part or area paikwikante(n)
syringe wihupi(n) ~ wihyupi(n)

T

table tipoh
tail kwasi [kwasintsi song form]
tail feather kwasi [kwasintsi song form]
take yaa" [hima" pl, -yaah comb],
    yaakka(n) [himakka(n) pl]; hannih;
    noo"; yunah
take (a person) paitse"
take aim aitiki(n); wapuih; yewampontsi
take away yunahku(n)
take away from yaanka(n) ~ yaanke(n)
    [himanka(n) himanke(n) pl]
take back noopite ~ nooppite
take care of mayekwi; mapitenka(n) ~
    mapitenke(n); manapuih ~
    manapunnih; mapaiah; temapaiah;
    nokatenka(n) ~ nokatenke(n)
take care of for temapaianka(n) ~
    temapaianke(n)
take care of oneself namanapuih(kan);
    namapaiah; namayekwi
take for yaanka(n) ~ yaanke(n)
    [himanka(n) himanke(n) pl]
take off kwaitu'a; tsakkwai'a;
    tsakkwaitu'ah
take off (e.g., pants, skirt) pikkwaitu'ah
take off of feet takkwaitu'ah
take off with tools wekkwaitu'ah
take out tsatto'ih [tsakkea pl]
taken care of temapaiappeh
[1]talk taikwa" [niweneh pl]; ninnaah
[2]talk taikwa(nna)
talk about nihannih [nimmeeh pl];
    tenisua"
talk to taikwanka(n)
talk with nimma'i(kki)
talker taikwawoppih
tall kepetaa(nten), kepetaa wenete(n),
    kekkepetaa; piante(n) [pia comb, pipia,
    pipiante(n) pl]; piappehte(n) [pia, pipia
    pl, pipiappete(n) pl]

tall grass whose seeds were harvested
sihu(n) ~ sihuh

tall rye grass piasonippeh

taller than ka'wi, makuppa(n)

tap wettantaki

tapaderos on saddle tahippa

taste kamma(n) ~ kammah; temmaih

taste bitter muha kamman(na)

taste of onion muha kamman(na)

taste rancid ta'oon kammanna

taste rotten pisikkamman(na)

taste salty ohakamma(n)

taste sour seken kamman(na)

taste sweet pihyaa kamman(na)

Taylor Canyon NV Pia Pohopi Hunupi(n)

tea tiih

teach teniwaah

teacher teniwaate(n)

teal duck sokopeliye(n)

tear siwah ~ si'wah; tsasiwah

tear with mouth or teeth kesi'wah

tease nisummaa

teenage girl naipi(n) [nai'yannee(n) pl]

tell niikwi"; natemu'i ~ nateme'i;
te'ahwaih, te'ahwainka(n) ~
te'ahwainke(n); ninnapunni ~ ninnapui;
nate'ahwaikka(n)

tell (how to) niyekwi

tell a lie isannai

tell a lie to isannainka(n) ~ isannainke(n)

tell a story natekwina

tell a story to natekwinanka(n) ~ natek-
winanke(n)

tell each other nanatemu'i ~ nanateme'i

tell to natemu'inka(n) nateme'inke(n) ~
nateme'inke(n)

tell to go away nimmawiih(tain)

ten seemaahte(n) [seemaah-,
seemaayente(n)]

tendon tammu

tent wanakahni

tepee wanakahni

termite aantsi'i

terrible natia(n), teittse

terribly natia(n), naketsa natia(n)

testicle noyo

than tempah

thank you Aise! (Aise!); aisem ma'i tsa'i

that (one) ote(n) [okka obj]; sote(n)
[sokka obj, sokka(n) poss]

that (one out of sight) ute(n) [ukka obj,
ukka(n) poss]; sute(n) [sukka obj,
sukka(n) poss]

that (which is said) semmai

that amount opaika(nten) ~ opika(nten),
sopaika(n)

that amount out of sight upaika(n) ~
upika(nten), supaika(n)

that amount yonder apika(nten) ~
apaika(nten); sapaika(n)

that is ma'i; kwa'i

that kind oitte(n), soitte(n)

that kind out of sight uitte(n), suitte(n)
[suittee(n) pl]

that kind yonder aitte(n), saitte(n)

that much opaika(nten) ~ opika(nten),
sopaika(n)

that much out of sight upaika(n) ~
upika(nten), supaika(nten)

that much yonder apika(nten) ~
apaika(nten), sapaika(n)

that not visible (is the) one use(n)

that (is the) one ose(n)

that place o'ana, so'ana

that place out of sight u'ana, su'ana
[su'anahtu(n)]

that place yonder a'ana, sa'ana

that time sopai; sapai; supai

that time long ago apaise(n)

that was it sunni taka

that way onni, sonni

that (particular) way suikkuh

that way out of sight unni, sunni
[sunnikku]

that way yonder anni, sanni

that yonder ate(n) [akka obj, akka(n)
poss]; sate(n) [sakka obj, sakka(n) poss]

that yonder (is the) one ase(n)

that's (that one's) okka(n), sokka(n);
akka(n); sakka(n); ukka(n), sukka(n)

that's all peai taka; usen taka

the best one tsaawoppih

the biggest one piawoppih

the end (e.g., of a story) Kaan kwasi
kwai'ahku!

The Point Tesi Koi

the right time tokaintempai ~
tokwaintempai
the same as pikase(n)
their matee(n)
their two matehe(n)
their own pemme(n), pemmese(n)
their own (dl) pehe(n)
them matii
themselves pemmese(n), pemmi
themselves (dl) peweh(sen), pehi
then wihnu; sipai, saipai, sopai, sapai,
supai
there okkuh ~ sokkuh
there are -pa'i(n), -kante(n)
there is -pa'i(n), -kante(n)
there out of sight ukkuh(ten); sukkuh
[sukkuhte(n), sukkuhtu(n) sukkuhse(n)]
there somewhere ana, o'ana ~ so'ana
there somewhere out of sight u'ana ~
su'ana
there somewhere yonder a'ana, sa'ana,
a'akkuh
there yonder akkuh, sakkuh(te(n)
thereabouts opi ~ sopi
thereabouts out of sight upi, supi
[supitte(n)]
thereabouts yonder api, sapi
therefore kwa'i, ma'i
therein ukkuhte(n), sukkuhte(n)
these matee(n) [matii obj]; itee(n) [itii obj,
itee(n) poss]; sitee(n) [sitii obj, sitee(n)
poss]
these near here aitee(n) [aitii obj,
aitee(n) poss]; saitee(n) [saitii obj,
saiteen poss]
these two mateweh [matehi obj]; iteweh
[itehi obj, itehe(n) poss]; siteweh [sitehi
obj, sitehe(n) poss]
these two near here aiteweh [aitehi obj,
aitehe(n) poss]; saiteweh [saitehi obj,
saitehe(n) poss]
they matee(n)
they say mai [maiti]
they two mateweh [matehi obj]
thick tenkwi; pohonte(n) ~ pohontante(n)
thicken tenkwito'ih; tsikkwintuihpui
thigh tohopi(n)
thin pasampeh

thing himpeh
thing(s) hii(n) ~ hinni [hinna obj, hinna(n)
poss]; noohii(n) [noohinna obj];
oyonte(n) ~ oyontettsi
think sua" [suan AUX]; suwai; suyekwi,
tesuyekwi; suhannih
think about suanka(n) ~ suanke(n);
summeeh(kan)
think angrily tuhusuahka(n)
think deeply teesuah(tekih)
think negatively of su'aipui
think of suanka(n) ~ suanke(n);
summeeh(kan)
think of oneself as nasuyekwi" ~
nasu'yekwi"
think through teesuah(tekih)
think well about tsaa suanka(n)
think well of tsaasuanka(n)
tsaasuanke(n); tsaa . . . sua"
thinking suanna, suante(n)
thirst taku"
thirteen seemayentem pahaittemman
to'inkanna
thirty pahaimaahte(n) [pahaimaah-,
pahaimaayente(n)]
this mate(n) [makka obj]; ite(n) [ikka obj,
ikka(n) poss]; site(n) [sikka obj, sikka(n)
poss]
this (is the one) ise(n)
this amount ipika(nten) ~ ipaika(nten),
sipaika(n)
this amount near here aipaika(nten) ~
aipika(nten), saipaika(n); aipaika(n),
saipaika(n)
this kind iitte(n), sitte(n)
this kind nearby aitte(n), saitte(n)
this much ipaika(nten) ~ ipika(nten),
sipaika(n); aipaika(n), saipaika(n)
this much near here aipaika(nten) ~
aipika(nten)
this near here aite(n) [aikka obj, aikka(n)
poss]; saite(n) [saikka obj]
this near here (is the) one aise(n)
this one's saikka(n)
this place i'ana, si'ana
this place near here ai'ana ~ sai'ana
this side ina; sainankuh [sainankuhten]
this time saipai

this time exactly sipai
this way a̲inni, sa̲inni
this way right here inni, sinni
thorn aikopi(n)
those otee(n) [otii obj, otee(n) poss];
   sotee(n) [sotii obj, sotee(n) poss]
those out of sight utee(n) [utii obj,
   utee(n) poss]; sutee(n) [sutii obj,
   sutee(n) poss]
those two oteweh [otehi obj, otehen
   poss]; soteweh [sotehi obj, sotehe(n)
   poss]
those two out of sight uteweh [utehi
   obj, utehe(n) poss]; suteweh [sutehi
   obj, sutehe(n) poss]
those two yonder ateweh [atehi obj,
   atehe(n) poss]; sateweh [satehi obj,
   satehe(n) poss]
those yonder atee(n) [atii obj, atee(n)
   poss]; satee(n) [satii obj, satee(n) poss]
though noo(n)
thought(s) suanna
thoughtless ka̲isuante(n)
¹thread tenkwisippeh, tammu
²thread tsakkenah [tsakkeni'ih pl],
   tetsakkenah; tenkwisi; tsiweh(ki)
three pahaitte(n) [pahai-]
Three Fork (on Duck Valley
   Reservation) Te'akate(n)
three hundred pahai pia seemaahte(n)
throat kuittseh ~ kuittsih, toyo(n)
through tu(n) (-ttun); mantu(n) [ma(n)]
through it or that umantu(n)
through that suttu(n); sumantu(n)
through there suttu(n), pentu(n)
through this area ittu(n), sittu(n)
through wherever hakattu(n)
through which pentu(n), penkahtu(n)
throughout kapa(n); attu(n)
throw tahwi ~ tawi [tappa̲itih ~ pa̲iti" pl];
   takkuhnai"; tepa̲iti"
throw aside or away towiih [toppa̲itih pl]
throw aside or down tawiih ~ tahwii
   [tappa̲itih ~ pa̲iti" pl]
throw away wiittai(n) ~ wiihtai(n)
   [pa̲itittai(n) pl]; tawiih(tain) [tappa̲itih(tain)
   ~ toppa̲itihtain pl]; tsawiihtai(n)
   [tsappa̲itihtai(n) pl]; wekkuhnai"

throw down or aside tsawiih [tsappa̲itih pl]
throw out towiihtain [toppa̲itihtain pl]
thumb mattoko
thunder toyakaite(n); toyakainnai
Thursday Wattsewin Nawookkah
thus ma'i; kwa'i; mase(n)
thus (something said) semma̲i
tie -tamah [-tami'ih pl]
tie (up) tsattamah [tsattami'ih pl]
tie in a bundle tsattempono'i
tie shoes tammuhkah
tie tight wettamah [wettami'ih pl]
tied up natsattamappeh [natsattami'ippeh
   pl]; natsattamahkante(n)
tighten tsannehki
till -yottah, weyottah, teeyottah
time pa̲i [pa̲ite(n)]
timepiece tapa̲i
times past uttuse(n)
tiny teaitettsi
tip katsu(n)
tiptop ko'i
tired (be) wemmiha", wemmihakkante(n);
   enuhi
to ka" [kai, kakku, kattu(n), katte(n), katti,
   kayente(n)]; nai [naiten]; mante(n) ~
   mantu(n) [ma(n)]
to (someone) waka(n) [wakante(n),
   wakantu(n), wakayente(n)]
to a lesser degree tsappe'a(n) ~
   tsappe'ase(n)
to him or her uwaka(nten), suwaka(n)
   [suwakanten]
to it or that umantu(n)
to one side senkwippu(n)
to that umantu(n), sumantu(n)
tobacco pahu(n)
today ekittsi, mai'ukka, tapa̲ima
toe taseki
toenail tasitoo(n)
together nana" [nahma(ten) dl];
   nanamma'ai ~ nanama'ai [nahma'ai dl]
toilet kwitakkahni
told te'ahwa̲ippeh, te'ahwa̲inkappeh ~
   teahwa̲inkeppeh
tomorrow imaa
tongue a̲iko(n)
Tonopah, NV Tonampaa

too tea(n) ~ tease(n); natia(n), naketsa
  natia(n)
tooth tama(n)
toothache taman kammanna
top of (hill or mountain) ana
torment nasuntsaa
tormented nasuntsaappeh
touch tsakkwaiha(n)
touch with behind pittekih
touch with feet tattekih
touch with nose mutekih
toward mante(n) ~ mantu(n) [ma(n)];
  nanku ~ nankwa; ka" [kai, kakku,
  kattu(n), katte(n), katti, kayente(n)]
toward (someone) waka(n) [wakante(n),
  wakantu(n), wakayente(n)]
toward him or her uwaka(nten),
  suwaka(n) [suwakanten]
toward it umantu(n), sumantu(n)
toward that umantu(n), sumantu(n)
toward the east tapaito'ippaitu(n)
toward the mountains toyapaitu(n)
toward the north kwinahaippaitu(n)
toward the south yu'aippaitu(n)
toward the west tapaiyuappaitu(n)
track (down) nayaa, nampuih,
  yewampontsi
trade nappihtuh ~ napittuh
trail po'i"
trample in tannehki
transparent papumpihte(n) [papun]
¹trap hea"; kwisinka(n) ~ kwisinke(n)
²trap wampu, wana
trap fish painkwihea
trap with words nikkwisinka(n) ~
  nikkwisinke(n)
trash teetto'ippeh ~ teetto'ihtaippeh
travel nemi [yeyenkah dl, yenka ~
  nayekwin pl]; yeme"
travel around neminemmi; nukkikki(nna)
treat manapuih ~ manapunnih; puhanai;
  nattahsu'a
treatment napuhakante(n)
tree huuppi(n) [huu"-]; sennapi(n);
  huukwitsappeh
¹trick isa(n),
²trick isannainka(n) ~ isannainke(n),
  itsapaikkah

trot poyokka
true tokai" ~ tokwai"; tukka(n),
  tukkukante(n)
truly tokainku ~ tokwainku, tokaise(n) ~
  tokwaise(n)
truthful tokaise(n) ~ tokwaise(n)
truthfully tokainku ~ tokwainku
try mapuih, matsu'ah
tuberculosis pasattukku
Tuesday Wahan Nawookkah
tule sai ~ saippeh
tule blackbird saipakantsukkih
tule hat saitetsoih
turkey tokkih
turkey vulture waikkumpittseh
turn metekki
turn a wrench wekkwinuhi
turn around kwinuhi; tsakkwinuhi
turn inside out tsammito'ih
turn inside out with something pointed
  tsimmito'ih
turn into tuah
turn key in lock wekkwinuhi
turn loose tsattoyah(tain)
turn over on face mukwantuah
turn over with foot tammetekki
turn over with hand tsammetekki
turn over with something sharp or
  pointed tsimmetekki
turn pale aato'ih
turned pale aato'ihtaippeh
Tuscarora, NV Tosa Konoki
twelve seemayente wahattemman
  to'inkanna
twenty wahamaahte(n) [wahamaah-,
  wahamaayente(n)]
Twenty-Five Mile Station Penka Tan
  Tapaitekka'inna
twin taka
twin(s) wawaha [wawahaneweh dl,
  wawahanee(n) pl]
twirl around pampunua
twist tsakkwintsunah [tsakkwintsuni'ih
  pl]
twist around kwinuhi
two wahatte(n) [waha-]
two bits tupittsih
two hundred waha pia seemaahte(n)

U

ugly atsa napuite(n) ~ atsa napunnite(n);
    kaitsaan napuite(n)
umbilical cord siku
unable to kai . . . -wa'i
unable to breathe suakkwaiyah
uncertain hakanni kia noo(n)
uncertain about kwa'i kia
uncertainly sampai noo(n)
uncle ata, haih
unclean tottsappeh ~ tuttsappeh
under tukka(n) [tukkai, tukkanku,
    tukkantu(n) tukkante(n)]
under it matukka(n), utukka(n)
under that utukka(n), sutukka(n)
under this matukka(n)
under which pentukka(n)
underarm ahnatukka
understand sumpana'ihki(n),
    nankasumpana'i, nankasumpaatu(n/h)
unpleasant teittse
up panai; pa'a(n) [pa'ai, pa'anku,
    pa'antu(n), pa'ante(n)]
upright wene" [tsatsakki dl; topo'ih(kan),
    tsattsakai, topihka pl]
upwards panai, panippu(n)
urinal siiawo
urinate sii" [sisiiwen pl distrib]
urinate all over or frequently si'si'we(n)
    ~ sisiiwe(n)
urine siippeh
us (excl) nemmi
us (incl) tammi ~ tai
us two (excl) nehi
us two (incl) tahi
use hannih, mee" ~ mehe(n)
used nahappeh
used to noha (kwa'i)
uterus no'ipeh

V

vagina ta'i"
value ninnakkih ~ ninnahki"
vein(s) paikwakkwapih ~ peekkwakwapih
venereal disease tempahai
very kettaa(n), kettaanku; natia(n);
    tepi(tsi); haiya

very few he'ehtettsi
very good tepitsi tsaa(n)
very much tukkumpai
violin ta weyakainkanna ~ ta
    weyakainkenna
visible napuippeh
visit wakapite
voice natempai
vomit wetto'ih; wetto'ippeh
vomit vigorously repeatedly
    wehuitsittsiki(n)
vomit violently wehuittsi
vulva ta'i"

W

wade pato'ih ~ patu'ih; nampatu'ih
wager tepaha; natepahappeh
wagon wopi(n)
waist pittsoka
wait for wesumpana'ih
wake up tepuih, nittepui
walk mi'ah ~ miah [mimi'ah dl]
walk along miannooh, mi'aki(n)
walk in ritual procession praying
    before round dance natayaa
walk in single file one behind the other
    woyoah(ka)
walk on tattekih
walk stooped over tu'ummi'akki(n)
walk wiggling the behind piyuppuki(n)
walk with a cane natsittoo
walk with head bobbing up and down
    winnooki(n) ~ wi'nooki(n)
wander nemi [yevenkah dl, yenka ~
    nayekwin pl]; yeme"
wander around neminemmi
want suwai, sua" [suan AUX]
war dance tan tase'yekwinna
war song tase'yekwi hupia
warm (be) yu'aih
warm up yu'ainka(n) ~ yu'ainke(n);
    kuyu'ainka(n) ~ kuyu'ainke(n)
warn against ninnatawi'i(n)
warrior hoakkante(n) ~ huakkante(n),
    hoawoppih ~ huawoppih
wash koitsoih ~ koitsohi
wash oneself nakoitsoih ~ nakuitsoih

washed koitsoippeh

wasp paina(n)

¹watch iya'ih, puikka(n)

²watch tap<u>ai</u>

watch (as entertainment) tempuih(kan)

watch closely puihtamah ~ puitamah

Watch out! eenee

watch over iya'ihka(n)

watch secretly watsippuih

¹water paa [pa- comb, pappa distrib]

²water hipinka(n) ~ hipinke(n), pamaka

water baby (mythological being) pa'ohaa

Water Baby's Bed Pa'ohaa'an Kapp<u>ai</u>

water basket osa ~ pa'osa

water bottle osa ~ pa'osa

water hemlock hattai

water jug osa ~ pa'osa

water snake patokoa

water spider (that runs on top of
    water) pasu'attsih

water willow paseepi(n)

water willow stand or place
    paseeweyaa

watermelon paatekkappeh

waterworn cobblestone patsittempi(n)

watery foam pasaattointsi

wave in the wind (as grass) yommann<u>ai</u>

way hakannikku

way (this/that) ni(sen) [-nni]; pu(n) ~ puhni

way back then aattuse(n), a'akkuse(n)

ways pakku

we (excl) nemme(n)

we (incl) tamme(n)

we two (excl) neweh

we two (incl) taweh

weak yu'ito'ihtaippeh

weaken yu'ito'ih

weakened yu'ito'ihtaippeh

wear on the head tsoyaah

wear out wihtuha ~ wituha

wear out (shoes) tawituha

weasel papitsii

weave kwisi"

weaving wanappeh

web wana

Wednesday Pahain Nawookkah

well tsaanku, tsaa(n), well maaikkuh

well-to-do tsaannaahkante(n)

well-worn footpath tetappo'ihapinkappeh
    ~ tetappo'ihapinkeppeh

wellness tsaayunna

west tap<u>ai</u>yuanankuhte(n)

westward tap<u>ai</u>yuappaitu(n)

¹wet patso'ippeh

²wet patekkih, weppatekkih

wet oneself neemapatekki(n),
    neeppatekki(n)

what hii(n) ~ hinni [hinna obj, hinna(n)
    poss]; hakai

what is said semm<u>ai</u>

what kind of hakaitte(n)

what time hakap<u>ai</u>, heettenka

what way hakanni

whatever noohii(n) [noohinna obj];
    noohakai; nanah hinna

whatever kind hakaitte(n), noohakaitte(n)

whatever time hakap<u>ai</u>

whatever way hakannikku,
    noohakanni(kku)

when himp<u>ai</u>; pemp<u>ai</u>; ukka

whenever noohimp<u>ai</u>

where haka'ana, hakattu(n), hakakka

where (rel) pempa'a(n), penka
    [penkayente(n)]

where from hakannai

where to hakappu(n)

wherever haka'ana, noohakattu(n),
    noohakka, noohimp<u>ai</u>ka

which direction hakannanku

which side hakannanku

while noo(n)

whip wettekwah [weppa'ih pl]

whirlpool pampunuaniite(n)

whirlwind wettso'appeh

whiskers motso(n)

whiskey ontempaa

white tosapihte(n) [tosa"-]

white (person) taipo

white chalky clay aipi(n)

White Gate (on the Duck Valley
    Indian Reservation) Tosan
    Natsattawih

White Knife Shoshoni Tosawihi(n)

White Wolf (= Jesus Christ) Tosa Isa

whitish aapihte(n) [aa-]

whitish gray aipuipihte(n) [aipui"-]

who hakate(n) [hakk<u>ai</u>" ~ hakki" obj]

whoever hakate(n) [hakk<u>ai</u>" ~ hakki" obj];
noohakate(n) [noohakk<u>ai</u> obj]

whoever else noohihiintsinee(n)

whoever's hakka(n)

whole ooyoku(sen) ~ oyoku(sen) ~
ooyote(sen)

whom hakk<u>ai</u>" ~ hakki"

whomever hakk<u>ai</u>" ~ hakki"

whose hakka(n)

[1]why hakanni, hakanniyun(ten) ~
hakanniu(ten)

[2]why sunni [sunnikku, sunniunte(n);
susunni pl]

wide piawaikite(n)

wide area piawaiku

widow kuhatiyainkappeh, tematiyainkappeh

widower kwehetiyainkappeh,
tematlyainkappeh

wife kwehe" ~ kwee"

wiggle yuppu

wild iyampeh

wild carrot yampa, payampa

wild iris tosittoya

wild onion kenka

wild parsnip haapp<u>ai</u>

wild rice piatetsii

wild rose blossom tsi'atontsia

wild rose hip tsi'ampih

wild rosebush tsi'api(n)

wild rye waata

wild tobacco newe pahu(n)

wildcat tukkupittseh

wilderness tepoo(n)

will (future tense) to'ih

Willis Meadows, NV Nakaha
Payuppuka

willow sehepi(n) ~ seepi(n); sakappi(n) ~
wakappi(n)

willow shoots patewintsi

willow stand or place seeweyaa

wilt takwittsih

win kwakkuhu(n) ~ kwakkwaha(n)

[1]wind nealppeh ~ neaippi(n) ~ neaite(n)

[2]wind tsakkwinuhi; wekkwintsunah
[wekkwintsuni'ih pl]

window panapui

wing kasa

winnings kwakkuhuppeh ~
kwakkwahappeh

winnow mayunaih, wettenta'ni,
weyannai, wettai(ni)

winnowing tray or basket yantu(n)

winter tommo; tommoh(ka)

winter house tookkahnih

wipe off patottsema, tottsema

wipe oneself off natottsema

with (accompaniment) ma'ai ~ mai ~
ma'i [ma'aihku, ma'aise(n)]

with (instrument) ma" ~ ma(n)
[mante(n), manku]

with (someone) waka(n) [wakante(n),
wakantu(n), wakayente(n)]

with back, behind, or butt pi"-

with cold se"-

with each other namante(n)
[namantu(n)]; na'ma'ai; nanamma ai
[nahma(ten) dl]

with face mu- ~ mo-

with feet ta"-

with fire ku"-

with fist or hand violently to"-

with hand ma-

with hand grasping tsa"-

with hard or rock-like object ta"-

with head tso"-

with heat ku"-

with long instrument we"-

with mind sun-

with mouth or teeth ke"-

with nose mu- ~ mo-

with sharp or pointed instrument tsi"-

with that (instrument) sama(n), ama(n),
uma(n); suma(n) ~ summa(n)
[sumanku, sumayente(n)]

with that (person) sama'ai, ama'ai,
suma'ai, uma'ai

with the night tukama(n)

with this (instrument) sima(n) ~
simma(n), s<u>ai</u>ma(n), <u>ai</u>ma(n)

with this (person) sima'ai

with which pemma" ~ pemma(n)

with whom pemma'ai

with words ni"-

within kuppa(n)

wolf isa ~ pia isa
woman wa'ippe
woman who has children tutuanaite(n) ~ tutuammi'ate(n)
woman's name Kiiki
womb no'ipeh
wonder kia ~ ki'a
wonder about sampai noo(n), nankasuanka(n) ~ nankasuanke(n)
wonderful nanasuwekai(n)
wood huuppi(n) [huu"-]
woodchuck yaha(n)
wooded place (end of) huummutsi
woodpecker putumpittsi ~ kuttumpittseh; wopin tottontaki; wampuni; woppimpono
Woods End, NV huummutsi
woodtick mittaa ~ mitteha
words taikwa(nna)
work teteai, wookkapi(n)
work for wages wookkah
worker teteaiwoppih, wookkawoppih
workhorse teeyaahpunku
worm wo'api(n)
worn out neewihtuhappeh
worthless nanahteppeh
wound e'attsih
wrap in a bundle wekkwantupi
wrap up tsattono'ih, tsakkwantupi
wreck wekkih ~ wikkah ~ wikkih, wekkisinah
wrestle nakwehe
wrist mawintsa, mattsinko'no
write pooh, tepooh
write on rocks tempimpooh
write Shoshoni newe tepooh
write with finger tsippooh
writer tepoowoppih
writing napooppeh
writing instrument tepoonnompeh
written tepooppeh
wrong kaikkaitsaa(n)
wrong way antananku

Y

yank out tsakkwai'a
yarrow patontsia
year tommo
yellow ohappihte(n) [oha"-]
Yellow Huni (north of Duck Valley Reservation) Waiki Hunupi(n)
yellow jacket paina(n)
yes haa('a)
yes/no question particle ha
yesterday kentu(n)
you e(n) ~ enne [emmi ~ e(n) obj]
you all memme(n) ~ mee(n) [memmi obj]
you all's memme(n) ~ mee(n)
you two meweh [mehi obj]
you two's mehe(n)
young eke
young (of animal) tuintsi
young (poetic) tuantsi
young daughter (prepuberty) paiteppe
young lady naipi(n) [nai'yannee(n) pl]
Young Ladies' Rock Peak Nai'yan Tekkoi
young man tuintsi, tuittsi(ttsi) [tuittsianee(n) pl]; tuipittsi [tuipittsi'anee(n) ~ tuttuipittsi'anee(n) pl]
young person ekepittseh [ekepittsehnee pl]
young son tuappe
younger brother tami
younger sister nammi
youngest (of offspring) nakaha
your e(n) ~ emme(n) ~ enne(n)
your two mehe(n)
your two selves mehese(n)
your (you all's) mee(n) ~ memme(n)
yourself ese(n) ~ eese(n), emmese(n)
yourselves memmese(n)
youth ekepittseh [ekepittsehnee pl]; tuintsi

Z

zenith tukuppeh